Reading and Understanding

ECONOMICS

Kevin Boakes

FT Prentice Hall
FINANCIAL TIMES

An imprint of **Pearson Education**
Harlow, England • London • New York • Boston • San Francisco • Toronto
Sydney • Tokyo • Singapore • Hong Kong • Seoul • Taipei • New Delhi
Cape Town • Madrid • Mexico City • Amsterdam • Munich • Paris • Milan

Pearson Education Limited

Edinburgh Gate
Harlow
Essex CM20 2JE
England

and Associated Companies throughout the world

Visit us on the World Wide Web at:
www.pearsoned.co.uk

First published 2009

© Pearson Education Limited 2009

ISBN: 978-0-273-72254-0

British Library Cataloguing-in-Publication Data
A catalogue record for this book is available from the British Library

Library of Congress Cataloging-in-Publication Data
A catalog record for this book is available from the Library of Congress

10 9 8 7 6 5 4 3 2 1
13 12 11 10 09

Typeset in Stone Sans 9pt by 3
Printed and bound by Henry Ling Ltd., at the Dorset Press, Dorchester, Dorset

The publisher's policy is to use paper manufactured from sustainable forests.

Dedication

To Sue who once again made an enormous contribution to the writing of this book

Table of Contents

Table of Contents

About the author

After graduating with a degree in Economics, and an MSc from the London School of Economics, Kevin Boakes started his working life on the bond trading desk at Greenwell Montagu Gilt-edged, which is now part of HSBC Investment Bank. As their Chief UK Economist he was responsible for giving on-the-spot advice to bond traders as soon as economic stories hit the news screens. He regularly contributed articles to newspapers including the *Times*, *Observer* and *Guardian* and appeared on the BBC's *Money Programme* and *The Financial World Tonight*. In the late 1980s he decided to make a radical career change and left the City to join Kingston University, initially in the Economics Department and then at Kingston Business School where he is currently a Senior Lecturer in the School of Accounting and Finance. In addition to his academic work he has run a number of economics and financial market training courses for various investment banks. In early 2008 his first book, *Reading and Understanding the Financial Times*, a practical analysis of financial articles from the FT, was published.

Preface

The book explains and analyses economics-based articles in the media. In doing so it aspires to bring the academic subject of economics to life. I want to show you that it is not only a fascinating subject but that it also provides a framework for understanding many key aspects of everyday life. I have not assumed that you have any previous knowledge of economics. Instead, I hope that this book will inspire you to increase your economics knowledge in the future through further reading or some form of study.

You will see that the book works by analysing a selection of articles from the *Financial Times*, the *Economist* magazine, and the *Guardian* and *Times* newspapers. The selected articles all relate to some of the most important issues in economics. I provide an analysis of each article, explaining how the subject matter reflects a key topic which will form an important part of any economics course.

How should you use the book? My suggestion is that you start by reading the actual source article. In some cases this will prove more challenging than in others. You should highlight all the main things that you do not understand at this stage. Then you can read my analysis of the article. You will see that I have attempted to focus on the key themes contained in the articles as well as explaining the major economic principles and concepts. At the end of the analysis you will find that I have provided a very accessible explanation of all the key terms used in the article. You can always refer to this section as you read through the article or my analysis. Next you might try any of the related exercises or the questions in the 'What do you think?' section. Finally, if you feel inspired, you can use the research references to seek out further useful reading.

I hope that the book is a handy size so that you can take it with you on buses ot the train as you travel into university or work. No article should take more than an hour or so to complete. The writing style is very informal and relaxed and I hope that you find it enjoyable to read.

My intention is that by reading the book you will acquire really useful transferable skills, which will help you engage with economics in any context such as television, radio reports or the internet. You will quickly learn how even some complex economic theory relates to the real world. Certainly by the end of this book I am confident that you will be able to give clear answers to some of the major economics questions that dominate our lives.

They include:

1. How do consumers react to uncertain economic times?
2. How did the credit crunch impact on small companies?
3. Should you send your children to a private school?
4. Why are the UK's airports such a disgrace?
5. Are you paying too much for electricity and gas?

6. Why are oil prices so high?
7. Should the government use the tax system to reduce carbon emissions?
8. How does Google make its money?
9. Is a national minimum wage a good thing?
10. Does privatisation always improve competition?
11. What is the best time to buy shares?
12. Why did Bear Stearns collapse?
13. Why does inflation seem to be much higher than the government says it is?
14. What is meant by a recession?
15. Does the US current account deficit matter?
16. What causes a currency to rise or fall?
17. Why are our top companies and brands being bought out by overseas companies?
18. What can shareholders expect from the companies they invest in?

Read this book and you will have the answers . . .

The main features of the book:

A selection of articles
The topics that have been selected for inclusion in the book will form the basis of any intro-ductory economics course. They also feature the key economic concepts and terms that are vital to understand. You will find a wide range of topical subjects covered. They include themes that recur regularly in the news so that once you have read through the analysis in the book these subjects will become much clearer.

All key terms explained
The specialised terms used in each article are clarified. The style of this explanation of terms is different from the standard approach of academic textbooks since practical analo-gies are drawn to help students from a variety of backgrounds understand the concepts.

An insider's view and self-review questions
Through a combination of practical and academic skills the articles are brought to life in a user-friendly way. Linked to each article is a selection of self-review questions, which can be used for self-study, or they can form the basis for further discussion activities in class.

Opportunities for further research
At the end of each topic there are useful suggestions for further reading in the main econ-omics textbooks. These references always include the relevant chapter and sometimes even particular pages from the chosen texts. I have attempted to highlight where certain economic concepts are particularly well explained.

Data exercises and web-based activities
In many cases a data exercise is also integrated which requires the analysis of certain sta-tistics related to the relevant topic. Where appropriate, there is also a web-based activity, which requires application of the newly acquired knowledge.

A message to the readers

Here are five reasons that I think that economics is an excellent subject to study at school, college or university, or in your own time.

1. It lies at the heart of a number of stories that dominate the news agenda every day. Just think about the Northern Rock crisis, the credit crunch, soaring domestic energy prices, rising oil prices, increasing globalisation, the costs of global warming and the ever-increasing wages that are being paid to top sports and music stars. Once you understand the basic tools of economics you will be in a position to comment effectively on these stories.

2. It should enable you to plan and organise your own personal finances for life. For example, you will have a view on whether you should take a risk and buy shares or take the traditionally safer option of leaving your money in a bank.

3. There is a good chance that your course will lead to a well-paid job at the end of your studies. If you get a good degree the investment banks will be queuing up to hire you!

4. Economics is so well covered in the written and visual news media. *The Economist* and the *Financial Times* are both great places to start to learn more about economics in practice. On the TV try *Channel 4 News* each night at 7 p.m. for some superb coverage of the main economics stories. And check out the Radio 4 website for a number of in-depth economics-based programmes. These include *Money Box* and many editions of *File on Four*.

5. Finally, it is just a fantastically interesting subject. Just pick up any good economics textbook and flick through a few pages. You are bound to find the answer to questions that have been intriguing you for ages.

I really hope that this book brings economics to life and I would like to wish you all the best with your studies and your future career.

If you have any comments or questions about the book feel free to e-mail me at: k.boakes@kingston.ac.uk

Best regards

Kevin

A message to the teachers

Firstly, I would like to thank you all for your support of my first book, *Reading and Understanding the Financial Times*. I received some really positive feedback from the academic users of the book. I hope that this book will prove equally useful to you. You will find a number of economics articles analysed in detail. This time I have added in more theory at the start of most articles, which I hope you will find useful.

I hope you enjoy using the book and that you will be able to use it as part of your teaching programmes. You may not want to use every item and there will probably be further topics that you would have liked to see included in this edition. This is inevitable as the aim was to keep the book fairly short and therefore I could not cover every possible economics topic. If you see a good article that you think would be appropriate for a further edition perhaps you could send it to me?

Thanks so much for using the book and I hope you continue to enjoy teaching economics.

If you have any comments or questions about the book feel free to e-mail me at:

k.boakes@kingston.ac.uk

Best Regards

Kevin

Kevin's blog

Go to www.pearsoned.co.uk/boakes to access Kevin's blog for additional analysis of recent news articles and post your own comments.

Find out more about the author

Click on the book cover of your choice to access the accompanying blog.

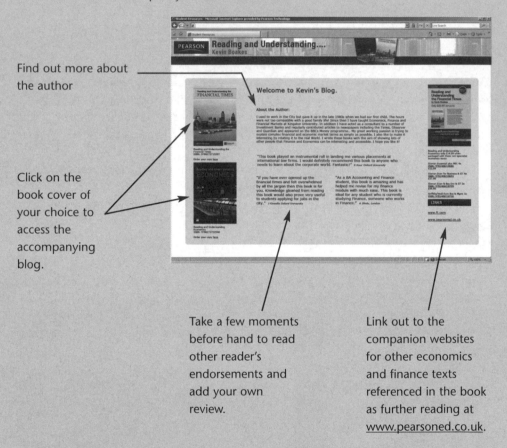

Take a few moments before hand to read other reader's endorsements and add your own review.

Link out to the companion websites for other economics and finance texts referenced in the book as further reading at www.pearsoned.co.uk.

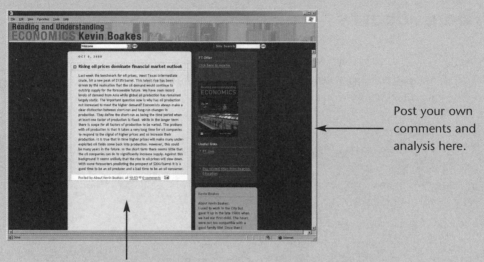

Post your own comments and analysis here.

Recent news articles are posted and analysed here by the author on a regular basis providing a further behind the scenes look at the economy.

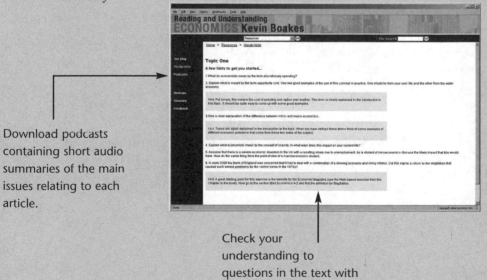

Download podcasts containing short audio summaries of the main issues relating to each article.

Check your understanding to questions in the text with the handy hints provided.

The podcasts

If you go the website that supports this book you will be able to download 23 podcasts in MP3 format. Each one provides a short audio summary of the main issues relating to each article.

I recommend that you start by reading the FT article and my analysis. Then you should listen to the podcast to hear the key points being reinforced. It is a good way to revise the key points in each topic.

The following podcasts are available to download at the book's website (you can also access them on itunes).

Podcast 1: Consumers cut back on the non-essentials.
Podcast 2: Falling supply forces oil prices to record highs.
Podcast 3: The economic price of a perfect education.
Podcast 4: BAA passes go and collects large price rises.
Podcast 5: The power of competition in the UK energy markets.
Podcast 6: The environmental impact of higher car taxes.
Podcast 7: Privatisation from Slovenia to Sweden.
Podcast 8: Google searching for new opportunities.
Podcast 9: A tale of unhappy shareholders at M&S.
Podcast 10: Small companies held in a bear squeeze.
Podcast 11: What price a national minimum wage?
Podcast 12: Iceland coming out of the winter darkness and into the chaos of spring.
Podcast 13: Inflation easy to define but harder to measure.
Podcast 14: US economy heading into recession.
Podcast 15: The rise and rise of Chinese inflation.
Podcast 16: Brown's golden rule under threat.
Podcast 17: Current account deficits and surpluses: a tale of two brothers.
Podcast 18: The end of the cash and carry trades.
Podcast 19: UK car industry goes up the junction as Jaguar and Land Rover are bought by Indian company.
Podcast 20: Time to go shopping for shares.
Podcast 21: Los endos for the monolines.
Podcast 22: Bear is all over the six o'clock news.
Podcast 23: Watching the ECB inside the Eurozone.

Acknowledgements

I would like to acknowledge the support of a number of people who helped me so much in writing this book.

First, I would like to thank a number of very good friends who gave me advice that helped me analyse some of the articles. I would especially like to thank David Franklin for spending so much time explaining the UK energy market to me. My thanks also go to James Watt who provided such useful feedback on some of the issues surrounding small companies and their finances. And last but not least, Lisa, who explained what a 'low-ball offer' was to me.

Secondly, thanks to my colleagues Bian Tan and Summer Wilson. Thanks also to Stuart Archbold, the Head of Accounting and Finance at Kingston University, for giving me his support with this project.

Thirdly, I would like to record my thanks to all the staff at Pearson Education who always make the whole writing process so easy. The many people involved include Emma Gibbs and Elizabeth Rix. I would also like to acknowledge the support of the Pearson representatives who go around the shops and the universities supporting the books on their list. They were very much responsible for the success of my first book and I would like to thank them in advance here for their help with this book.

Once again I would like to give a special thanks to the book's editor, Ellen Morgan. Her continued enthusiasm and support have been a key factor in enabling me to write two books over the last couple of years.

A special thanks to everyone at the FT for their support of my first book and the permission to use their articles again here. The quality of the writing and the analysis in the paper always impresses me. It was a well-deserved winner of the 'newspaper of the year' award in 2008.

Finally, I would like to thank my great family. I do appreciate that they have had to put up with a great deal during the writing of this book. I simply could not have got it done without their support. So, thanks to my wife Sue and my special daughters Katy and Rachel.

With thanks

Kevin

Publisher's Acknowledgements

We are grateful to the following for permission to reproduce copyright material:

Article 1 from Britain cuts back – but still goes on holiday, *The Guardian*, 27th May 2008, © Guardian News & Media Ltd 2008; Article 3 from Is it worth it? As the cost of private schools soars, we look at what parents get for their money, 28th February 2008; Article 4 from Inside the Googleplex, 30th August 2007; Article 8 from Crude Measures: Not everybody is paying higher oil prices, 29th May 2008; Article 18 from Are rising prices in China driven by the supply of meat or money?, 13th March 2008; Article 22 from How far can the dollar fall before Japan feels the need to intervene?, 19th March 2008; Article 24 from Time to go shopping?, 23rd March 2008; Article 25 from A monoline meltdown?, 26th June 2007 © *The Economist Newspaper Limited*, London; Article 7 from Petrol price rises and penalties for gas-guzzlers as Chancellor Alistair Darling goes green, *The Times*, 10th March 2008; Article 20 from Brown's golden rule threatened by red ink, *The Guardian*, 20th October 2006, © Guardian News & Media Ltd 2006.

We are grateful to the Financial Times Limited for permission to reprint the following material:

Article 2 Supply-side squeeze explains oil's relentless rise into record territory, © Financial Times, 16 April 2008; Article 5 BAA monopoly on airports under fire, © FT.com, 11 March 2008; Article 6 Lack of wholesale competition blamed, © Financial Times, 9 April 2008; Article 9 Privatisation: One step forward, © Financial Times, 17 December 2007; Article 10 Sweden privatisation scheme faces delay, © FT.com, 11 March 2008; Article 11 Investor fury at M&S role for Rose, © Financial Times, 10 March 2008; Article 12 M&S to placate investors over Rose, © FT.com, 2 April 2008; Article 13 Small companies face cash squeeze, © Financial Times, 28 March 2008; Article 14 Minimum wage increases by 3.8%, © Financial Times, 6 March 2008; Article 15 German minimum wage ruled illegal, © Financial Times, 8 March 2008; Article 16 Inflation jumps to 9-month high on data move, © Financial Times, 19 March 2008; Article 17 Overview: Recession fears rise after US employment fall, © FT.com, 7 March 2008; Article 19 Concern grows for Iceland as rates hit 15%, © Financial Times, 26 March 2008; Article 21 Why the US current account deficit is a cause for concern, © Financial Times, 25 August 2004; Article 23 Tata's bid promise to keep UK car plant open won over unions, © Financial Times, 27 March 2008; Article 26 Fed leads Bear Stearns rescue, © Financial Times, 15/16 March 2008; Article 27 JPMorgan lifts Bear offer fivefold, © FT.com, 24 March 2008; Article 28 Bear and the moral hazard, © Financial Times, 25 March 2008; Article 29 Eurozone set to receive more liquidity, © Financial Times, 29/30 March 2008.

In some instances we have been unable to trace the owners of copyright material, and we would appreciate any information that would enable us to do so.

Part **A**

Microeconomics

Introducing economics: scarcity and choice

■ Scarcity

In a world of unlimited goods and services there would be no economics courses and even more worryingly for me, no economists. Everyone would be able to buy as much as they wanted without any need to think about what they could really afford. In the real world we are forced to make economic choices every day of our lives. For most of us these are trivial issues while for others they can be a matter of life and death:

> **The unimportant decisions:**
> Can we afford to buy a newspaper today?
> Can we afford to stop off at Prêt à Manger for an expensive sandwich, drink and cake?
> Can we justify spending £65 for a ticket to see our favourite band in a few weeks' time?

> **The important decisions:**
> We must always remember that for other people in the world these decisions are much more important.
> Should a pensioner on a low income spend his last £5 this month on electricity to heat the home or on food?
> Should a family in sub-Saharan Africa risk drinking water that is highly polluted?

■ The factors of production

So if economics is about one thing, this is scarcity. Most of us have almost unlimited desires that are satisfied by ever-increasing amounts of spending. However, if you look around you will quickly see that the world has very limited resources. Economists have a term for these resources. They call them the 'factors of production'. These are:

a) Land and raw materials

A perfect example is oil. This is a finite resource where demand from ever-growing industrialised economies was far outstripping the available supply during the first half of 2008. The result was a sharp rise in oil prices.

b) Labour

The size and the skills of the available workforce is always a limited resource. Why do sports stars and music performers earn so much? The answer is simple. They are a scarce resource and so they can demand an enormous wage premium for their services.

c) Capital

This refers to the availability of factory units, industrial machinery and the transport infrastructure which are all vital components of the production process. What is the use of hiring 100 people and buying in the necessary components to make a car if you do not have the factories and the required machinery available? A company has to raise funds to finance the development of a manufacturing complex.

■ The economic choices and their impact

With all three factors of production you can see that the price mechanism plays a key role in deciding what goods and services will be produced. So as crude oil prices rise the oil companies will undertake new exploration projects around the world to discover new supplies. Similarly as the wages paid to soccer stars in the Premiership rise this acts as an inducement for the best players from around the world to join an English soccer team. Finally, if consumers decide that they want to buy less polluting cars the manufacturers will quickly switch production to those vehicles with lower carbon dioxide emissions. The price mechanism is central to driving the changes in the range of goods and services that are being offered. With the pace of technological development getting ever faster the range of products on offer changes almost on a daily basis.

A good example is the development of the television market. As someone born in 1960 my early TV watching was 100% on a black-and-white screen with just three available channels. The first time I saw colour a colour television was at a friend's house for the first World Cup Cricket final in the summer of 1975. In more recent years we have seen the onset of satellite digital TV and HD screens. The TV consumer now has much more choice in terms of the number of channels they can watch and the way they choose to view them. This situation has come about because of a multitude of economic decisions made by consumers (what they want to watch), manufacturers (what goods and services they want to produce) and the government (how it regulates the market).

Take Sky TV which currently has around 8m subscribers in the UK paying between £192 and £540 per year for their various bundles of channels. Economists would argue that this is a classic example of discretionary spending in the sense that it is not a necessity of life. This is in contrast to the more basic things like food and heating. We might enjoy watching a big soccer match live on TV but we do not need to watch it. In the wake of the 2008 credit crunch this is very much the type of spending that consumers might choose to cut back on. If they did there would be a profound impact on the economy.

Here are just three examples of how . . .

The value of BSKYB as a business might fall sharply. It makes most of its money from subscriptions. Take a significant number of these away and the profits of the business collapse. As the company's share price is driven by the profitability of the business the value of its share price would be much lower.

The value of TV sports deals would be lower. The Premiership sold its UK TV rights for the three years from 2007/08 for about £1.7bn. With lower subscriptions the next contract would be worth much less.

The wages of Premiership footballers would be reduced. Their value owes much to the value of the TV contracts. There might be second-hand Ferraris and Bentleys for sale!

■ Opportunity cost

This brings us to another key concept in economics, opportunity cost. Put simply, this means the cost of selecting one option over another. If we cancel our subscription to Sky TV we might instead spend the money on watching sport live or even playing it. Similarly, if a company produces cosmetics this might be at the cost of not manufacturing clothes. If you are studying for a degree you are facing an opportunity cost of not going straight out to work. This financial sacrifice will be considerable in the short term. Hopefully, in the longer term the higher salary you can command as a graduate will more than offset this cost.

There was a perfect example of the opportunity cost in action during 2008. Due to environmental pressures, farmers had been encouraged to use their farms to grow crops like rape seed and corn to be used in the production of biofuels. However, as food prices rose sharply governments around the world began to question this strategy and instead started to encourage them to switch back to food production. It might be good for the future of the planet to use less fossil fuels but maybe not if this is at the cost of even more of the world's population going hungry. As we said at the start economics is all about choices.

■ Micro- and macroeconomics

So in a world of scarcity economics is the subject that examines the choices that governments, companies and ordinary people make every day. It is normal to divide most economics courses and books into two sections covering micro- and macroeconomics.

Microeconomics covers all the aspects that deal with the behaviour of individuals and companies as economists try to explain how markets operate. It shows us how the supply and demand for a particular good or service determines its price. The study of microeconomics will enable us to have a better understanding of a whole range of subjects all the way from why a particular food item costs more in one shop than in another to what determines the value of a company's shares. The articles chosen for this section include ones on the UK energy market, the market for education and the role of government intervention in the economy.

Macroeconomics takes a look at the economy as a whole. In the articles analysed in this book you will see that macroeconomists are interested in the total number of people unemployed in the United States or the general level of price inflation in China. In essence they are concerned with the bigger picture.

■ Financial markets and institutions

The final section of the book covers financial markets and institutions. This is because when you read about economics in the newspapers these subjects tend to play a key role. This section also shows the international dimension of the book. The featured topic focuses on the reasons for and the consequences of the failure of Bear Stearns, the US investment bank.

I have analysed the following article, 'Britain cuts back – but still goes on holiday', *The Guardian*, 27 May 2008, to illustrate the basic concepts you have just been introduced to, as well as a few more.

These include:

■ What is economics?

■ Micro- and macroeconomics

■ The economic problem of scarcity

■ Discretionary and basic consumption

■ Consumer services

■ The International Monetary Fund

■ Economic slowdown

■ Stagflation

■ Inflation.

A question of choice?

Normally the first person who sees the initial draft of my writing is my ever-patient wife who reads it through and offers her comments. She is a perfect critic: sympathetic and supportive but always willing to tell me if something I have just written makes no sense. With this article I will have to resist the temptation to show it to her for at least a couple of weeks. The problem is that it is her birthday very soon and I have arranged for her to go to London and have a really special haircut at a top salon. I have to admit that the idea for this came from one of those Sunday newspaper supplements where people write in to an agony aunt for advice. In this case a worried man felt that he had been neglecting his wife a little recently and he wanted to use the occasion of her forthcoming birthday to make amends. The magazine's relationship expert gave him this advice:

1. Go to the make-up counter in a good department store and find the smartest, best-dressed assistant on show. Tell her that you want to get a really nice selection of make-up products and leave the choice entirely to her. Believe me, she will know best.

2. Most women love a fantastic haircut. So find a top London stylist and book your wife in for the haircut of her life. Meet her afterwards tell her she looks amazing and then take her for a fantastic dinner in a romantic restaurant.

3. With this strategy you cannot go wrong. All your recent neglect will be forgotten and a few months of marital bliss are guaranteed.

That sounded simple so the expensive hairdresser and restaurant are all booked for the big day . . .

Article 1

Guardian, 27 May 2008

Britain cuts back – but still goes on holiday

Mark Milner, industrial editor

Holidays are still being taken despite the gloomy economic picture.

British consumers are tightening their belts in the face of economic uncertainty, spending less on eating out, going to the cinema, working out at the gym or having their hair done, according to the CBI.

Consumer services companies are suffering their worst period since the end of 2001, with business volumes and values slumping over the past three months at a time when costs have risen rapidly.

The latest CBI services sector survey, published today, shows professional services companies – such as lawyers, architects, IT companies, accountants and head hunters – fared better. They continued to grow but at well below previous levels.

'Service sector firms are concerned about their business prospects,' said Ian McCafferty, the CBI's chief economic adviser. 'Consumers are reining in spending on leisure, entertainment and eating out, while professionals offering services such as accountancy, property and law have seen their profits flatten off as costs continue to grow.'

Within the consumer services sector, the CBI said that only travel firms saw business grow but with costs rising rapidly and little scope for passing on the increase to consumers, profitability fell at a record rate.

'Travel companies reported healthy demand for holidays in the past three months, with people more inclined to take a well-earned break as rising costs put greater demands on household spending,' McCafferty said.

Companies providing transport for goods and post were hard hit, with volumes falling at their fastest rates since the CBI survey began in 1998 and employment levels plummeting.

The survey showed the telecommunications and IT sector saw sharply higher volumes driven by aggressive price-cutting while marketing companies saw profitability rising at a record rate.

The latest evidence of the uncertainties facing the economy comes days after the International Monetary Fund predicted slower growth in Britain, urged the government to press on with planned tax increases and warned there was little scope for further interest rates cuts.

In an interview published yesterday George Soros added to the gloom, warning that the soaring oil price was a bubble that would be deflated only by recession in the US and Britain.

'Speculation is increasingly affecting the price,' the financier told the Daily Telegraph. 'The price has this parabolic shape which is characteristic of bubbles.'

Soros, best known for his role in helping drive the pound out of the exchange rate mechanism on Black Wednesday, warned that the economic outlook was bleak.

'I think the dislocations will be greater because you also have the implications of the house price decline, which you didn't have in the 1970s – so you had stagflation and transfer of purchasing power to the oil-producing countries, but here you also have the housing crisis.'

Oil prices, which had reached a record $135 last week, climbed back above $133 on supply worries yesterday after an explosion at a facility in Nigeria and a shut-in at a field in the North Sea.

Norwegian oil and gas producer StatoilHydro said Statfjord A in the North Sea, which produces 19,000 barrels of oil a day, remains closed after an oil leak on Saturday. The leak halted output of about 138,000 barrels a day at Statfjord and two linked fields. Output at the other two fields has since been restored.

Oil prices have climbed by about a third this year as investors seeking a hedge against inflation and the falling dollar have switched into commodities. Worries that supply will struggle to keep up with demand over the next few years also continue to support prices.

On Sunday the United Arab Emirates said it was ready to boost output if necessary. 'We are always happy to put more oil in the market if the market needs more,' oil minister Mohammed al-Hamli said. He declined to say if the UAE planned to boost output in June.

■ The analysis

In the first half of 2008 the UK economy began to show clear signs that the credit crunch was biting hard with economists watching consumers' buying decisions closely. When economic activity slows and unemployment increases economists expect us all to behave far more cautiously. The consumer shows this in terms of lower spending on all the goods and services that can be classified as discretionary items in the sense that they are 'nice to have' rather than 'need to have'. So we might cancel the trip to the pub, a meal out and the subscription to the DVD rental service. However, the weekly food shop is secure.

This article suggests that the biggest losers in the latest downturn were the restaurants, hairdressers and gyms. 'Consumer services companies are suffering their worst period since the end of 2001, with business volumes and values slumping over the past three months at a time when costs have risen rapidly.'

In contrast, according to the latest survey by the Confederation of British Industry (CBI), the downturn had not yet translated itself into an adverse impact on the professional services companies such as accountants and lawyers. Their businesses were still growing albeit at a slower rate than in the recent past.

As we saw in the introduction to this topic, economics is all about the choices we make. This is perfectly illustrated here with the claim that the one thing that appeared to be sacrosanct to UK consumers was their annual holiday. It might well be a case of consumers wanting to escape their economic problems for at least a few days in the sun. As a result the travel companies were able to report a continued strong demand for the holiday packages that they were selling on their internet sites and in their brochures and shops.

However, looking further ahead, even this sector could not be too confident. The latest survey of the UK economy from the highly influential International Monetary Fund (IMF) forecasts much slower economic activity in coming months. With the government's finances also in a poor state the IMF urged it to persist with planned increases in taxes which could only further damage consumer spending in the year ahead. There looked to be no respite available from lower interest rates as the IMF warned that there was little prospect of further interest rate cuts ahead.

When the UK economy is in crisis it seems that the newspapers always turn to one man for his view. His name is George Soros and he was the founder of Soros Fund Management and the Quantum Fund in particular. He came to prominence in 1992 on the so-called Black Wednesday (16 September 1992) when he made a fortune from the collapse of sterling on the foreign exchange markets. In this latest crisis he was reported as saying that the soaring oil price bubble would only be deflated by a recession in both the US and the UK. He offers a very gloomy outlook for the UK economy. He contrasts the present situation with the 1970s when, in the wake of the oil crisis, stagflation occurred with a combination of an economic slowdown and very high price inflation. He speculated that this time it could be even worse with the same factors present but now combined with the fallout from the crisis in the housing market where prices were falling sharply.

Against this background UK consumers seemed about to face a severe lesson in the realities of economics. They were confronted for the first time in many years with hard choices between what they needed to have and what they actually could afford. I think I had better end this now as I need to make a couple of quick phone calls to a hairdresser and a restaurant. Anyway I am sure my wife would rather have a nice new pair of socks and a jumper!

■ Key terms

1. **Economic uncertainty**

   This is when there the future course of economic activity cannot be predicted with any degree of confidence. There might be a strong chance of a severe downturn but there is a doubt about the timing and the severity of this outcome.

2. **Consumer service companies**

   Put simply these are businesses that make their living by supplying services to their customers. In this article good examples include hairdressers and gym instructors.

3. **Confederation of British Industry**

   The Confederation of British Industry (CBI) is widely described as the employers' organisation. It is a voluntary group made up of around 1500 UK-based manufacturing companies. It carries out a wide range of surveys to gauge its members' views on the current state of economy activity. In this article the focus is very much on its survey of the services sector.

4. **International Monetary Fund**

   The IMF is a large international organisation with some 1801 members. It was set up in the mid-1940s with the aim of

   'Promoting international monetary cooperation, exchange stability, and orderly exchange arrangements; to foster economic growth and high levels of employment; and to provide temporary financial assistance to countries to help ease balance of payments adjustment.'

5. **Recession**

   A severe economic slowdown normally defined as two or more successive quarters of negative economic growth.

6. **Stagflation**

   This is the nightmare combination for macroeconomists. An economy goes through a period of very weak economic growth combined with high unemployment. This is accompanied by a continued significantly high level of price inflation.

7. **Purchasing power**

   Economists normally use this term to define the value of money in terms of the quantity and quality of goods it can be used to purchase. In this article it is being used to refer to the shift in national wealth from the rich industrialised countries of the 1970s (like the United States) to the oil producers (like Saudi Arabia).

8. **Hedge**

   This term is widely used in financial markets to indicate that an investment in a financial market product is being made to minimise the risk of any unfavourable movement in the price of a particular financial asset. In the context of this article it seems that some investors have been specifically investing in commodities (like oil) to protect themselves against a rise in inflation.

9. **Inflation**

This is normally defined as any sustained increase in the general level of prices for goods and services. It is normally measured by a consumer price index that records the monthly changes in a basket of goods and services reflecting typical spending patterns across different time periods and in different countries.

■ What do you think?

1. What do economists mean by the term discretionary spending?
2. Explain what is meant by the term opportunity cost. Give two good examples of the use of this concept in practice. One should be from your own life and the other from the wider economy.
3. Give a clear explanation of the difference between micro- and macroeconomics.
4. Explain what economists mean by the concept of scarcity. In what ways does this impact on your current life?
5. Assume that there is a severe economic downturn in the UK with a resulting sharp rise in unemployment. As a student of microeconomics discuss the likely impact that this would have. Now do the same thing from the point of view of a macroeconomics student.
6. In early 2008 the Bank of England was concerned that it had to deal with a combination of a slowing economy and rising inflation. Did this signal a return to the stagflation that caused such severe problems for the central banks in the 1970s?

■ The Web

Go to the website for *The Economist* magazine.
This is at: **www.economist.com**.
Now go to the section titled 'Finance and Economics'.
Select the section within this called Economics A–Z.
Find the definitions here for the following key economic concepts:

1. Positive economics
2. Command economy
3. Mixed economy
4. Demand
5. Supply
6. Consumption.

You are required to read this and now make sure you understand them by putting them in your own words.

■ Research

Begg, D. and Ward, D., (2007) *Economics for Business*, 2nd edition, Maidenhead: McGraw-Hill. You should look at Chapter 1.

Begg, D., Fischer, S. and Dornbusch, R., (2008) *Economics*, 9th edition, Maidenhead: McGraw-Hill. You should look at Chapter 1. The major economic issues are set out on pages 4–7.

Gillespie, A., (2007) *Foundations of Economics*, 1st edition, Oxford: Oxford University Press. You should focus on Chapter 1 for an excellent introduction to economics. There is a good account of the key terms and concepts in economics starting on page 11.

Sloman, J., (2007) *Essentials of Economics*, 4th edition, Harlow: Financial Times Prentice Hall. You should look at the Introduction (Economic issues). The distinction between micro- and macro-economics is well explained on pages 6–7.

Sloman, J., (2008) *Economics and the Business Environment*, 2nd edition, Harlow: Financial Times Prentice Hall. Chapter 1 looks at some of these issues from the viewpoint of businesses.

Sloman, J, and Hinde, K., *Economics for Business*, 4th edition, Harlow: Financial Times Prentice Hall. You should look at Chapter 2, page 21 for a clear outline of the difference between macro-economics and microeconomics.

Go to **www.pearsoned.co.uk/boakes** to access Kevin's blog for additional analysis of recent topical news articles and to post your own comments. Download podcasts containing short audio summaries of the main issues relating to each article and check your understanding of in-text questions with the handy hints provided.

The economics of demand and supply

The opening chapters in most economics textbooks are devoted to explaining how markets work. In the model of supply and demand a market is simply a place where buyers and sellers are brought together. This might be a very visible place like an auction room selling antiques or an Internet-based marketplace like eBay. In either case the price is set by the balance between demand and supply. In economics we define demand as the quantity of a good or service that a consumer wishes to buy at a particular price. In the same way the supply is defined as the quantity of a good or service that a producer wishes to make available at a particular price.

The level of demand will normally decrease as the price rises. In the same way the level of supply will normally increase as the price rises. The price is the mechanism to provide incentives to the market participants to get them to change the quantities that they want to buy or sell.

Economists arrive at the market equilibrium price where the quantity demanded equals the quantity supplied. In reality of course most markets reach this level only fleetingly. Instead they are in almost permanent imbalance with either excess demand forcing prices up or excess supply resulting in falling prices. Economists view these price changes as important signals to return us nearer to that equilibrium state. So a higher price acts as a stimulus to either reduce demand or raise supply, or some combination of the two.

We look at this issue in detail in the first article in this section which examines the economic reasons for a surge in oil prices to over $110/barrel. In the second article in this section we look at the specific factors that influence the amount of a good or service that consumers wish to purchase in the context of the demand for private education in the UK.

The following articles are analysed in this section:

Article 2
Supply-side squeeze explains oil's relentless rise into record territory,
Financial Times, 16 April 2008.

Article 3
Is it worth it? As the cost of private schools soars, we look at what parents get for their money,
Economist, 28 February 2008.

These articles address the following issues:

- The problem of short-run and long-run changes in production
- Demand and supply

Article 2 Supply-side squeeze explains oil's relentless rise into record territory

- Equilibrium prices
- Elasticity of demand
- Cartels in action (OPEC)
- The economic choices
- Consumption and investment goods
- The earnings premium.

Falling supply forces oil prices to record highs

In the spring of 2008 the oil market was far from being in equilibrium. In this article the FT looks at the factors which caused the price of crude oil to shoot up to over $110/barrel. This latest rise was being driven by the realisation that oil demand would continue to out-strip supply for the foreseeable future. We had seen record levels of demand from Asia while global oil production remained largely static. The important question then was why had oil production not increased to meet the higher demand? Economists always make a clear distinction between short run and long-run changes in production. They define the short run as being the time period when at least one factor of production is fixed, while in the longer term there is scope for all factors of production to be varied. The problem with oil production is that it takes a very long time for oil companies to respond to the signal of higher prices and so increase their production. It is true that in time higher prices will make many under-exploited oil fields come back into production. However, this could be many years in the future. In the short term there was apparently little that the oil companies could do to significantly increase supply. Against this background it seemed unlikely that the rise in oil prices would slow down.

The impact of this latest price rise was being felt severely by consumers and businesses that rely on this precious commodity in their daily lives. This is clear from the rise in petrol prices to over $3.50 a gallon in the US and to well over £1 a litre in the UK. It has long been recognised that the elasticity of consumer demand for petrol is very low. This means that car drivers will still try to fill their cars up each week almost no matter what level the price hits. However, it still has a serious impact on economic activity in other areas as consumers look to make savings elsewhere In order to maintain their spending on petrol. The winners from higher prices are the oil giants like BP and ExxonMobil as well as the oil producing nations.

| Article 2 | Financial Times, 16 April 2008 |

Supply-side squeeze explains oil's relentless rise into record territory

Javier Blas

The rise in crude oil prices in recent weeks has appeared to defy the conventional wisdom that says prices should fall as the world economy – and particularly the US – slows and energy demand decelerates.

This has led to warnings that the oil market could have become the latest asset bubble following the boom in dotcom shares and house prices.

But that is to focus too much on

→

demand. What is arguably driving the market to record highs is supply.

Non-Opec production is growing far less than expected just a few months ago, weighed down by the first fall in Russia output in a decade and a sharp supply drop in other mature areas, including the North Sea and Mexico.

At the same time, Opec, the oil producer's cartel, has started to cut output, reducing production by about 350,000 barrels a day between January and March, according to the International Energy Agency, the western countries' oil watchdog.

Traders say Opec's cuts are likely to deepen in April after the cartel yesterday highlighted its concerns about the strength of oil demand during the spring.

The slower growth in non-Opec supply and the cartel cuts have offset the impact of lower demand growth, analysts say, tightening the market and boosting prices.

West Texas Intermediate crude oil yesterday jumped to an all-time closing high of $113.79 a barrel, up more than $2 on the day.

Paul Horsnell, head of commodities research at Barclays Capital in London, acknowledges that the growth in demand has been fairly slow in the past three years, but he adds that it has risen much faster than the growth in non-Opec supply.

The IEA says global oil demand will grow by 1.3m b/d this year, while non-Opec supply, including a large addition from biofuels, will increase by about 800,000 b/d. Additional Opec output will have to close the gap.

'Global demand growth has outstripped non-Opec supply growth in each of the last five years and 2008 is set to become the sixth year,' Mr Horsnell says. He expects the imbalance to continue.

Long-dated oil futures already reflect the market's fears that demand growth,

led by the industrialisation of emerging countries in Asia, will continue to exceed non-Opec supply, forcing the world to rely more on the cartel.

The five-year forward crude oil future yesterday surged above $100 a barrel, having jumped 32.8 per cent in the past six months. Over the same period, spot prices have risen 29.8 per cent to yesterday's intraday high of $113.99 a barrel.

The entire forward curve, which extends to December 2016, is trading above $100.

That increase reflects, in part, a structural shift that makes the current boom different to previous ones.

In the late 1970s oil companies were able to expand geographically, oil fields were conventional and production was located close to the main consuming centres. Today, most of the reserves are in countries, such as Saudi Arabia or Mexico, that ban foreign investment, in challenging environments such as east Siberia or in politically inhospitable countries such as Iran. Otherwise, there are fields producing non-conventional oil such as Canada's tar sands.

One reason for the long-dated futures price jump is that cost inflation is eating into international oil companies' extra investment in exploration, according to a recent analysis by the International Monetary Fund.

It found that nominal investment surged in 2006 to about $250bn from about $80bn in the early 1990s. But surging costs 'meant that this did not translate into large real investment increases', the IMF said, pointing out that real investment, adjusted for inflation costs, moved from about $80bn in 1994 to $115bn in 2006.

Adam Sieminski, chief energy economist at Deutsche Bank in Washington, says that the exploration and development costs for US-based international oil companies have risen from a low of $5.4 a barrel in 1995 to about $22.8 a barrel in 2007.

'The pace of the rise in price since the mid-1990s has been a stunning development that mirrored the impressive decline in costs from $20 a barrel in 1980,' he says.

Meanwhile, fears that the world's biggest oil producers cannot keep up with demand have escalated after the warning from a senior Russian oil executive that the country's output has peaked.

Leonid Fedun, vicepresident of Lukoil, Russia's largest independent oil company, told the Financial Times that he believed last year's Russian oil production of about 10m b/d was the highest he would see 'in his lifetime'.

If Mr Fedun's warning proves correct – and analysts say this year's production declines support his view – medium-term oil supply and demand forecasts that rely on further Russian oil output growth could be wrong.

The IEA's latest medium-term outlook, published in July, points to Russia as the third largest contributor to an expected 2.6m b/d increase in non-Opec supply, just behind Brazil and biofuels. It said that Russia would increase its production to 10.5m b/d in 2012, about 600,000 b/d above last year's level.

But it is not only Russian production that could fall short. Analysts believe that the current rise in food prices raises questions over whether biofuels will contribute as much as expected to fuel needs if acreage devoted to biofuels is reduced. If that is the case, it is all too likely that the world will become more dependent on new supplies from Opec, Brazil, Canada, Kazakhstan and Azerbaijan.

■ The analysis

This article examines the various factors that contributed to the latest sharp spike in world oil prices and resulted in the price of a barrel of West Texas Intermediate crude oil, the benchmark for global markets, breaking through the important $110 barrier. This was a little surprising as economists might have expected a period of softer prices in the wake of the worldwide economic slowdown. However, this was very much a case of the rising price reflecting a lack of supply which more than offset any slight fall in demand.

When you examine the supply of oil it makes sense to split this into that from the Organization of Petroleum Exporting Countries (OPEC) and the rest from the non-OPEC producers. The International Energy Agency (IEA) carefully monitors the activities of OPEC. It reported a fall in their supply of some 350,000 barrels per day in the first quarter of 2008. Unfortunately this was coming at a time of falling non-OPEC production with lower levels reported from Russia, Mexico and the North Sea. This had resulted in a serious shortfall in the supply of oil when compared to the level of demand which was still strong partly due to the increased usage by former emerging economies, which had become industrialised.

The FT article quotes Paul Horsnell, head of commodities research at Barclays Capital, as saying that while global oil demand will increase by 1.3m barrels a day this will not be satisfied by a growth of just 800,000 in non-OPEC supply. The question is whether OPEC will be willing to raise production to make up this shortfall. As Mr Horsnell says, 'Global demand growth has outstripped non-OPEC supply growth in each of the last five years and 2008 is set to become the sixth year.'

At this time there was also a growing move to view commodities like oil as an additional vehicle for investors who were fleeing the financial markets that were tied to a falling dollar. It certainly looked more attractive than the US stock market which had fallen sharply in the last year. These new investment trends combined with long-term supply fears were reflected in the oil futures markets. In these markets the buyer agrees to take delivery and the seller agrees to supply a fixed amount of oil for some set dates in the future and at a set location. The most commonly traded futures contract in the oil market would be for delivery in the next month. However, at this time even the five-year forward crude oil price was above the $100/barrel level. Indeed, the level of all futures contracts extending all the way to 2016 was now above $100/barrel.

What were the chances that higher oil prices would lead to increased supply in coming years? The truth was that investment spending on oil exploration projects had shot up to $250bn in 2006, but this gave a somewhat misleading picture. Much of this spending had been offset by rising cost pressures which meant that the real increase in investment was much less. The chief energy economist at Deutsche Bank in Washington highlighted this trend, pointing to the development costs of a barrel of oil which had soared from $5.4/barrel in 1995 to nearer $23/barrel in 2007.

There were two more good reasons for oil consumers to worry about the future. First, it had been reported that one of the main non-OPEC producers, Russia, was now seeing a decline in its oil production levels. This was particularly serious as the IEA's latest medium-term outlook was based on Russia remaining the third largest contributor to an expected 2.6m barrels/day increase in non-OPEC supply. Finally, with world food prices on the rise oil consumers could not rely on a sharp rise in biofuels production to meet any shortfall in supply. Farmers might be tempted to return their fields to conventional food production rather than the rapeseed or sugar cane needed to produce biofuels. Against this background the economic power of OPEC looked as strong as ever and consumers would seemingly have to get used to permanently high petrol prices.

■ Key terms

1. OPEC and non-OPEC (oil production)

OPEC is the most important example of a cartel operating in practice. This is where a group of suppliers come together to create a formal agreement to control the volume delivered into the market. The members of OPEC have been meeting in Vienna since the mid-1960s to set the level of their output and to influence the level of world oil prices. Each OPEC member is allocated a specific quota that they are allowed to produce. The members include Algeria, Indonesia, Iran, Iraq, Saudi Arabia and Venezuela.

The non-OPEC producers include Mexico, Russia and Norway.

2. International Energy Agency (IEA)

The IEA has the role of providing independent advice to its twenty-seven member countries. It was founded as a result of the 1973 oil crisis in an attempt to coordinate the supply of oil in emergencies.

3. **West Texas Intermediate (WTI)**

   There are many different types of crude oil. They are differentiated in terms of their specific gravity and sulphur content which is largely determined by the origin of the oil. WTI is a light crude oil and it is the standard benchmark for oil trading and pricing in the US.

4. **Biofuels**

   These are types of fuel made from crops like sugar cane, corn or rapeseed. One of the main factors driving their development was the view that they were more environmentally friendly than traditional fossil fuels.

5. **Oil futures**

   Like most other commodity markets there is a very liquid futures market for oil trading. In these markets the buyer agrees to take delivery and the seller agrees to supply a fixed amount of oil for some set dates in the future and at a set location. The most commonly traded futures contract in the oil market would be for delivery in the next month. The minimum size of contract is 1000 barrels.

6. **Industrialisation (emerging economies)**

   This refers to an economy that has a very well-developed industrial sector. At this time we were seeing many former emerging economies go through this process and as a result become large users of oil as well as other commodities.

7. **Cost inflation**

   This simply refers to the higher charges being faced by the oil exploration companies. This would include labour (wages) as well as materials and transport costs.

8. **Nominal and real investment**

   The term 'nominal' means before we allow for inflation. The term 'real' means after allowing for inflation. For example, a company might spend £500m more on new investment this year compared to last year. However, if the costs of investment have increased by £400m over this time period, the real increase in investment is only £100m.

■ What do you think?

1. What are the main functions of OPEC?

2. What are the main economic reasons that the oil companies could not respond to the signal of higher prices and increase production much more quickly?

3. Why can it be very difficult to maintain a cartel in the long term?

4. Why might you expect to see a fall in oil prices as a result of the slowdown in international economic activity?

5. The article reports that there has been a sharp surge in nominal investment in new oil

exploration projects. Why has this not translated into a large increase in real investment spending?

6. Why might the new market in biofuels not contribute as much as expected to meeting the needs of energy consumers?

■ Data exercise

At the time of writing this article the level of fuel duty was set at 47.1p/litre of unleaded petrol. The retail price includes VAT charged at a rate of 17.5%.

If the retail price of unleaded petrol in a UK garage is set at 90p/litre:

1. How much is the total level of tax paid to the UK Treasury on a litre of petrol?

   Hint: work out the VAT payable/litre and then add this to the fuel duty.

2. If it costs the garage 23.2p/litre to buy the petrol what is the profit per litre. In addition calculate the percentage margin.

■ The Web

Go to the official website of the International Energy Agency.
This can be found at **www.iea.org**. Read the latest 'oil market report'.
Produce a short summary (one page of A4) outlining the current position in the crude oil market.

■ Research

Begg, D. and Ward, D., (2007) *Economics for Business*, 2nd edition, Maidenhead: McGraw-Hill. You should look at Chapter 6. A cartel is discussed on page 126.

Begg, D., Fischer, S. and Dornbusch, R., (2008) *Economics*, 9th edition, Maidenhead: McGraw-Hill. You should look at Chapter 9. There is a good discussion of the activities of cartels starting on page 171.

Gillespie, A., (2007) *Foundations of Economics*, 1st edition, Oxford: Oxford University Press. You should examine Chapter 5 to see the concept of supply explained. In addition Chapter 4 has a good discussion of the elasticity of demand.

Sloman, J., (2007) *Economics and the Business Environment*, 2nd edition, Harlow: Financial Times Prentice Hall. Chapter 5 has a good explanation of cartels on page 136.

Sloman, J. and Hinde, K., (2007) *Economics for Business*, 4th edition, Harlow: Financial Times Prentice Hall. You should look at Chapter 5. There is a useful discussion of 'adjusting to oil price shocks' on pages 96–97.

The economic price of a perfect education

It is safe to say that if you were eavesdropping on a typical middle-class dinner party the main topics of conversation would be either the rise and fall of house prices or some aspect of the British education system. As one previous prime minister famously said, 'education, education, education' is the priority of most families. The puzzling thing is that at a time of ever-increasing government spending on education there has still been a record amount spent on private education. It seems that many parents see this as a good-value purchase. It is seen to be a way of securing for their children access to the best universities and later on to the most lucrative careers.

Article 3

Economist, 28 February 2008

Is it worth it? As the cost of private schools soars, we look at what parents get for their money

Fee-paying schools have long played a giant part in public life in Britain, though they teach only 7% of its children. The few state-educated prime ministers (such as the current one) went to academically selective schools, now rare; a third of all MPs, more than half the appointed peers in the House of Lords, a similar proportion of the country's best-known journalists and 70% of its leading barristers were educated privately. There is no sign that the elevator from independent schools to professional prominence is slowing: nearly half of the undergraduates at Oxford and Cambridge were privately schooled too.

Many ambitious parents would like to set their children off on this gilded path. But there is a problem: the soaring cost. Fees at private day schools have more than doubled in the past 20 years, in real terms; those at boarding schools have risen even faster (see chart). Since 2000 fees have risen by at least 6% every year,

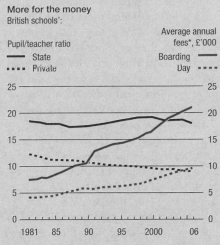

More for the money
British schools':

Pupil/teacher ratio
— State
···· Private

Average annual fees*, £'000
Boarding —
Day ····

Source: Centre for the Economics of Education

according to Horwath Clark Whitehill, a consultancy – double retail-price inflation and half as much again as the growth in wages. If this continues, a four-year-old embarking on a career in private day schools this autumn will have cost his parents around £170,000 ($335,000) in today's money by the time he completes secondary school. So even though more Britons than ever before describe themselves as comfortably off, the share of children being educated privately is barely higher than it was two decades ago.

Yet as the cost grows, so do the incentives. It is increasingly hard to be sure of securing an acceptable alternative. State-financed schools for the gifted are now scarce. Other time-honoured routes, such as finding God (and a place in a religious school packed with the offspring of similarly provident parents) or buying a house next to a good state school (the price will be hefty, but can be recouped by selling once the children have grown), are becoming harder. Ed Balls, the schools secretary, has signalled a shift away from increasing state-funded religious education, and many schools are thinking of choosing students by lottery rather than proximity.

On March 3rd parents all over England will get letters telling them which schools their 11-year-olds are to go to – and many will be watching with interest to see what happens in Brighton, on the south coast. For the first time, places in its eight secondary schools will have been allocated randomly within each catchment area.

Already the benefits are being felt by local private schools. Brighton College, in the town centre, has seen the number of 11-year-olds taking its entrance test rise by almost half. Its head teacher, Richard Cairns, says he is thinking of expanding.

Just what will these refugees from randomness be getting for their money? Researchers at the Centre for the Economics of Education have used data on earnings, social class and education to distinguish the effects of private schooling from other advantages that students at such schools may enjoy (such as having richer, better-educated parents). Those who left private schools in the 1980s and

early 1990s can expect to earn 35% more in life than the average product of a state school, they found, around half of which can be attributed to education, not background. That, they calculated, means parents achieved an average 7% return on their investment in fees.

If that were the entire benefit their children received, it would not be bad – but there is more, says Francis Green, one of the researchers. 'Private education is a consumption good, not just an investment. Long gone are the days of spartan dormitories and cold showers – kids in the private sector now have fabulous science labs and sports facilities, and access to a huge range of subjects and activities.'

The researchers also managed to pinpoint the way private schools work their magic: through better exam results, rather than through networking opportunities or better teaching of soft skills, such as etiquette or leadership. Once they compared state- and private-school leavers with identical qualifications, the earnings premium disappeared. 'In the past few decades, private schools have transformed themselves into highly effective exam-passing machines,' says Mr Green. They hire better-qualified teachers, and more of them, offering higher salaries to lure those with qualifications in difficult subjects such as physics, mathematics and foreign languages, and now have twice as many teachers per pupil as state schools do.

Whether today's parents can expect similar returns on their investment depends partly on whether fees continue to grow at a similar pace. One insider thinks this unlikely: many parents have remortgaged to pay fees, and with house prices shaky and banks tightening their lending criteria, this route is fast closing off.

But parents willing to take a riskier route could reap greater rewards. Another group of researchers interviewed parents and children from 124 well-off white middle-class families in three English cities. The parents had made the decision to send their children to poorly-performing local comprehensives. The children did well, with excellent exam results and plenty of places offered by highly-regarded universities, including Oxford and Cambridge.

One reason for their success, the researchers suggest, is that the schools, mindful of their positions in official league tables, were keen to keep these valuable clients. Teachers paid the youngsters more attention in class than they did to dozier students and arranged extension activities for them. One school, desperate to keep a bright child in the sixth form, even ran an A-level drama course especially for her.

The parents were delighted by their huge savings. But they had to work hard. More than half became school governors, and all monitored their children's progress relentlessly. 'They thought their children would do well being exposed to a more socially and ethnically diverse educational experience,' says David James, one of the researchers. 'But as people must do with more volatile, risky investments, they watched closely and were ready to pull out if needs be.' So parents inclined to take this route must ask themselves two things: what their risk profile is, and whether they are willing to be activist investors.

■ The analysis

There is no doubt that paying for a private education has never been so expensive. As *The Economist* article reports, the level of fees at private day schools has more than doubled in the past 20 years while those at boarding schools have been rising even faster. Indeed, the fees have risen way above the annual rate of inflation. A quick survey around the Net reveals that the average fees for private day schools are running at £10,000 per year as compared with more than £20,000 for boarding schools. Assuming a child was entirely educated in the private system from age 5 to 18 (13 years) this could amount to a total cost of around £250,000 (including extra costs) in today's money. Despite the cost the article reports record demand from families wanting to buy their children what they believe are the best educational opportunities. In response to this the private sector is looking to increase the supply of private school places with schools like Brighton College looking to expand to meet the higher demand.

So what are they buying? A quick survey of a few friends with children in the private system suggested that the following are the key factors:

■ smaller class sizes (less than 20 compared to 30+ in the state system);

■ better exam results (virtually everyone achieving good exam grades compared to the upper percentile, or the high achievers, in the state system who achieve a similar standard);

■ less tied into a rigid curriculum and strict testing regime;

■ superior extra-curricular activities and resources (e.g. sports, drama and music);

■ better chances of securing a good university place;

2

THE ECONOMICS OF DEMAND AND SUPPLY

- improved career chances;

- a school's stated aim of developing skills and confidence of each individual pupil is more likely to be realised in the smaller setting of a private school;

- networking opportunities later in life through the 'old boy (or girl) network' may be of benefit particularly in the world of work.

The above list reveals education to be both a consumption and an investment good. It is a consumption good in the sense that it can be viewed as being an end in itself. Pupils can simply enjoy the process of being educated well without any thought being given to their future economic success. They might for example enjoy being taught to appreciate great literature or to have access to superb sports facilities. At the same time the attraction of a private education definitely suggests that buying this service has been viewed by many parents as an investment in their children's economic future. They clearly see the years spent on 'the playing fields at Eton' as being useful in getting their children into a top university and later into a career that is well paid. It may be the perfect route to becoming a barrister, a City financier or even a future prime minister.

Economists try to measure this benefit by investigating the 'earnings premium' enjoyed by privately educated pupils compared to their state-educated counterparts. This article intriguingly suggests that private schools achieve this success by increasing the 'value added' for their pupils which equates to a significant improvement in their exam results. They quote the economist Francis Green as saying that 'private schools have transformed themselves into exam-passing machines'. How have they done this? They have hired better-qualified teachers and employed many more of them than a state school could ever afford. According to the article, their consumers (the pupils) get more individual attention and support and better-quality teaching.

Is there any hope for the pupils left behind in the state system? The answer is a definite 'yes' as long as they can maximise the opportunities available at their schools and achieve good exam results. The article suggests those children who can secure those excellent GCSEs and three top-grade A-levels within the state system perform just as well as those educated privately at great expense. However, this requires much more effort by the pupils and their parents. The latter must spend time ensuring that their children remain well motivated and that the performance of the state schools that they use is adequate. The article adopts a term widely used in economics and describes these parents as 'activist'. It is vital that those families that keep their faith in state education continue to assess the risks involved and, in extreme circumstances, be willing to withdraw their children from a school that is failing.

■ Key terms

1. Private and state schools

In the UK we use the term 'private' to cover schools that are not funded by the government. As a result they generally require the parents to pay fees before their children can be educated in these schools. In contrast state schools are fully funded by the government so that their pupils can be educated free of charge.

2. Retail-price index (RPI)

This was the main measure of UK inflation used in the UK until 2003. The RPI measures inflation by looking at the prices of a wide group of goods and services. Unlike the consumer price index (CPI) it includes certain important costs such as council tax and mortgage interest payments.

3. Randomness

This is where the outcome of some event lacks any predictability or pattern. In this context many local authorities introduced a lottery to determine which pupils would be accepted into a particularly popular school. This meant that the schools could no longer use set entry criteria such as religious affiliation, academic ability or location to influence their selection decisions.

4. Consumption good

Economists use this term to define the purchase of certain goods or services that give pleasure in their own right. The consumer does not purchase these items in order to derive any future gains. For example, I might spend £20 on a ticket to go and see my favourite football team. In contrast, I could use this money to buy a new textbook that promises to increase my knowledge of economics and improve my chances of securing a well-paid job in the future.

5. Investment good

Economists use this term to define the purchase of certain goods or services that they hope will result in a significant future financial gain. It can be compared to similar investments in physical capital (a new machine) or some kind of financial assets (some shares).

6. Earnings premium

In simple terms this is the wage differential enjoyed by one person compared to another. It is used to calculate the value of different stages of educational attainment. For example, you can calculate the earnings premium enjoyed by graduates compared to non-graduates.

7. Activist investors

We use this term in finance to cover groups of shareholders that range from private investors with small stakes in the business right up to the large financial institutions that often own a significant percentage of the equity of a business. It is normally among these larger shareholders that we find the activist shareholders. These are the shareholders who believe that the managers are not doing a good job and as a result they will attempt to alter company policy and even possibly seek to replace existing senior managers with new people who they think will do a better job. In this article it is being used to cover the investors in the similarly risky product which is state education. So that the parents in this situation must monitor their children's education at all times and if necessary pull them out of the state system if their children's education is failing.

2

THE ECONOMICS OF DEMAND AND SUPPLY

■ What do you think?

1. In what circumstances would spending on private education be a particularly good economic investment?

2. Explain what the difference is between consumption goods and investment goods.

3. What is meant by the term earnings premium?

4. If your child was clearly a gifted mathematician at a young age would it be better to educate them privately or in the state system? (Make sure you relate your answer to economic theory.)

5. If you were considering educating your child at a private school what specific research would you undertake?

■ Data exercise

Back in 2006 in a parliamentary answer Bill Rammell, the Minister of State (Lifelong Learning, Further and Higher Education: Department for Education and Skills) said that the government 'carefully monitors the labour market for graduates, including the earnings premium'. He went on to say that the latest estimate was that the average premium remained well over £100,000 across the lifetime of a graduate (in today's money) compared to a similar individual with 2+ A-levels.

You are required to try to find the latest best estimate for this graduate earnings premium. Explain why it is expected that this premium might fall in coming years.

■ Research

Begg, D. and Ward, D., (2007) *Economics for Business*, 2nd edition, Maidenhead: McGraw-Hill. You should look at Chapter 4.

Begg, D., Fischer, S. and Dornbusch, R., (2008) *Economics*, 9th edition, Maidenhead: McGraw-Hill. You should look at Chapter 20. Pages 399–401 define consumption demand and investment spending.

Gillespie, A., (2007) *Foundations of Economics*, 1st edition, Oxford: Oxford University Press. You should focus on Chapter 3 for a good introduction to demand. There is a particularly clear discussion of the factors that impact on the level of demand on page 29.

Sloman, J., (2007) *Essentials of Economics*, 4th edition, Harlow: Financial Times Prentice Hall. You should look at Chapter 1.

Sloman, J. and Hinde, K., (2007) *Economics for Business*, 4th edition, Harlow: Financial Times Prentice Hall. You should look at Chapter 6 to see a discussion of the factors that impact on the level of consumption.

Go to **www.pearsoned.co.uk/boakes** to access Kevin's blog for additional analysis of recent topical news articles and to post your own comments. Download podcasts containing short audio summaries of the main issues relating to each article and check your understanding of in-text questions with the handy hints provided.

Costs: in the short and the long run

At the time of writing this topic the rising level of costs was a subject of hot debate in the media across the globe. One example came from the UK with the government publishing data showing that higher prices for food, oil and raw materials had resulted in a sharp rise in manufacturers' input and output prices. The input prices are the prices of raw materials being used in factories. The output prices are the prices of goods as they leave the factories. The annual rate of inflation for input prices reached 28% in May 2008. This was the highest level since the 1970s. The annual rate of output price inflation over the same period jumped to 9%. These data were quite shocking to the economists who are paid by investment banks to assess the significance of such releases. As a result they entirely changed their view on the course of UK interest rates for the next year or so. The expectation had been for further interest rate cuts. This was now replaced by the near certainty that the Bank of England would now be raising interest rates.

At a more micro level the control of a company's costs is a crucial function for the production managers in any business. There is no point in the sales team winning new contracts if this additional business results in significant additional costs that make the extra production unprofitable. For any business to be successful in the long term a good understanding of the control of its cost structure is central to the financial health of the business. Before we begin to look at the article chosen for this topic let us define some key terms that economists use in relation to this subject.

■ Key terms

1. **Opportunity costs**

   When economists are examining the costs of a particular activity they like to apply the concept of opportunity costs. This is simply the cost of doing something measured in terms of what must be sacrificed in order to do this activity. For example, if you decided to undertake some paid bar-work this evening you would make a financial gain; however, there would be an opportunity cost because you would be forgoing the chance to have some leisure or possibly study time. In this sense everything that we do has a cost. It is the opportunity cost that we incur.

2. **Short-run costs**

   Economists define the short run as being the time period when at least one of the factors of production is completely fixed. For example, for a particular company this might mean that they have reached full capacity in a warehouse or at a factory site.

These short-run costs consist of both fixed and variable costs. These are both defined fully in the next 'Key terms' section.

3. **Long-run costs**

In contrast, economists define the long run as being the time period when all the factors of production can be changed. So in the example above, the company can now look to expand its warehouse or factory capacity without any problems.

4. **Average cost**

This can be defined as the cost per unit of production.

5. **Marginal cost**

This can be defined as the additional cost of producing one extra unit of production.

6. **Total cost**

This can be defined as the sum of total fixed costs and total variable costs.

7. **Economies of scale**

Put simply this is the reduction in unit costs that comes about from an increase in production. Let us assume that we have a textile factory that is able to produce 5000 packs of curtains per day. It costs the factory just £2 for the raw materials needed to produce each pack. However, the company has a factory that is a fixed cost of £5000 per day and this is completely independent of the production level. If the company produces 1000 pairs of curtains the total cost is £5000 for the factory plus £2000 for the raw materials, making a total of £7000 or £7 per set of curtains. However, if the company can raise production to the maximum level of 5000 units per day the total costs are now the £5000 fixed costs (for the factory) and the £10,000 variable costs (for the raw materials), making a total of £15,000 or £3 per pair of curtains. This reduction in the total costs per pair of curtains is due to the economies of scale.

8. **The law of diminishing returns**

We start with the production process being made up of fixed and variable units.

For example, for a particular company: the factory might be the fixed factor; the supply of labour might be the variable factor. If the company adds extra labour (more staff or existing staff working overtime) this will result in an increase in the amount being produced. However, in the end the company will reach a certain production level where as they add an additional unit of the variable input this starts to result in less and less extra output being produced. Put simply, their level of total output is still increasing but now it is at a reduced rate. This is the impact of the law of diminishing returns in action. This phenomenon might be caused by the difficulties in managing an ever-growing labour force at the point that it goes above a certain crucial level.

In the article from *The Economist* that is discussed in this section we see the importance of costs with a real example. This is for the Internet search engine Google where most of its costs are fixed. These result from establishing and maintaining its sophisticated network of super-computers. In contrast Google's variable costs are virtually zero. With this in mind there is a strong economic argument for the managers of this business to diversify into as many new areas as possible. This is because the additional revenue will translate straight into higher profits, which will be very good news for its shareholders.

The following article is analysed in this section:

Article 4
Inside the Googleplex,
Economist, 30 August 2007.

This article addresses the following issues:

- Stock market listing

- Advertising

- Profit margins

- Fixed costs

- Variable costs

- Profitability

- Diversification

- Incremental revenue.

Google goes searching for new business opportunities

In years to come it is quite possible that historians will divide this period that we are living through as BG and AG. So that any date from the late 1990s onwards will be AG. This will denote that it was after the birth of Google, the world's favourite Internet search engine. Just ask yourself this question. How many times have you accessed Google in the last week to find out some important piece of information? I sometimes wonder how we all survived in those distant days BG. When its founders, Larry Page and Sergey Brin, met as graduate students at Stanford University they could not have guessed at the global impact they would have in just a few years. As a business they fascinate economists for many reasons. This is not least because they absolutely dominate their market but claim not to be motivated by money. I guess it is easy to say that when they are each worth some $16bn.

Article 4   *Economist*, 30 August 2007

Inside the Googleplex

It is rare for a company to dominate its industry while claiming not to be motivated by money. Google does. But it has yet to face a crisis

In America a phenomenon might claim to have entered mainstream culture only after it has been satirised on 'The Simpsons'. Google has had that honour, and in a telling way. Marge Simpson types her name into Google's search engine and is amazed to get 629,000 results. ('And all this time I thought "googling yourself" meant the other thing.') She then looks up her house on Google Maps, goes to 'satellite view' and zooms in. To her horror, she sees Homer lying naked in a hammock outside. 'Everyone can see you; get inside,' she yells out of the window, and the fumbling proceeds from there.

And that, in a nutshell, sums up Google today: it dominates the internet and guides people everywhere, such as Marge, to the information they want. But it also increasingly frightens some users by making them feel that their privacy has been intruded upon (though Marge, technically, could not have seen Homer in real time, since Google's satellite pictures are not live). And it is making enemies in its own and adjacent industries. The grand moment of Marge googling herself, for example, was instantly available not only through Fox, the firm that created the animated television show, but also on YouTube, a video site owned by Google, after fans uploaded it in violation of copyright.

Google evokes ambivalent feelings. Some users now keep their photos, blogs, videos, calendars, e-mail, news feeds, maps, contacts, social networks, documents, spreadsheets, presentations, and credit-card information – in short, much of their lives – on Google's computers. And Google has plans to add medical records, location-aware services and much else. It may even buy radio spectrum in America so that it can offer all these services over wireless-internet connections.

Google could soon, if it wanted, compile dossiers on specific individuals. This presents 'perhaps the most difficult privacy issues in all of human history,' says Edward Felten, a privacy expert at Princeton University. Speaking for many, John Battelle, the author of a book on Google and an early admirer, recently wrote on his blog that 'I've found myself more and more wary' of Google 'out of some primal, lizard-brain fear of giving too much control of my data to one source.'

Google itself has been genuinely taken aback by such sentiments. The Silicon Valley company, which trumpeted its corporate motto, 'Don't be evil', before its stockmarket listing in 2004, considers itself a force for good in the world, even in defiance of commercial logic. Its founders, Larry Page and Sergey Brin, and Eric Schmidt, its chief executive, have said explicitly and repeatedly that their biggest motivation is not to maximise profits but to improve the world.

Too many sermons

Such talk can make outsiders wince. Book and newspaper publishers, media companies such as Viacom, businesses which depend on Google's search rankings and a lengthening queue of others are tired of moralising sermons. Some feel their own livelihoods are threatened and are suing Google. Even some employees (called 'Googlers') or former employees ('Xooglers') are cynical. Google is 'arrogant' because it feels 'invincible', says a Xoogler who left to run a start-up firm. The internal attitude towards customers, rivals and partners is 'you can't stop us' and 'we will crush you', he says. That 'kinder, gentler' image is 'mythology' and, he reckons, Google gets away with it only because of its impressively high share price.

That share price has quintupled since 2004, making Google worth $160 billion. The company has not yet had its tenth birthday. Yet Piper Jaffray, an investment bank, expects it to have revenues of $16 billion and profits of $4.3 billion this year. With so much money pouring in sceptics say it is easy to ignore shareholders and talk about doing good instead of doing well. But what happens when earnings fall short of Wall Street expectations or some other disaster strikes? Yahoo! and other rivals have gone through such crises and been humbled. Google has not.

Fifty cents at a time

Google's success still comes from one main source: the small text ads placed next to its search results and on other web pages. The advertisers pay only when consumers click on those ads. 'All that money comes 50 cents at a time,' says Hal Varian, Google's chief economist. For this success to continue, several things need to happen.

First, Google's share of web searches must remain stable. Thanks to its brand, this looks manageable. Google's share has steadily increased over the years. It was about 64% in America in July, according to Hitwise. That is almost three times the volume of its nearest rival, Yahoo!. In parts of Europe, India and Latin America, Google's share is even higher. Only in South Korea, Japan, China, Russia and the Czech Republic does it trail local incumbents.

Second, Google must maintain or improve the efficiency with which it puts ads next to searches. And here its dominance is most impressive. In a recent analysis by Alan Rimm-Kaufman, a marketing consultant, it took a whopping 73% of the budgets of companies that advertise on search engines (versus 21% and 6%, respectively, for Yahoo! and Microsoft). It charged more for each click, thanks to its bigger network of advertisers and more

→

competitive online auctions. And it had far higher 'click-through rates', because it made these ads more relevant and useful, so that web users click on them more often.

Perhaps most tellingly, advertisers do better with Google. Mr Rimm-Kaufman found that Google's ads 'converted' more often into actual sales, which tended to be larger than those originating from Yahoo! or Microsoft. This is astonishing, given that Yahoo! has just spent a year on an all-out effort, codenamed Panama, to close precisely these gaps.

But even lucrative 'pay-per-click' has limits, so Google is moving into other areas. It is trying (pending an antitrust inquiry) to buy DoubleClick, a firm that specialises in the other big online-advertising market, so-called 'branded' display or banner ads (for which each view, rather than each click, is charged for). And Google now brokers ads on traditional radio stations, television channels and in newspapers of the dead-tree sort.

Sceptics point out that with each such expansion, Google reduces its profit margins, because it must share more of the revenues with others. If a web surfer clicks on a text ad placed by Google on a third-party blog, for instance, Google must share the revenue with the blogger. If Google places ads in newspapers or on radio stations, it must share the revenues with the publisher or broadcaster.

Yet Google does not look at it that way. Its costs are mostly fixed, so any incremental revenue is profit. It makes good sense for Google to push into television and other markets, says Mr Varian. Even if Google gets only one cent for each viewer (compared with an average of 50 cents for each click on the web), that cent carries no variable cost and is thus pure profit.

The machinery that represents the fixed costs is Google's secret sauce. Google has built, in effect, the world's largest supercomputer. It consists of vast clusters of servers, spread out in enormous data-centres around the world. The details are Google's best-guarded secret. But the result, explains Bill Coughran, a top engineer at Google, is to provide a 'cloud' of computing power that is flexible enough 'automatically to move load around between datacentres'. If, for example, there is unexpected demand for Gmail, Google's e-mail service, the system instantly allocates more processors and storage to it, without the need for human intervention.

This infrastructure means that Google can launch any new service at negligible cost or risk. If it fails, fine; if it succeeds, the cloud makes room for it. Thus Google can redefine its goals almost on a whim. Its official strategy recently became 'search, ads, and apps' – the addition being the apps (i.e., software applications). Sure enough, after a string of acquisitions, Google now offers a complete alternative to Microsoft's entrenched Office suite of programs, all accessible through any web browser. A new technology, called Google Gears, will make these applications usable even when there is no internet connection. And Google is hawking these applications not only to consumers but also to companies. Ultimately it does so because, thanks to its supercomputer, it can.

With Google's cashflow and infrastructure, the freedom to do anything it fancies gives rise to constant rumours. Often, these are outrageous. It used to be conventional wisdom that Google would build cheap personal computers for poor countries. This turned out to be nonsense, because Google does not want to make hardware. Now there is talk of a 'Gphone' handset. This is also unlikely because Google is more interested in software and services, and does not want to alienate allies in the handset industry – including Apple, which shares board directors with

Google and uses Google software on its iPhone.

Sometimes the rumours are both outrageous and true. Google is experimenting with new ways of bringing broadband connections to consumers, by blanketing parts of Silicon Valley with Wi-Fi networks. It is planning to enter an auction for valuable radio spectrum in America, and thinking of radically new business models to make money from wireless data and voice networks, perhaps a free service supported by ads.

If it goes wrong, how?

Beyond its attempts to expand into new markets, the big question is how Google will respond if its stunning success is interrupted. 'It's axiomatic that companies eventually have crises,' says Mr Schmidt. And history suggests that 'tech companies that are dominant have trouble from within, not from competitors'. In Google's case, he says, 'I worry about the scaling of the company.' Google has been hiring 'Nooglers' (new Googlers) at a breathtaking rate. In June 2004 it had 2,292 staff; this June the number had reached 13,786.

Its ability to get all these people has been a competitive weapon, since Google can afford to hire talent pre-emptively, making it unavailable to Microsoft and Yahoo!. Google tends to win talent wars because its brand is sexier and its perks are fantastically lavish. Googlers commute on discreet shuttle buses (equipped with wireless broadband and running on biodiesel, naturally) to and from the head office, or 'Googleplex', which is a photogenic playground of lava lamps, volleyball courts, swimming pools, free and good restaurants, massage rooms and so forth.

Yet for some on the inside, it can look different. One former executive, now suing Google over her treatment, says that the firm's personnel department is 'collapsing' and that 'absolute chaos' reigns. When she was hired, nobody knew when or where she was supposed to work, and the balloons that all Nooglers get delivered to their desks ended up God knows where. She started receiving detailed e-mails 'enforcing' Google's outward informality by reminding her that high heels and jewellery were inappropriate. Before the corporate ski trip, it was explained that 'if you wear fur, they will kill you'.

Google is a paradise only for some, she argues. Employees who predate the IPO resemble aristocracy. Engineers get the most kudos, people with other functions decidedly less so. Bright kids just out of college tend to love it, because the Googleplex in effect replaces their university campus – with a dating scene, a laundry service and no reason to leave at weekends. Older Googlers with families tend to like it less, because 'everybody, even young mums, works seven days a week'.

Another Xoogler, who held a senior position, says that by trying to create a 'Utopia' of untrammelled creativity, Google ended up with 'dystopia'. As is its wont, Google has composed a rigorous algorithmic approach to hiring, based on grade-point averages, college rankings and endless logic puzzles on whiteboards. This 'genetic engineering of their workforce,' he says, means that 'everybody there is a rocket scientist, so everybody is also insecure' and the back-stabbing and politics are reminiscent of an average university's English department.

Then there is the question of what all these people are supposed to do. 'We kind of like the chaos,' says Laszlo Bock, the personnel boss. 'Creativity comes out of people bumping into each other and not knowing where to go'. The most famous expression of this is the '20% time'. In theory, all Googlers, down to receptionists, can spend one-fifth of their time

→

33

exploring any new idea. Good stuff has indeed come out of this, including Google News, Gmail, and even those commuter shuttles and their Wi-Fi systems. But it is not clear that the company as a whole is more innovative as a result, as it claims. It still has only one proven revenue source and most big innovations, such as YouTube, Google Earth and the productivity applications, have come through acquisitions.

In practice, the 20% time works out to be 120% time, says another Xoogler, 'since nobody really gets around to those projects for all their other work'. The chances of ideas being executed, he adds, 'are basically zero'. What happens to the many Googlers whose ideas are rejected? Once their share options are fully vested they consider leaving. The same phenomenon changed Microsoft in the 1980s, when allegedly T-shirts popped up saying FYIFV ('Fuck you, I'm fully vested'). Already some are going to even 'cooler' start-ups, such as Facebook or Twitter.

This week George Reyes, Google's finance chief, said he would retire. At 53, he is a multi-millionaire. Mr Reyes has maintained the company's policy of not providing guidance to Wall Street on future earnings, although his comments on growth prospects have moved its share price.

As Nick Leeson was to Barings . . .

Besides the slow risk of calcification that comes with growth, there is also the risk that Nooglers will dilute Google's un-evil values. Worse, Google might inadvertently pick up a rogue employee, as the late Barings Bank notoriously did with Nick Leeson. Indeed, Google is fast becoming something like a bank, but one that keeps information rather than money. This applies equally to its rivals, but Google is accumulating treasure fastest. Peter Fleischer, Google's privacy boss, argues that the risk of a malicious or negligent employee leaking or compromising the data, and thus the privacy of users, is minimal because only a 'tiny' number of engineers have access to the databases and everything they do is recorded.

But the privacy problem is much subtler than that. As Google compiles more information about individuals, it faces numerous trade-offs. At one extreme it could use a person's search history and advertising responses in combination with, say, his location and the itinerary in his calendar, to serve increasingly useful and welcome search results and ads. This would also allow Google to make money from its many new services. But it could scare users away. As a warning, Privacy International, a human-rights watchdog in London, has berated Google, charging that its attitude to privacy 'at its most blatant is hostile, and at its most benign is ambivalent'.

At the other extreme, Google could decide not to make money from some services – in effect, to provide them as a public benefit – and to destroy data about its users. This would make its services less useful but also less intrusive and dangerous.

In reality, the balance must be struck somewhere in between. Messrs Schmidt, Page and Brin have had many meetings on the subject and have made several changes in recent months. First, says Mr Fleischer, Google has committed itself to 'anonymising' the search logs on its servers after 18 months – roughly as banks cross out parts of a credit-card number, say. This would mean that search histories cannot be traced to any specific computer. Second, Google says that the bits of software called 'cookies', which store individual preferences on users' own computers, will expire every two years.

Not everybody is impressed. The server logs will still exist for 18 months. And the cookies of 'active' users will be automatically renewed upon expiry. This includes everybody who searches on Google, which in effect means most internet users. Then there is the matter of all that other information, such as e-mail and documents, that users might keep in Google's 'cloud'. Mr Schmidt points out that such users by definition 'opt in', since they log in. They can opt out at any time.

As things stand today, Google has little to worry about. Most users continue to google with carefree abandon. The company faces lawsuits, but those are more of a nuisance than a threat. It dominates its rivals in the areas that matter, the server cloud is ready for new tasks and the cash keeps flowing. In such a situation, anybody can claim to be holier than money. The test comes when the good times end. At that point, sharcholders will demand trade-offs in their favour and consumers might stop believing that Google only ever means well

■ The analysis

This article begins by linking two of the most iconic US brands of the 21st century. They are Google and the Simpsons. The claim is made that you know that your business has hit the mainstream in the US when it is satirised on this show. In this case the all-important moment is when Marge types her name into the search engine and gets 629,000 hits. This story shows how in just a few short years Google has come to completely dominate its market. It is almost impossible to imagine Marge using any other search engine. Many people now use Google for a range of other related activities. As *The Economist* says,

> 'some users keep their photos, blogs, videos, calendars, e-mails, news feeds, maps, contacts, social networks, documents, spreadsheets, presentations and credit-card information – in short much of their lives on Google's computers'.

However, this almost total success has come at a price. It seems that some consumers are now becoming concerned about just how much of their everyday activities are effectively being controlled by Google. As a result some consumers have concerns about how effectively their privacy is being protected. In addition there are some latent worries about the power of this business. While it was a privately controlled business the owners could reasonably argue that they did not have to aim to maximise profits. However, once the business was floated on the stock market in 2004 such sentiments became much less convincing. The company's initial share price was just $85. At the time of writing this article this had grown to nearly $600. Such an astonishing performance must primarily come from keeping their shareholders happy. This will largely be in financial terms.

How does Google make its money? This is quite simple: it earns money from all the adverts you see when the results of the search are displayed. Google earns on average 50 cents from the advertisers every time a person clicks on one of these links. With Google taking nearly two-thirds of the US internet search engine market alone this is a very profitable business. It has revenues of some $16bn per year, generating profits of over $4.3bn. Eric Schmidt, the Chief Executive of Google, is now keen to find new business opportunities to exploit. This diversification makes sound business sense to economists because of the structure of its costs. Google is unusual because virtually all

3

COSTS: IN THE SHORT AND THE LONG RUN

of its costs are fixed. They are represented by the world's largest super-computer made up of a 'vast cluster of servers, spread out in enormous data centers around the world'. In contrast any extra business will not result in significant additional variable costs so every 1 cent earned will translate straight into profits. This means that it is very worthwhile for Google to enter new markets even where the additional revenue is much less impressive than its core business.

So what is the future for Google? According to this article the company is now committed to push ahead into many new market sectors including mobile phones, television and radio and software products. This suggests that soon it might be the biggest business in the world, which will add many more billions to the net worth of its founders.

■ Key terms

1. **Stock market listing**

   This is the process of a company selling its shares on a recognised stock market. The company in question will be required to sign a listing agreement which commits its directors to certain standards of behaviour especially in relation to reporting to their shareholders.

2. **Fixed costs**

   Economists use the term 'fixed costs' to denote those that must be paid by a company no matter what their level of production. For example, a company might employ a member of staff to deal with all health and safety issues in all their factories. Her salary must be paid no matter what the production levels might be. Indeed, even if the factory's production ceases all together it will continue to be paid until the company decides that this position can be terminated.

3. **Variable costs**

   In contrast to fixed costs, these are the costs that are entirely dependent on the level of production. For example, for a company manufacturing curtains and other textile products these costs will come mainly from the factory's inputs like material and cotton. If the company receives a new large order from a customer the resulting increase in production will see a sharp rise in the variable costs.

4. **Incremental revenue**

   This refers to the extra revenue that a company generates by going ahead with a new investment project.

■ What do you think?

1. What is meant by the term 'opportunity cost'?
2. Explain the difference between short-run and long-run costs?
3. What is meant by the term 'economies of scale'?
4. Explain the law of diminishing returns.

5. What is the difference between fixed and variable costs? Illustrate your answer in relation to any company other than Google.

6. What is the difference between manufacturers' input and output prices?

■ The Web

Go to the website for *The Economist*. This is at **www.economist.com**.
Now go to the section titled 'Finance and Economics'.
Select the section within this called 'Economics A-Z'.
Find the definitions here for the following key economic concepts:

1. Marginal

2. Economies of scale

3. Division of labour.

You are required to read these and now make sure you understand them by putting them in your own words.

■ Research

Begg, D., Fischer, S. and Dornbusch, R., (2008) *Economics*, 9th edition, Maidenhead: McGraw-Hill. You should look at Chapter 7.

Gillespie, A., (2007) *Foundations of Economics*, 1st edition, Oxford: Oxford University Press. You could look at Chapter 9. Short-run costs are well explained on page 119.

Sloman, J., (2007) *Essentials of Economics*, 4th edition, Harlow: Financial Times Prentice Hall. You should look at Chapter 3.

Sloman, J., (2008) *Economics and the Business Environment*, 2nd edition, Harlow: Financial Times Prentice Hall, Chapter 4.

Sloman, J. and Hinde, K., (2007) *Economics for Business*, 4th edition, Harlow: Financial Times Prentice Hall. You should look at Chapter 9. Opportunity costs are explained on page 173.

PODCAST Go to **www.pearsoned.co.uk/boakes** to access Kevin's blog for additional analysis of recent topical news articles and to post your own comments. Download podcasts containing short audio summaries of the main issues relating to each article and check your understanding of in-text questions with the handy hints provided.

Competition policy in action

The satisfaction of participating in sport comes from playing someone who is of a similar standard. If you were to draw Tiger Woods in the first round of the World Match Play Golf Championship he would surely gain no fun from winning by ten holes with eight still left to play. Now if he gave you a four shot advantage each hole then the match might be slightly more competitive and you might even take him to the 12th or 13th green before he won!

Competition is also a very important concept in economics. It is all about the battle that takes place in the marketplace as one supplier takes on another. Economists regard effective competition as a necessary precondition to creating a fair market for consumers. The extreme form which is called 'perfect competition' exists where the following conditions are met:

a) There are a large number of buyers and sellers. This means that nobody is in a position to have dominant market power. They are all just price-takers. Each supplier controls a small share of the total market so that they cannot impact on the price by changing the amount of supply available. Each consumer buys such a small share of the total market that they cannot impact on market prices by changes in their demand.

b) There must be no barriers to entry for new buyers and sellers. This means they can enter and leave the market as they wish.

c) All firms in the industry must make an identical product. This means that if one producer raises their prices the consumers can simply switch to another source.

d) There is full information available to all buyers and sellers. For example, buyers must know what prices are being charged so that they can move to the cheapest available supply.

For economists these conditions define perfect competition as a situation where the suppliers and consumers are all price-takers.

While this concept is relatively easy to define and explain it is much harder to assess the relative competiveness of a real market in reality. In the first article we see how consumers can suffer where a particular producer has a monopoly of supply. This example focuses on the British Airports Authority (BAA) which was being allowed to raise prices at a level well in excess of the rate of inflation. This was particularly controversial at the time since the level of consumer service being offered by BAA was coming in for severe criticism as the opening of Terminal 5 had gone very badly wrong. There were calls from the airline industry for BAA to be broken up into different businesses to increase competition. In the second article included in this section of the book we examine the issue of the wholesale supply of energy in the UK. We will soon discover that the market for gas and electricity is extremely complex with many participants and various trading arrangements. This will make it a tough task for the official regulator, the Office of Gas and Electricity Markets (OFGEM) which was just about to start work on yet another investigation into this market. Its remit was to judge the level of competitiveness in the UK energy market.

The following articles are analysed in this section:

Article 5
BAA Monopoly on airports under fire,
Financial Times, 11 March 2008.

Article 6
Lack of wholesale competition blamed,
Financial Times, 9 April 2008.

This article addresses the following issues:

- The economic impact of a monopoly
- Impact on consumers
- Regulation through the Competition Commission
- Government regulation
- The impact of competition
- Price caps
- Defining perfect competition
- What defines a competitive market?
- The wholesale market in gas and electricity
- Changes in the wholesale market
- What factors define a liquid energy market?
- Excess profits
- Trading platforms
- New Electricity Trading Arrangements.

Monopoly: BAA passes go and collects large price rises

Whenever I have to fly into Heathrow Airport I cannot help but wonder what first-time travellers to the UK think when they see the squalor of the infrastructure and then experience the chaos of the baggage collection system. An honest slogan might be 'Fly from New York to London in seven hours and then wait ten hours to be reunited with your bags at carousel 7'. At the time of writing this article there was great hope of the rebirth of Heathrow with the state-of-the-art Terminal 5 being unveiled. Sadly, within hours of its opening this dream fell apart, leaving both British Airways and the airport's owner, British Airports Authority (BAA), to face the ultimate humiliation of both customer and media criticism.

This article looks at the public outcry that existed at this time as BAA was being allowed to significantly increase the charges on each passenger that landed at their airports. This subject was of great interest to economists as it was claimed that BAA was taking advantage of its monopoly position to make unreasonable profits at the expense of the airlines and their long-suffering customers.

Article 5

Financial Times, 11 March 2008

BAA monopoly on airports under fire

Kevin Done, Aerospace Correspondent

Airlines on Tuesday launched a fierce attack on the economic regulation of the three leading London airports, as the Civil Aviation Authority announced a big increase in the charges BAA, the airport operator, can set at Heathrow and Gatwick.

The attack came as a CAA official disclosed that BAA would be unable to meet its original aim of completing the planned £1bn Heathrow East terminal in time for the London Olympics in the summer of 2012.

Four of the largest airlines operating from the UK – BMI British Midland, EasyJet, Ryanair and Virgin Atlantic – joined forces in an unusual display of unity to demand an overhaul of the regulatory system and a break-up of the BAA London airports monopoly.

BAA's structure is already being investigated by the Competition Commission.

The airlines also called for Ruth Kelly, the transport secretary, to intervene to resolve the CAA's failings and demanded a moratorium on the price increases. The 'failing finances' of BAA, which operates seven UK airports, should also be made public, they said.

The four airlines said the 'dramatic' price rises at Heathrow and Gatwick showed the system was 'broken and needs to be changed'.

They complained the CAA was allowing charges at Heathrow to increase by 86 per cent from £10.36 to £19.31 per passenger during the next five years, while charges at Gatwick would rise by 49 per cent from £5.61 to £8.36.

The airlines said the increases would 'inevitably hurt consumers'.

Any rise in fares as a result of the higher charges is likely to be limited by competition between the airlines, however, and would be dwarfed by the impact of higher oil prices on airline finances and ticket prices.

The CAA said it was increasing the Heathrow price cap – the maximum fee the airport can charge the airlines – by £2.44, or 23.5 per cent in real terms, to £12.80 per passenger for the coming year from April 2008. Charges in the four subsequent years could rise 7.5 per cent a year above inflation.

Harry Bush, CAA group director for economic regulation, said improvements in airport facilities and service standards including £5bn of investment over the next five years and a halving of security queuing times 'have to be paid for in increased charges'. The outcome for passengers should be 'decently modern airports and consistently high service standards'.

Mr Bush maintained that the need for the capital investment – £4.79bn at Heathrow and £920m at Gatwick in the next five years – and increased spending on security had broadly been agreed between the airlines and the airports, but the carriers were not happy to have to pay for the investment.

He revealed that BAA would be unable to meet its original aim of completing Heathrow East in time for the London Olympics in 2012. Phase one of the project, which is eventually to replace Terminals 1 and 2, would not be completed until the end of 2012, he said.

The CAA said it had toughened the standards of service BAA must meet at Heathrow and Gatwick and had more than doubled the maximum penalties it would incur for missing targets.

Mr Bush refuted claims by the airlines that the CAA had given in to BAA pressure by agreeing excessive charges to help finance debts loaded on to the company when it was acquired in 2006 in a highly leveraged take-over by a consortium led by Spain's Ferrovial.

Analysts have expressed fears about BAA's ability to finance investment commitments, but it said on Tuesday it remained committed to spending £4.8bn in the next five years on UK airports.

■ The analysis

Almost exactly a year before this article was published the UK's Office for Fair Trading had referred BAA to the Competition Commission. This body has the task of investigating whether a monopoly or a possible monopoly is acting against the public interest. It was due to unveil its provisional findings in August 2008, with a final definitive report being available in December 2008. At this time concern centred on the decision by the Civil Aviation Authority (CAA) to allow BAA to make significant increases in the charges that they levied on airlines for every passenger that used their airports. This contributed to the widespread feeling that BAA was exploiting its market position to overcharge airlines at a time when its standards of passenger service were falling way behind an acceptable level. If BAA was not quite the UK's public enemy number one it was very close to it.

The anti-BAA campaign was being led by the airlines, which included BMI Midland, easyJet, Ryanair and Virgin Atlantic, who were united in their attempt to urge a major change in the regulation of BAA and a break-up of its monopoly at the London airports. The airlines complained that these price rises would be against the interest of passengers who now faced inflation-busting increases in their air fares as a result. Even the fierce competition among the airlines could not hold down air fares in the face of both these higher charges and the rising cost of aviation fuel. It was clear that UK passengers would have to pay a great deal more in order to fly in and out of London.

So how were BAA's operations regulated at this time? The main body involved was the CAA which had the task of being the main economic regulator for airports in the UK. It was permitting BAA to raise the landing charges at Heathrow and Gatwick by 23.5% and 21% respectively. It was widely thought that one reason for the CAA's perceived generous settlement for BAA was the recognition that BAA's relatively new owner, Grupo Ferrovial, the Spanish construction group, had vast debts, amounting to over £20bn. Indeed the company had taken out £10bn worth of additional debt just to fund the acquisition of BAA.

In June 2006 Ferrovial had combined with the Singapore government's investment arm and Quebec's state pension fund to purchase BAA. Despite reassuring words to the contrary the management of Ferrovial must have deeply regretted that decision. One problem was they had acquired BAA in a very different financial climate to the one that existed in March 2008. Back in 2006 the credit boom had been at its height with lots of cheap debt available and company valuations sky-high. In the much harsher financial realities prevalent in the spring of 2008 Ferrovial was struggling to refinance this huge debt burden. It was a terrible time to own a company with large borrowings and significant operational problems. Its newly acquired business, BAA, was a company in urgent need of substantial investment to make its airports fit for purpose. One additional and unpredicted complication was that BAA had been landed with much higher security costs in the wake of the heightened terrorist threats.

For economists the major interest in this case stems from the extent to which BAA was exploiting a monopoly position to the detriment of its customers, the airlines using the airports. BAA was regulated by the price cap system which was effectively a ceiling on price rises placed on most UK utility businesses that had been privatised since the mid-1980s when British Telecom became the guinea pig for this process. Under the price cap arrangement a limit was placed on the highest price rise allowed for these companies. The aim of this type of regulation is to protect consumers and to force companies to make efficiency savings which they can use to increase the rewards to their shareholders. One key aspect of the official regulation system employed to control BAA's activities was that the return on its capital was pegged at just over 6% per annum at both Heathrow and Gatwick. The limits on price rises ensured that BAA's return on capital would be below their preferred figure of 7.75%.

The CAA announced that it was raising the Heathrow price cap by £2.44 to £12.80 per passenger from April 2008. In addition there would be increases of inflation plus 7.5% in the next four years. These increases were justified by the expectation that they would help fund major capital expenditure projects to improve the operations at the London airports. Greatly enhanced security measures would also be high on the agenda. As a result the CAA would impose much higher standards of service on BAA. Despite these assurances the

CAA's decision on prices came in for fierce criticism from the airlines, passenger groups and the House of Commons's Transport Committee which called for the break-up of BAA.

In response to these charges Harry Bush, the CAA's group director, was quoted as saying:

> 'Passengers and airlines deserve better than they have been provided with at Heathrow and Gatwick in recent years. However, the resulting improvements in airport facilities and service standards – £5bn of investment over the next five years and a halving of security queuing times – have to be paid for in increased charges'.

If one result of the higher air fares was to be a reduction in air travel in the future at least the environmentalists who worry about global warming might sleep easier in the beds. That is unless they happen to live close to one of these airports!

■ Key terms

1. **Economic regulation**

   This refers to some form of government intervention that is intended to impact on the behaviour of firms and individuals in the private sector.

2. **Civil Aviation Authority (CAA)**

   The CAA is the UK's independent regulator of the aviation sector. According to its website its activities include economic regulation, airspace policy, and safety regulation and consumer protection.

3. **Monopoly**

   In economics a pure monopoly exists where only one single supplier exists in the marketplace. This gives them considerable control over the price that is being charged. It should not be confused with monopsony, where there is only one buyer of a particular good or service.

4. **Competition Commission**

   This is an official UK body that investigates whether a monopoly or possible monopoly acts against the public interest. It replaced the Monopolies and Mergers Commission in 1999. It can only make investigations following referrals by the Office for Fair Trade (as in this case) or the Secretary of State for Trade and Industry.

5. **Competition**

   In economics we use this term to refer to the battle between companies to win market share. For this to be the case there have to be enough buyers and sellers in a market to ensure that no single player has so much power that they can influence the price of the good or service. Economists define perfect competition as existing where many companies operate, there are no barriers to entry into the sector, the product or service is identical and the companies must all be price-takers. In contrast to this we sometimes have a monopoly.

6. **Price cap (Heathrow)**

   The main tool used to regulate former publicly owned utilities now operating in the private sector. It is effectively a price ceiling placed with a limit imposed on the highest price rise allowed to be made by these companies. The aim of this type of regulation is to encourage these companies to seek efficiency savings as they can take advantage of any additional gains to their shareholders.

7. **Capital investment**

   This term is used to cover any money that is invested in a business to buy new fixed assets like machinery, technology or industrial buildings. The aim of this expenditure is to enable the company to increase production of goods or services and generate higher income in future years. Economists see this type of investment as being vital in terms of securing higher rates of economic growth in the future.

8. **Leveraged takeover**

   This term is used in the context of management buyouts and it suggests that the new company will be financed largely with debt capital.

■ What do you think?

1. In the context of BAA explain what is meant by the term 'monopoly'. How might this company be using its market position to the detriment of its customers (the airlines) and air passengers?

2. In economics what is meant by the term 'a natural monopoly'? Do you think that BAA's role in owning and managing UK airports is a good example of a natural monopoly?

3. Define the term 'price cap' in the context of the regulation of former state-owned UK utility companies. What purpose does such a mechanism serve?

4. What is the role of the Competition Commission in the UK? Give an example of how it has encouraged greater competition in the supply of a UK product or service.

5. What are the possible reasons that the CAA might have awarded such large price increases to BAA?

6. What types of economic regulation can governments use to ensure that a company under public ownership operates more efficiently?

■ The Web

Go to the official website of the UK's Competition Commission.
This can be found at **www.competition-commission.org.uk**.
Now select a recent investigation that the Competition Commission has carried out. You are required to write a short summary of its findings.

■ Research

Begg, D. and Ward, D., (2007) *Economics for Business,* 2nd edition, Maidenhead: McGraw-Hill. You should look at Chapter 7. The role of the Competition Commission in action is well shown on the top of page 148 (Heinz deal).

Begg, D., Fischer, S. and Dornbusch, R., (2008) *Economics*, 9th edition, Maidenhead: McGraw-Hill. You should look at Chapters 8 and 17. Competition policy is well explained on pages 349–351.

Gillespie, A., (2007) *Foundations of Economics*, 1st edition, Oxford: Oxford University Press. You should focus on Chapter 16. The role of the Competition Commission is explained on page 210.

Parkin, M., Powell, M. and Mathews, K., (2008) *Economics*, 7th edition, Harlow: Addison Wesley. You should see pages 327–328 for the economic impact of price cap regulation. It is very well explained.

Sloman, J. and Hinde, K., (2007) *Economics for Business*, 4th edition, Harlow: Financial Times Prentice Hall. You should look at Chapter 11.

The power of competition in the UK energy markets

At the time of writing this article UK energy prices were big news. In the previous few months there had been significant increases in the retail prices of both gas and electricity. In the early months of 2008 British Gas, RWE npower, Scottish Power, E.ON and EDF Energy all announced that they would be making a double-digit increase in their electricity and gas prices. One company, Scottish and Southern Energy, initially used the gains from its successful trading strategy in the market to resist this pressure before also announcing increases for its electricity and gas customers from 1 April. As a result the average annual combined fuel bill in the UK would rise to over £1000 per year. The pressure group Energywatch responded to these price rises by claiming that the market was not competitive enough and that consumers were paying too much. Under pressure from the media the official energy regulator, OFGEM, announced that it would once again be investigating the UK's gas and electricity supply market.

Article 6

Financial Times, 9 April 2008

Lack of wholesale competition blamed

Ed Crooks

Customers are paying too much for their power because competition in the wholesale market has declined steeply in the past decade, small energy companies have told the FT.

Despite the widespread view that household bills are rising because retail energy companies are making excess profits, some experts say the real problems lie in the wholesale market.

Smaller companies argue that this should be the focus of the inquiry into the market by the regulator Ofgem, announced in February after sharp rises in gas and electricity prices provoked a public outcry.

The roots of the problems in the wholesale market lie in three changes over the past decade: the decline of independent power generation, the disappearance of a liquid trading market and the introduc-

tion of the New Electricity Trading Arrangements (Neta) to replace the old electricity 'pool' in 2001.

Independent power generation has been in decline in Britain since very low power prices in the first half of the decade forced many companies out of the market, including US groups such as *AES*, *AEP* and *TXU*. Today about 60 per cent of Britain's electricity is generated by the 'big six' integrated suppliers.

Electricity trading has been in decline since the failure of Enron, which played an important role in creating liquidity in the UK power market.

An initiative led by generators and investment banks to set up a new power exchange or trading platform has been making progress, but is still looking at possible designs.

Neta (later reformed and renamed the

→

British Electricity Trading and Transmission Arrangements, or Betta) is a freer market than the pool it replaced. But Dieter Helm of New College Oxford says it gave 'enormous benefits' to the big integrated suppliers.

'Once the market is voluntary, there is no compulsion to sell power at market prices and no ability to buy power at the market price,' he says. 'Neta is not a market that lends itself to transparent competition.'

Keith Munday, commercial director of Bizzenergy, Britain's biggest independent energy supplier, says: 'The wholesale market is not deep or liquid or reliable.' Bizz-energy has no generation of its own but buys power to sell to businesses.

Mr Munday says that while relatively large volumes of electricity are sold in the 'prompt' markets for delivery in the next month or two, very little power is traded further into the future.

'That means you don't have a reliable price marker and nobody knows how much money the integrated companies are making in each of their businesses,' he says.

Integrated suppliers such as *Eon* and *Centrica* argue that the wholesale market is working well. They accept that liquidity has fallen since 2002 but argue that it is still high enough to set realistic prices that reflect the costs of generation.

For Bizzenergy, the only way to be sure that the market is working is to force a formal separation of the integrated companies' generation and supply businesses.

When a company's generation arm sells power to its supply business, it would have to declare its selling price and give rival suppliers the chance to buy it, too.

Graham Paul, sales director of Electricity4Business, another small supplier, agrees.

'If the government really wants a market with true competition, power stations and supply businesses can be owned by the same organisations but would need some public gap between their generation and retail businesses,' he says.

Such a move would be a radical restructuring of the market.

Smaller energy suppliers argue that the lack of competition in the market could get worse if one of the leading players, such as Electricité de France or *RWE* of Germany, is allowed to buy *British Energy*, the country's biggest generator.

The government is considering the sale of all or part of its 35 per cent stake in British Energy, and *EDF* and RWE are both believed to be in talks about a possible bid for the entire company.

If British Energy ends up in the hands of a single buyer, tying up another 15 per cent of the UK's generation capacity in an integrated company, the pressure for reform of the market to mitigate the impact could be hard to resist.

Copyright The Financial Times Limited 2008

■ Analysis

This article will be analysed by answering four questions:

1. What were the main concerns about the state of competition in the UK energy market?

This was written at a time when energy prices were rising sharply. The reasons for this upward trend were rather complicated. One factor was the impact of the depleted North Sea and Irish Sea gas reserves which led to much higher levels of demand for the more expensive imported supplies. This was combined with a surge in oil prices with a barrel of crude pushed well above the $100/barrel level. One of the main reasons for this increase in international energy prices was that demand was at a record level. This had been fuelled by much higher usage in the former developing nations in the Indian subcontinent and south-east Asia. Against this background it was hardly surprising that consumer prices were rising strongly as the retail prices had to reflect higher costs of supply.

This FT article analysed the UK energy market in an attempt to discover whether ordinary retail customers were paying too much and, if they were, then who was to blame. The general perception as portrayed in the media at this time was that rising prices were in part due to the greed and the excess profits of the domestic retail suppliers of energy in the UK. The market was dominated by the 'big six': British Gas, RWE npower, Scottish Power, E.ON, EDF Energy and Scottish and Southern Energy. These companies certainly argued strongly that the supply of energy was competitive. In support of this view the companies could point to the much increased 'rate of customer churn' with figures showing that 5m homes had switched suppliers in 2007. This trend had been encouraged by the growth of price-comparison sites such as uswitch.com. The whole process of changing suppliers had also been greatly simplified to encourage this process. Certainly if you can assess the level of competiveness from the amount of doorstep selling and high-pressure phone selling there appeared to be a fierce battle for retail customers at this time.

It might be argued that the UK energy market was simply a good example of a high-volume and low-margin business. In these types of businesses when the cost of supply increases then all the main suppliers are affected immediately. As a result it was not surprising that the big six raised their prices at much the same time. This might be compared to the UK supermarket sector. When the cost of basic food supplies like bread increase you will see that Tesco, Sainsbury's and Asda will all announce increases in their retail prices. This was not a sign of market manipulation or collusion but rather the inevitable consequence of higher supply costs being passed on to the consumers.

2. How competitive was the wholesale energy market?

If the problem of lack of competition did not appear to lie with the retail energy market it might instead be in the wholesale markets. These are the markets where the energy suppliers themselves must secure the gas and electricity that they need for their own customers. Before commenting on competition in these markets it might be worth setting out some details on how the wholesale market for gas and electricity works in the UK.

Firstly, how does a retail gas company obtain its supply?

The market for gas is characterised by its large size and international scope. The way it works is set out in Exhibit 4.1. A retail supplier like Scottish Power will go to an independent energy broker who in turn will find the cheapest buying price and highest selling price available from one of their counterparties in the gas market. This might be a large producer like ExxonMobil, a bank that takes a trading position in the market or another retail supplier that wants to deal in the market.

Where did the gas supplies come from? They used to come predominantly from the North Sea but these domestic reserves were now in decline. So the bulk of gas supplies had to be imported from Russia or Norway. The balance came in the form of liquefied natural gas (LNG) which is a gas that is converted to liquid so that it becomes easier to transport. The UK government had invested large amounts of cash building new LNG capacity at Milford Haven. The new Langaled pipeline was intended to give the UK access to the continental European supplies including the massive Norwegian gas fields. Despite this expenditure imports of LNG fell to a record low in the spring of 2008. This was in part because LNG supplies were very price-sensitive and the UK had to compete internationally with countries like Japan that were often willing to pay much higher prices to guarantee that their needs were met first. The LNG suppliers viewed the UK very much as a secondary market compared to the various continental European countries that had longer-term supply contracts.

Exhibit 4.1

A retail gas company like Scottish Power . . .

Goes to a specialised broker (like ICAP or Tullet Prebon) who will search the market and find the lowest buying price or highest selling price for gas from one of the counterparties.

These will be one of:

a) The large producers like ExxonMobil, Statoil or BP
b) One of the banks or other financial institutions that trade in the gas market
c) Other retail companies that are either long of supply (they have a surplus) or short of supply (they have a shortage).

Looking at this structure it did not seem as if the wholesale market in gas was uncompetitive. There certainly seemed to be a good range of suppliers and they all seem to be 'price-takers' in a large international market. If the supply of gas in the UK market had a problem it was more likely to be because it had increasingly become the swing market in terms of international players. If European supplies were short the UK tended to suffer most as it faced the shortfall and consequent sharp rise in price. On the other hand when there was a surplus the UK market benefited more than most from lower prices. In this sense it could be argued that the UK wholesale gas market was actually more competitive than that in other European countries.

The way the wholesale electricity market works is set is out in Exhibit 4.2. On the face of it, it looks rather similar to the gas model. The two major differences are:

i) This was a market that was largely dominated by domestic suppliers. Although some electricity could be exported and imported via underground cables through France this was a small percentage of the total UK electricity market.

ii) There was a much greater role for the integrated companies that combined electricity generation with retail customers.

As a result it would seem to be fair to conclude that the wholesale market in electricity was certainly less competitive than the wholesale gas market.

> **Exhibit 4.2**
>
> A retail electricity supplier like Scottish Power goes to a specialised broker who will go into the market and find the lowest buying price or highest selling price for electricity from one of the counterparties.
>
> These will be one of:
>
> a) The independent generators like British Energy or Drax. The latter company owned the largest coal-fired power station in the UK.
> b) One of the integrated suppliers who combine generation and retail.

3. What did the FT article think was wrong with the wholesale energy market?

The FT article identifies three changes in the market that had inhibited competition:

a) The decline in independent power generation. This was apparently due to low energy prices in the first half of the decade that led to the exit of many companies from the market. As a result energy supply was now dominated by the big six integrated companies that combine wholesale and retail supply.

   From what we have seen above this seems to be a fair comment in terms of the wholesale electricity market but not for the gas market.

b) The absence of a liquid energy trading market. This might be partly due to the corporate failure of Enron in 2001. This business started out as an energy producer but was soon transformed into an energy trader. It was the first company to treat energy just like any other financial market security (shares or bonds). When it collapsed it left debts of $21bn, twenty thousand employees out of work and a large hole in the energy supply market.

   Again in the electricity market it would seem to be fair to argue that while there were large volumes of electricity being traded for 'immediate' delivery the market for delivery a few months out was relatively small. The contrary view was offered by two of the integrated companies that supplied the wholesale market. While both E.ON and Centrica conceded that liquidity in the market had fallen they still believed that those volumes were high enough to result in fair prices being set.

c) The introduction of the 'New Electricity Trading Arrangements (NETA)' which took over from the old electricity pool at the start of this decade. According to Diter Helm of New College Oxford:

   'Once the market is voluntary, there is no compulsion to sell power at market prices and no ability to buy power at the market price. NETA is not a market that lends itself to transparent competition.'

   The previous system, called the 'Electricity Pool of England and Wales', required all electricity generators to put all their electricity into a central pool. The retail suppliers would then place bids to obtain the amount that they wanted at this price. A 'system

4

COMPETITION POLICY IN ACTION

marginal price' was then set. This was the highest price that you needed to go to in order to obtain all the electricity that was required. Just like other auction systems used in financial markets all the electricity generators would receive this higher price for all the electricity that they supplied. This system was felt to be inflexible and uncompetitive and was replaced by NETA in 2001. The FT article quotes the expert from New College as saying that this replacement system was actually less competitive in practice.

4. Was there a new threat to the wholesale electricity market?

In the long term the FT article quotes Graham Paul of electricity4business as saying that

'If the government really wants a market with true competition, power stations and supply businesses can be owned by the same organisations but would need some public gap between their generation and retail businesses.'

This would be a radical step, requiring the separation of existing businesses into the wholesale and retail operations. It is unlikely that any government would be keen to take such a controversial step. Indeed, in the short term one action of the current government might actually pose an even greater threat to competition. The government was looking to improve the state of public finances by selling its remaining 35% stake in British Energy. If this were sold to EDF or RWE then it would push one of the last two independent wholesale electricity suppliers into the hands of the integrated companies. Not for the first time a government might be about to do something that makes financial sense in the short term but could have serious longer term consequences for UK energy consumers.

Wholesale gas markets: an interesting aside!

Arbitrage trading in the gas markets

Arbitrage is a very important concept in economics and financial markets. There is a particularly good example in the wholesale gas market.

The national balancing point is the prevailing price for gas in the UK. This is derived from the wholesale trade between producers and the retail companies.

The equivalent wholesale gas trading hub in Holland is called TTF.

Sometimes the prices in these two markets move out of line. As a result traders will arbitrage between them. This means they will buy supply where it is cheap and sell it where it is high. The result of this 'arbitrage trading' activity is that prices move back into line.

■ Key terms

1. Competition

Economists use the term 'competition' to refer to the level of rivalry between the suppliers in a particular market. It is suggested that a high level of competition is in the best interests of consumers by ensuring that prices remain as low as possible. You will also see this concept discussed in the previous article.

2. Wholesale market (energy)

We use the term 'wholesale' to refer to the supply of energy to the retail energy companies. These companies purchase gas and electricity from the wholesale markets.

3. Excess profits

Economists measure these as any profits earned by a company that are above the normal level of profits. This normal level offers a fair return on capital employed. It is accepted that a major cost for companies is the opportunity cost of not using their time and money in doing something else. They are taking far more risk than they would be if they simply left their money in a bank. So economists allow for this cost when they decide on a reasonable rate of return for them to earn. The normal profit will be made up of the riskless return plus some extra amount to offset this risk they take. Any level of profit above this normal level is termed excess in the sense that it is more than can be justified by the costs incurred by the business.

4. OFGEM

This is the body that regulates the UK's gas and electricity companies. It is supposed to protect the interests of consumers, ensuring that the supply of energy remains competitive.

5. NETA (pronounced 'neater') (New Electricity Trading Arrangements)

This was a new market mechanism that replaced the 'Electricity Pool of England and Wales'. Under this older system all electricity generators had to put all their electricity into a central pool. The retail suppliers would then place bids to obtain the amount that they wanted at this price. A 'system marginal price' was arrived at. This was the highest price that you needed to go to in order to obtain all the electricity that was needed. All the electricity generators then received this higher price for all the electricity that they supplied. This system was felt to be inflexible and uncompetitive and was replaced by NETA in 2001.

6. Liquid (trading market)

A liquid trading market refers to the level of trading that takes place in this market. The more trading there is, the more liquid the market.

7. Integrated suppliers

In terms of the energy market this refers to vertical integration. This is where a firm owns its upstream suppliers and its downstream buyers. So you have Centrica that both owns production platforms in the North Sea (upstream) and supplies its retail gas customers. This is very common in other markets. For example, BP is involved in oil exploration and supply while at the same time owning petrol stations supplying retail customers.

8. Trading platform

In finance we use the term 'trading platform' to describe the market where buyers and sellers can operate. It might be an official marketplace like the official list (London Stock Exchange) or a less structured market.

■ What do you think?

1. Give some reasons for the reported surge in international energy prices.

2. Explain the difference between the wholesale and retail energy markets.

3. What conditions are necessary to create perfect competition? Should we see the practice of the retail energy companies all increasing prices at the same time as being clear evidence of anti-competitive practices at work?

4. What factors does the FT article suggest have resulted in reduced competition in the wholesale energy market?

5. To what extent is it fair to conclude that the wholesale market in gas is much more competitive than the wholesale market for electricity?

6. Why might the UK government's sale of the rest of its stake in British Energy further erode competition in the UK energy market?

7. How could you test the relative competitiveness of the UK retail energy suppliers?

■ Data exercise

It has long been recognised that producer price inflation provides a good early warning indicator for consumer price inflation. The idea is that higher producer prices will be passed on to retailers who will in turn impose these on the consumers. In mid-April 2008 the UK Statistics Authority released the latest data for March 2008.

The two main tables (taken from the UK Statistics Authority's release) are shown below. Table 4.1 shows output prices (these are the prices of goods as they leave a factory).

Table 4.1 Output prices (home sales)

	All manufactured Products		Excluding food, beverages, tobacco and petroleum		All manufactured products excl. duty	
	12 months (NSA)	1 month (NSA)	12 months (NSA)	1 month (SA)	12 months (NSA)	1 month (SA)
Percentage change						
2007 Oct	4.0	0.7	2.3	0.3	3.8	0.7
Nov	4.7	0.7	2.2	0.2	4.7	1.0
Dec	5.0	0.4	2.4	0.3	5.1	0.6
2008 Jan	5.7	1.0	3.2	0.9	6.1	0.9
Feb	5.9	0.5	3.1	0.2	6.1	0.4
Mar	6.2	0.9	3.1	0.3	6.2	0.4

NSA/SA not/seasonally adjusted

Table 4.2 shows input prices (these are the prices of raw materials that will be used in manufacturing process).

Table 4.2   Input prices[1,2]

	Materials and fuels purchased			Excluding food, beverages, tobacco and petroleum industries		
	12 months (NSA)	1 month (NSA)	1 month (SA)	12 months (NSA)	1 month (NSA)	1 month (SA)
Percentage change						
2007 Oct	8.9	2.4	2.2	2.8	1.1	0.6
Nov	10.9	3.6	2.2	2.2	1.7	0.3
Dec	12.2	1.8	1.6	3.9	1.5	1.1
2008 Jan	18.9	2.8	2.7	7.5	2.1	2.3
Feb	19.7	1.5	1.9	8.7	1.3	1.3
Mar	20.6	2.9	1.8	9.7	1.8	1.5

NSA/not/seasonally adjusted
1 These indices include the Climate Change Levy which was introduced in April 2001
2 These indices include the Aggregates Levy which was introduced in April 2002

You are required to study the data above and then answer the following questions:

a) What is the latest annual rate of increase for producer input and output prices?

b) What has been the recent trend in these data series?

c) Why do think that the data that excludes petroleum had been showing a much smaller rise during this period?

■ The Web

Go to the official website of OFGEM.
This can be found at **www.ofgem.gov.uk/Pages/OfgemHome.aspx**.
Now go to the Markets section.
You are required to explain OFGEM's role in terms of the UK's energy wholesale and supply markets.

■ Research

Begg, D. and Ward, D., (2007) *Economics for Business*, 2nd edition, Maidenhead: McGraw-Hill. You should look at Chapter 8. Market power and competition power are discussed on pages 184–187.

Begg, D., Fischer, S. and Dornbusch, R., (2008) *Economics*, 9th edition, Maidenhead: McGraw-Hill. You should look at Chapter 8.

4

COMPETITION POLICY IN ACTION

Article 6 Lack of wholesale competition blamed

Gillespie, A., (2007) *Foundations of Economics*, 1st edition, Oxford: Oxford University Press. You could look at Chapter 8, page 104 to see a nice discussion of the European Commission and energy markets. In addition Chapter 11 sets out the conditions for perfect competition (see page 154).

Sloman, J., (2007) *Essentials of Economics*, 4th edition, Harlow: Financial Times Prentice Hall. You should look at Chapter 4.

Sloman, J. and Hinde, K., (2007) *Economics for Business*, 4th edition, Harlow: Financial Times Prentice Hall. You should look at Chapter 11.

Go to **www.pearsoned.co.uk/boakes** to access Kevin's blog for additional analysis of recent topical news articles and to post your own comments. Download podcasts containing short audio summaries of the main issues relating to each article and check your understanding of in-text questions with the handy hints provided.

Market failure and government intervention

For economists market failure occurs when the allocation of goods and services that is achieved through market forces is not efficient. This is seen to arise in three main situations:

1. The first relates back to the previous topic of competition policy. We saw then that it is possible for one company to exploit a monopoly position to allow it to set higher prices than would be the case if more competition existed. This is clearly damaging for all consumers in that market.

2. The second example of market failure relates to the presence of externalities. These occur when the actions of either consumers or producers has an impact on people other than themselves. These consequences for others are sometimes referred to as 'third-party or spin-off effects'. The existence of externalities creates a clear divergence between the private and the social cost of production. For example, a company might knock down an existing house and replace it with a new larger dwelling. The private cost to the house builder could be £1m. However, once we take account of the noise pollution and the generally negative impact on the nearby homeowners the full cost (including this social cost) might be nearer to £1.25m.

3. Lastly, market failure exists in the provision of so called public goods. These are products where one person's consumption does not result in less being available for others. In addition it is impossible to exclude certain individuals from the consumption of these goods. For example, the protection afforded by the armed forces, police and fire services are all public goods.

Despite the existence of these failures we have seen in recent years a growing consensus among politicians of nearly all mainstream parties that when it comes to economics the market nearly always knows best. This has led to the widespread reduction in the public provision of a range of goods and services. In this world where market economics dominates, the forces of supply and demand are used to determine the optimum level of production. However, there are still some areas where the government is seen to play an important role. This leads to the use of the term 'mixed economy' to describe a state where some goods and services are provided by the government while the rest come from private-sector provision.

What areas does the government normally intervene in?

a) The supply of certain essential goods and services. For example, this generally includes some kind of National Health Service and a system of state education. The important question is what level of service should the state supply and when should the private sector step in to offer additional provision. This normally comes down to cost, and the level of state services will be driven by what the government can afford to provide.

b) The government can also attempt to use a system of taxes and subsidies to correct any perceived market imperfections. For example, a tax may be levied on the amount of refuse that a household generates. This might encourage the family to put more effort into recycling.

c) Most governments will also use the legal system to prohibit certain kinds of behaviour that it considers to be undesirable. For example, we have seen a number of legislative measures brought in to control the activities of companies.

d) Finally, governments have a long record of trying to influence the behaviour of their citizens via the use of publicity and information. The classic example would be the campaigns to show the adverse effects of smoking on public health. Anyone who watched the US TV series *Mad Men* shown on BBC4 in the UK in the first half of 2008 could not help but be struck by the widespread smoking that was prevalent in the 1960s. In the context of today's smoking bans this behaviour would now be considered totally unacceptable.

In the first article discussed here we see how the UK government was attempting to use the tax system to try to persuade us all to become a little more environmentally friendly. This might be easy in theory but achieving the desired outcome is much harder in practice. The second article focuses on the use of fuel subsidies across the world. It shows that a number of emerging economies were devoting a significant share of their national income to maintaining petrol prices at a lower level for their citizens.

The following articles are analysed in this section:

Article 7
Petrol price rises and penalties for gas-guzzlers as Chancellor Alistair Darling goes green,
The Times, 10 March 2008.

Article 8
Crude measures: not everybody is paying higher oil prices,
The Economist, 29 May 2008.

These articles address the following issues:

- Market failure

- Government intervention

- Examples in practice

- Green budgets

- The use of taxes and subsidies

- Improving social inequality.

The last days of the Chelsea tractors!

If you pick up any quality newspaper and turn to the business section you will quickly see that the government plays a key role in many aspects of economic policy. If food prices are sharply increasing and as a result inflation is rising, all eyes quickly turn to the politicians to see what they propose to do about it. Similarly if the banking system is facing difficulties the population expect the government to do something to sort it out fast. In recent years we have seen the government starting to use its tax system in order to discourage various types of environmentally damaging activities. The use of so-called green taxes and subsidies has long impacted on the motorist with a clear differential between leaded and unleaded petrol duties. This was taken a step further in the 2008 Budget when the Chancellor unveiled plans to vary the level of vehicle excise duties according to the level of carbon emissions produced by the particular car. This was to prove a highly controversial measure as motorists began to see the higher costs that they would face as a result. It seems that we all like the idea of green taxes unless we have to pay them ourselves!

Article 7   *The Times*, 10 March 2008

Petrol price rises and penalties for gas-guzzlers as Chancellor Alistair Darling goes green

Philip Webster, political editor

Alistair Darling will increase petrol duty and impose swingeing penalties on high-emission cars this week in what ministers will call 'the green Budget'.

He will give tax incentives to companies that opt for greener vehicle fleets. And in a further move to show his green credentials Mr Darling will announce that Britain's first five-year carbon budget, setting out the way independent experts believe that the country should meet the target of reducing emissions by 60 per cent by 2050, will be published next year alongside the main Budget.

The move is designed to show that meeting climate change objectives is now at the heart of the Government's economic policy.

Mr Darling will try to repair his damaged relations with the City with concessions over his plans to tax non-domiciles, including a deal with Washington that will mean thousands of American bankers and businessmen working in Britain can set their annual £30,000 charge against their US tax bills. He will also change the rules relating to non-residents qualifying to pay tax, freeing thousands from the British tax net.

The Chancellor is also expected to use his legal powers to prevent pay-as-you-go gas and electricity customers being unfairly treated by energy companies, compared with those who pay by direct debit. The disparity, where poorest customers are charged up to £330 a year more than internet customers, was revealed by *The Times* on Thursday.

The Budget will also highlight measures to tackle child poverty as Mr Darling responds to growing Cabinet calls for him to do more to more to enable Labour to meet its target of halving child poverty by 2010. There will be changes to the tax credit system to help working families.

The Chancellor is set to announce a shake-up of car taxation, with people buying the most polluting vehicles heavily penalised and those who go for green alternatives paying less tax. Buyers of 'gas-guzzlers' in car tax Band G will be confronted with a first-year charge of more than £1,000 in vehicle excise tax, before it reverts to the current level of £400. Mr Darling will also increase the number of bands from the current seven. Drivers in the lower bands will pay less tax than at present. The higher the emissions, the higher the first year excise duty.

One of his most controversial moves will be to go ahead with the 2p-a-litre rise in the price of petrol that was announced last year. Motoring organisations have been calling on him to defer it because of the present high prices. But to do so would leave him short of much needed revenue and go against the grain of his emphasis on environmental measures.

As *The Times* disclosed on Saturday implementation of many of the tax increases, including those on cars, will be delayed for a year. But he will raise duties on alcohol, ending the ten-year freeze on spirits duty.

Mr Darling needs to show the markets that, over time, he will act to bring down borrowing, but he does not want to tighten the economy at a time when it is expected to slow down. He will revise his growth forecast down by a quarter of a percentage point to 1.75 per cent on Wednesday.

Mr Darling's moves on non-doms will be welcomed in the City, even though he is refusing to back down over introducing the new charge. He will say that he is confident that an agreement with the US will ensure that the £30,000 charge on Americans working in Britain does not amount to double taxation.

American citizens are taxed on their worldwide income. The changes to rules for non-residents will also be welcomed by those who commute to London. Originally the plan was for days spent travelling to and from Britain to count towards the limit of 183 days a year to qualify as non resident. Now it will be based on overnight stays.

George Osborne, the Shadow Chancellor, called for corporation tax to be curbed to help to revive the economy. He said that the main rate should be cut from 28p to 25p and a planned increase in the small companies rate from 20p to 22p abandoned. Mr Osborne said that Britain currently had 'one of the most uncompetitive corporate tax rates in the world'.

The Institute for Public Policy Research, the left-leaning think-tank, said that this Budget was the Government's 'last chance' to take the steps needed to meet its goal on child poverty. It urged Mr Darling to increase working tax credit for couples to £91.31 a week, introduce a personal tax credit allowance so that each adult in eligible families would be able to earn £100 a week before losing credits and raise the child element of child tax credit by £8 a week.

■ Analysis

In March 2008 the Chancellor, Alistair Darling, unveiled what was generally perceived to be a 'green budget' explicitly designed to change people's behaviour in a number of areas. The key economic aspects of these proposals can best be analysed by answering three questions:

1. How was the UK government attempting to use the tax system to curb the use of high-emission cars?

Substantial reforms to vehicle excise duties were made in an attempt to curb the use of 4×4s and other so-called gas-guzzlers. The latest announcements built on previous moves that had introduced a range of bands for different types of cars based on their polluting characteristics. The 2008 Budget increased the number of these bands from seven to thirteen with the new top 'M' band resulting in an annual charge of £440. This applied to those vehicles whose emissions exceeded 255g of carbon dioxide per kilometre. This included many of the ubiquitous 4×4s as well as the high-performance sports cars like Ferraris. At the other end of the scale there was a new lower annual levy of just £20 on the least polluting cars including the Toyota Prius.

2. In what ways were various measures in this budget being used to promote greater fairness in society?

At the time of this budget there was growing unease about the sharp increases in energy bills facing domestic customers. Customers were affected unequally by these increases. More affluent customers who had access to the internet and paid by direct debit were able to seek out the cheapest deals, whereas energy companies were charging the highest prices to their poorest households who were unable to take advantage of these discounts. As a result the industry regulator estimated that there were around 4m households living in fuel poverty in the UK. They used the following measure to arrive at this figure.

> 'Households are deemed to be living in fuel poverty if they spend more than 10% of their income on heating and lighting bills.'

The Chancellor suggested that he would use his legal powers to stop the practice of the energy companies charging their 'pay as you go' customers a higher charge than the direct debit ones.

If this was designed to alleviate some aspects of poverty for the poorest members of society the Chancellor also unveiled some measures to curb the excesses of the super-rich. Back in October 2007 he had announced that adult non-domiciles (the so-called non-doms) who had been UK residents for more than seven years would have to pay £30,000 tax per year or face a tax on any of their overseas income above £2000 per year. In the 2008 Budget he reacted to some concerns that these moves would lead to a mass exodus of some important super-rich individuals from the UK. This was seen as a particular threat to the City of London. Following some particularly strong lobbying there were concessions made to American citizens who were resident in the UK.

3. Can the tax and subsidies system be an effective way to change people's behaviour?

There is little doubt that taxes and subsidies can be a very useful way for the government to intervene and correct some market imperfections. It can force an individual or a company to take account of the overall social impact of their behaviour. In this case the UK government is trying to persuade certain car drivers to change their vehicle of choice. It is hoping that by imposing higher taxes on high-polluting cars consumers will think twice before buying them. In this case it might well turn out that the new duties imposed will be too small to have much of an impact. The problem in practice is that the political impact of imposing even higher deterrents on 4×4s and other similar vehicles would be considered too big a risk by all political parties. Therefore it is unlikely that we will see fewer 'Chelsea tractors' on our roads as a result of this tax in the near future.

■ Key terms

1. **Green budget**

   Economists use the term 'green budget' to refer to any measures that are designed to have a beneficial impact on the environment. This could include policies to discourage the frequent use of air travel or to encourage greater use of recycling.

2. **Non-domiciles**

   These are people who are granted 'non-domiciled' status by the UK tax authorities. They will normally be from abroad but be living and working in the UK. They must pay tax on any UK earnings but not on any money earned overseas. It is estimated that there are as many as 110,000 such people in the UK.

3. **Vehicle Excise Tax**

   An annual charge levied by the UK tax authorities on car drivers. There are now thirteen different tax bands with the annual charge varying from £0 to £950 per year.

4. **Corporation tax**

   A direct tax charged on the profits made by limited companies. In the UK this is split into a main corporation tax rate (charged at 28%) and a small company's corporation tax rate (charged at 21%).

5. **Institute for Public Policy Research**

   This is a UK-based think tank founded in the late 1980s which has strong links with the UK Labour Party. On its website it describes itself as: 'The UK's leading progressive think tank, producing cutting edge research and innovative policy ideas for a just, democratic and sustainable world'.

6. **Working Tax Credits**

   These credits are part of a complex system of welfare reforms introduced in 2003. Under the credits scheme those people who are in low income work receive extra payments from the state. It is a means-tested benefit designed to provide such individuals or families with an incentive to work rather than just rely on government aid.

■ What do you think?

1. Explain what is meant by the term 'green budget'.

2. Discuss four ways that governments frequently intervene to correct so-called market imperfections.

3. What are the advantages and disadvantages of using taxes and subsidies to correct market failures?

4. Select any two types of services that are normally provided by the government. Explain why it is a good thing for the state to offer these particular services.

5. Explain how the government could discourage the provision of free plastic bags by retailers to their customers.

■ The Web

Go to the official website for the Institute for Fiscal Studies (IFS). This can be accessed at: **www.ifs.org.uk**.
Find the section on Budgets.
Now select Green Budget (select the latest one available).
This is where the IFS sets out the background to the official budget that is about to be published.
Choose any section that relates well to the economics of market failure and write a short review explaining the economics that lie behind this topic. For example, the 2008 Green Budget had an outline of the economic principles of aviation taxes. This would have been a very good topic to analyse.

■ Research

Begg, D. and Ward, D., (2007) *Economics for Business*, 2nd edition, Maidenhead: McGraw-Hill. You should look at Chapter 8. Market failure is discussed on pages 179–180.

Begg, D., Fischer, S. and Dornbusch, R., (2008) *Economics*, 9th edition, Maidenhead: McGraw-Hill. You should look at Chapters 15 and 16. Section 16.2 clearly sets out the role of the government in the economy.

Gillespie, A., (2007) *Foundations of Economics*, 1st edition, Oxford: Oxford University Press. You could look at Chapter 8, page 103 for a clear discussion of government intervention in practice.

Sloman, J., (2007) *Essentials of Economics*, 4th edition, Harlow: Financial Times Prentice Hall. You should look at Chapter 6.

Sloman, J. and Hinde, K., (2007) *Economics for Business*, 4th edition, Harlow: Financial Times Prentice Hall. You should look at Chapter 20.

5

MARKET FAILURE AND GOVERNMENT INTERVENTION

Why does petrol cost just 5 cents per litre in Venezuela?

This article appeared in *The Economist* at a time when rapidly rising petrol prices were dominating the news. With crude oil prices hitting ever higher levels the impact was being felt by motorists who were devoting an increasing percentage of their disposable income to keeping cars on the road. As a result we started to see stories appearing in the press that showed that there was a wide range of petrol prices being paid by car owners across the world. This was due to a complex range of fuel subsidies being offered by governments that kept petrol prices relatively low in several countries. For example while motorists in Germany paid as much as $2.35 a litre those in Venezuela enjoyed the lowest price of just 5 cents per litre.

Article 8   *Economist*, 29 May 2008

Crude measures: not everybody is paying higher oil prices

Half of the world's population enjoys fuel subsidies. This estimate, from Morgan Stanley, implies that almost a quarter of the world's petrol is sold at less than the market price. The cheapest petrol is in Venezuela, at 5 cents per litre. That makes China's pump price of 79 cents seem expensive, but even this is a bargain compared with $1.04 in the United States and $2.35 in Germany (see chart).

As the gap has widened between soaring international prices and fixed domestic prices, so has the cost of subsidies. Indeed, budgetary strains are now forcing some governments to lift prices. On May 24th Indonesia raised fuel prices by around 30%. This was the first increase since 2005, but it still leaves petrol too cheap at 65 cents a litre. Dearer oil is likely to push up inflation from 9% to 12%. But without the increase, the government's subsidy bill was heading for an alarming 3% of GDP this year. In the past week Taiwan has also raised petrol prices by 13% and Sri Lanka has lifted them by 24%.

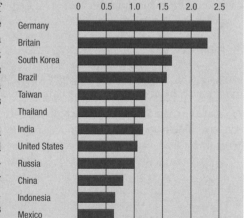

Tax and spend
Retail petrol prices, $ per litre, latest

Germany, Britain, South Korea, Brazil, Taiwan, Thailand, India, United States, Russia, China, Indonesia, Mexico, Malaysia, Saudi Arabia, Venezuela

Source: Morgan Stanley; *The Economist*

Malaysia has one of the biggest fuel-subsidy bills in the world, estimated at as much as 7% of GDP this year. By holding down the price of petrol, Malaysia now has the lowest inflation rate of all the 32 emerging economies tracked by *The Economist*. But the government is expected to allow prices to rise soon to curb its widening budget deficit.

In theory, rising crude-oil prices should reduce global demand. But if domestic prices are capped, then emerging economies will continue to guzzle oil, pushing world prices still higher. Emerging economies accounted for more than the whole increase in world oil consumption last year – because demand in the rich economies fell. But recent price increases will make little difference to global consumption unless China and India follow suit.

India's state-owned oil companies face mounting losses, as they are forced to sell fuel at fixed prices below cost. Petrol prices are actually slightly higher in India than in the United States, because Indian motorists pay much higher fuel taxes, but diesel is about 40% cheaper than in America. The oil firms are partly compensated by bonds which the government issues to them – a trick which allows the government to keep the subsidy off its books. At today's prices, the total subsidy (including the full losses of oil companies) could be as much as 2–3% of GDP this year. Morgan Stanley estimates that the government's total budget deficit (central and state governments and all off-budget items) is running at 9% of GDP in this fiscal year. The government must hold an election by May next year, so it is reluctant to raise fuel prices by much. It is thought to be considering a modest rise combined with a cut in excise duty.

In early 2008 Chinese motorists paid roughly the same for their petrol as Americans did. Whereas the pump price in America has since jumped by 33%, Chinese prices have remained fixed, swelling the losses of state-owned refiners. According to Dragonomics, a Beijing-based economic research firm, the retail price for diesel is about 40% below that in America. To cut their losses, oil firms have reduced supply, causing shortages at some petrol stations. However, China is less likely than other countries to lift prices soon. Oil subsidies are estimated at less than 1% of GDP, and its budget surplus and small public debt mean that the government can afford to keep prices down for some time. Most likely, it will delay increasing fuel prices until food-price inflation has eased.

Across the emerging world, governments fear that lifting fuel prices will hurt the poor and so trigger social unrest. Yet fuel subsidies are an inefficient way to protect the poor: they mainly benefit the richer owners of cars and air-conditioners, and favour energy- and capital-intensive industries, rather than those that create most jobs. An IMF study of five emerging economies found that the richest 20% of households received, on average, 42% of total fuel subsidies; the bottom 20% received less than 10%. That money would be better spent on health, education and infrastructure. Not only would this benefit the poor, but higher prices would also help to dampen global oil consumption, and hence the price of oil.

■ The analysis

Governments across the world use subsidies to encourage the consumption of a wide range of goods and services. In general they are used to provide an incentive to raise demand for what economists call 'merit goods'. These are simply items that the government wants people to consume in much larger quantities than they would if they were left to their own devices. There was a perfect example in June 2008 when the UK government announced plans to provide free access to swimming for everyone aged over 60 in the run-up to the London Olympics in 2012. In contrast the consumption of demerit goods is generally discouraged by governments. They include legal products like cigarettes and some illegal ones like heroin or crack cocaine.

The level of fuel subsidies as shown by the article might come as a surprise to most readers. It indicates that Malaysia devotes as much as 7% of its total national income to promoting lower petrol prices for its consumers.

There seem to be two main arguments in favour of this form of government intervention.

1. To lower inflation:

   There is no doubt that all governments worry if inflation starts to rise sharply. During 2008 we saw that escalating crude oil prices were having a significant impact on inflationary pressures across the world. Why is inflation so sensitive to oil prices? First, this is because higher petrol and aviation fuel prices will directly feed through into consumer price inflation. These items make up a significant percentage of the basket of goods and services included in a consumer price index. Secondly, there is the indirect impact that will come from higher transportation costs which feeds through to virtually every category of inflation. Every good that is produced has to be moved to the final consumer. So if higher oil prices cause inflation the use of government fuel subsidies must have a powerful effect in terms of keeping price rises more subdued.

2. Protecting the poor and preventing social unrest:

   A second argument in favour of fuel subsidies would be that they keep petrol prices within the budget of the poorer members of society. *The Economist* article argues: while this might be true it is 'an inefficient way to protect the poor'. It suggests that these subsidies will be of greater benefit to the rich. The more affluent are certainly more likely to be owners of larger higher-fuel-consumption cars. *The Economist* reports the latest research from a survey by the International Monetary Fund that looked at five emerging market economies. This showed that the richest 20% of households received, on average, 42% of total fuel subsidies; the bottom 20% received less than 10%. It is hard to argue against the view that the resources spent on these subsidies could do more to improve the life chances of the poor with higher government spending on such basic services as health and education.

If fuel subsidies are a bad way of combating inequality there is another important reason that they seem to be a bad use of public funds. This is due to their unfavourable impact on the environment. We are all living through a time of great concern about the adverse effect on climate change from emissions of carbon dioxide from cars. One good effect of higher oil prices should be that they eventually result in lower demand as consumers are forced to cut back on their use of expensive oil-based products. However, with the demand for oil largely being increasingly driven by the new and emerging economies the existence of these generous subsidies would counter this trend. The message from *The*

Economist could not be clearer: it is time to end these fuel subsidies and the governments of the emerging economies should spend their money on the people who really need it.

■ Key terms

1. Merit (and demerit goods)

Merit goods can be defined as any that are more highly valued by society than they are by individual consumers. As a result the government would like people to consume them in much larger quantities than they would if they were left to their own devices. A good example of a merit good might be art and culture. In contrast demerit goods are those items that we tend to consume without taking full account of their negative impacts. Examples of demerit goods include smoking or drinking to excess.

2. Subsidies

This is a financial inducement that governments can offer to encourage the consumption of particular goods or services. They can also be used for a number of other purposes:

a) To keep the prices of some basic food items as low as possible.

b) To maintain the production of a particular good or service. For example, in agriculture or certain industries.

c) To encourage the employment of a particular group of individuals. For example, the long-term unemployed.

3. Inflation

This is normally defined as any sustained increase in the general level of prices for goods and services. In Iceland, as in most other countries, it is measured by a consumer price index that records the monthly changes in a basket of goods and services reflecting typical spending patterns within the country.

4. Gross domestic product

This is a measure of the total level of income earned within a country's national boundaries.

5. Emerging economies

This term is used to denote the generally fast-growing economies of the newer nations around the world. They tend to be characterised by high growth but much greater political and social risk.

6. Budget deficit

A budget deficit is where the government spends more than it receives in tax revenue. The reverse is a budget surplus where tax receipts exceed government spending.

7. International Monetary Fund (IMF)

This international body was set up in the 1940s with the aim of running the new fixed exchange rate system. These days it has a membership that runs to over 180 countries. The IMF plays an important role in terms of working with these economies and advising them on their fiscal and monetary policies.

5

MARKET FAILURE AND GOVERNMENT INTERVENTION

■ What do you think?

1. What are the arguments in favour of the emerging market economies using fuel subsidies to keep petrol prices at an artificially lower level?

2. Explain what is meant by the term 'merit good'.

3. *The Economist* article argues that fuel subsidies are 'an inefficient way to protect the poor'. Do you agree with this viewpoint?

4. How else could governments use subsidies to have a beneficial impact on the environment?

■ The Web

Go to the IMF's website.
You can access this at **www.imf.org/external/index.htm**.
Now locate the IMF Survey Online Magazine.
Find the edition published on 20 March 2008.
The main article is titled 'Managing surging oil prices in the developing world'.
This article considers the use of fuel subsidies. It concludes with this view:

'Countries should pass through increases in world petroleum prices, both to preserve economic efficiency and avoid excessive fiscal costs. This requires overcoming political constraints, but is critical since oil importers are facing greater financing requirements as a result of the negative terms-of-trade shock they are suffering. Greater pass-through also implies the need for expanded safety nets, particularly in the light of higher food prices.'

Read the article and comment on this viewpoint.

■ Research

Begg, D. and Ward, D., (2007) *Economics for Business*, 2nd edition, Maidenhead: McGraw-Hill. You should look at Chapter 8. Market failure is discussed on pages 179–180.

Begg, D., Fischer, S. and Dornbusch, R., (2008) *Economics*, 9th edition, Maidenhead: McGraw-Hill. You should look at Chapter 15 which examines welfare economics.

Gillespie, A., (2007) *Foundations of Economics*, 1st edition, Oxford: Oxford University Press. You could look at Chapter 8, page 103 for a clear discussion of government intervention in practice.

Sloman, J., (2007) *Essentials of Economics*, 4th edition, Harlow: Financial Times Prentice Hall. You should look at Chapter 6, pages 204–206.

Sloman, J. and Hinde, K., (2007) *Economics for Business*, 4th edition, Harlow: Financial Times Prentice Hall. You should look at Chapter 20.

Go to **www.pearsoned.co.uk/boakes** to access Kevin's blog for additional analysis of recent topical news articles and to post your own comments. Download podcasts containing short audio summaries of the main issues relating to each article and check your understanding of in-text questions with the handy hints provided.

The role of government in the economy (privatisation)

In the previous topic we introduced the economic concept of market failure. We now move on to see how governments can intervene to correct these inefficiencies. A good example is in relation to so called public goods. These are simply the goods that everyone consumes and benefits from. In addition it is impossible to prevent a non-contributor from enjoying their benefits. Some examples are law and order and national defence. In most countries the government will directly provide these services. The government will also be involved in managing various publicly owned resources including national parks and the coastline. In addition, the government is actively involved in terms of the tax and benefit system. This is partly with the aim of achieving a fairer distribution of income in society. Finally, the government is expected to intervene when the economy faces a particularly serious problem. A good example of this was when they were forced to protect Northern Rock's depositors by taking this financial institution into public ownership.

This action was to some a throwback to past times when the government was considered to be the best provider of many of the goods and services that people consumed. For example, in the aftermath of the Second World War the new Labour government undertook the widespread nationalisation of British industry. From coal-mining to electricity and from railways to gas the government set about bringing huge sectors of industry under its control and ownership. Later, in the 1960s and 1970s we saw a second period of widening state ownership as various industries that were in decline came under state control. This included ship building and car manufacturing.

However, during the 1980s 'nationalisation' became something of a dirty word. The Conservative government under Mrs Thatcher had a very different philosophy as she believed that these industries belonged in the private sector. Within a short space of time we saw the privatisation of British Telecom, British Airways, British Steel, regional water companies and the electricity industry amongst others.

The entire subject of privatisation is a very controversial area. As a result I have set out below the main advantages of this policy together with the counter-argument in each case.

1. Raising revenue for the government

   The cash that can be generated from the sale of former state assets can be used to either lower taxes or increase government spending. It has been estimated that the UK government raised a total of £50bn between 1984 and 1996 alone.

   The counter-argument:

   Critics of privatisation would argue that is in many ways a case of the 'family selling the family silver'. The government can only sell these very valuable assets once and it may live to regret this course of action in the future.

2. Stimulus to industrial competition

This can be from the introduction of private-sector services into the public sector. A good example might be allowing companies to tender for school meal services or cleaning contracts in the National Health Service.

The counter-argument:

It should be said, however, that that process has been very controversial. Critics would point to evidence that this process has led to a reduction in the quality of such services. This prompted Jamie Oliver to lead a very powerful campaign against the school meal service in the UK where the average spend per pupil had been cut to just 37p.

3. Widen share ownership across the population

There is little doubt that the UK programme of privatisations in the 1980s and 1990s certainly produced a generation of individuals who were far more willing to try this form of investment.

The counter-argument

The downside of this policy is that it might have persuaded private investors to buy shares in former state-owned industries by selling them far too cheaply. As a result such individuals were convinced that investing in shares was an easy route to great riches. Sadly, these same investors may have lost large amounts of money when the dot-com boom of the late 1990s ended.

4. Offer access to better financing opportunities

The government will always face many different demands for additional funding. This can have the consequence that some important investment projects cannot easily be undertaken in the public sector. In contrast it might be easier for a private sector company to obtain the finance as long as it can demonstrate that the investment is financially sound.

The counter-argument:

In the case of some privatisations the effect has been merely to replace a state-owned monopoly with a privately owned one. If you refer back to Article 5 on BAA you will see the problems in practice with the government having to regulate the privately owned company that operates most of the UK's airports.

Despite the controversial nature of this policy there is no doubt that many other countries have followed the UK's example in this field. This has included many European countries that have emerged out of the break-up of the old Soviet Union and the development of a new and vibrant Eastern Europe. In this section we examine privatisation policy in Slovenia and in Sweden. Both countries have seen a radical shift in policy with their governments now looking to take more of a back seat in terms of economic policy making.

The following articles are analysed in this section:

Article 9
Privatisation: one step forward,
Financial Times, 17 December 2007.

Article 10
Sweden privatisation scheme faces delay,
Financial Times, 11 March 2008.

These articles address the following issues:

- The role of government in the national economy
- Public goods
- Privatisation
- Role of investment banks in managing these transactions
- Valuation of former state companies
- Process of organising public sales
- Rights of new shareholders
- Regulation of these enterprises.

6

THE ROLE OF GOVERNMENT IN THE ECONOMY (PRIVATISATION)

Privatisation from Slovenia to Sweden

My most memorable day spent working as a financial markets trainer in an investment bank came one Friday in the mid-1990s. I had been hired by an investment bank to run a one-week introductory course for a large group of their Eastern European clients. There were people from the Czech Republic, Poland, Hungary and Russia. To be honest it had been hard work as the level of English language skills among the group was rather mixed. While some delegates were almost fluent I am not sure that some of the others understood anything I said all week! However, they were incredibly polite and listened patiently to what I had to say.

By the Friday afternoon I was looking forward to the course ending and the weekend arriving. Just as we were getting ready to break for some refreshments there was a knock at the door. I opened it and was somewhat surprised to see a group of balding older men led by a more youthful head of corporate finance from the bank. As they came into the room there was a sharp intake of breath from the delegates which I could not understand. To be honest they all looked like they had seen a ghost or even more accurately a group of them. The visitors talked to some of the delegates in their native languages. I kept my fingers crossed hoping that they were confirming that the course had been going well. After about ten to fifteen minutes the men all left with the head of corporate finance shaking my hand and telling me that I should call him later with a list of relevant finance books so that the bank could go out and buy a selection for every delegate.

As I prepared to start the course again one of the delegates asked me if I knew who the visitors had been. I gave the honest answer: no! He then told me that it had included presidents, prime ministers, government ministers and heads of central banks from each of their countries. In that moment two things became clear to me. First, this explained the surprise of the delegates when the guests walked in and secondly the whole point of the course was at last clear. The bank had wanted to impress this group of eminent decision-makers. In running the course the bank was saying 'look, we are working to improve the financial knowledge of people from your countries'. It had been an astute piece of long-term marketing from the bank. In the coming months when I was reading the FT I would see many privatisation transactions from these countries with the bank in question often acting as lead manager and in the process pocketing millions of pounds in fees. I had a wry smile as I thought back to that Friday afternoon in the city when I had met some of the most powerful and influential leaders from Eastern Europe without knowing who they were!

Article 9

Financial Times, 17 December 2007

Privatisation: one step forward

Thomas Escritt

For Slovenes, privatisations of state companies are something of a novelty. When shares in NKBM, a bank based in Maribor, the second city, were offered to the public last month, queues snaked out of the doors.

'The public have this perception that if the government is selling and people are queuing up, then it must be a good deal,' says Uros Marter, director of Arkas, a boutique corporate finance advisory firm in Ljubljana.

Enthusiasm for the privatisation has been fuelled by the Ljubljana stock exchange's strong performance over the past year. Average price-earnings ratios stand at between 22 and 25 times, compared with 12 or 13 times on the S&P500, according to Mr Marter. 'The returns on the Slovenian stock market are incredible,' he says.

The Ljubljana stock exchange has been a star performer this year, although analysts agree that growth is likely to be slower than in recent years. One reason for 2007's strong returns was the one-time impact of Slovenia's entry into the eurozone. This brought the country's stocks into the eurozone indices, attracting a flood of mutual fund and tracker money.

Shortness of supply is another reason. The Slovene state has been loath to follow the privatisation prescription meted out to much of eastern Europe.

Many former state enterprises are listed and traded on the stock exchange but the state retains sizeable positions in many of the largest companies, either directly or through two state-owned investment funds.

Slovenia's government has also adopted an unconventional approach to privatisation.

In the case of NKBM, for example, no new capital was raised. Rather, 75 per cent of the shares held by the state were placed in an initial public offering. Half the shares were allocated to members of the public, who were individually limited to purchases worth €50,000. The state has committed itself to selling its final 25 per cent tranche in due course though this promise may raise eyebrows at KBC, the Belgian bank.

In 2002, it bought a 34 per cent share in Nova Ljubljanska Banka (NLB), the country's largest. It has been waiting five years to exercise pre-emption rights should the state sell a further tranche. Meanwhile KBC remains a minority shareholder, while the state and its investment funds control a full 45 per cent.

Many of these companies have proven good investments. Darko Kovacic, an equity analyst with the local subsidiary of Raiffeisen, the Austrian bank, says: 'Former state-owned companies have had pretty good performance since privatisation.'

Attitudes towards state ownership are changing, however, insists Peter Groznik, head of asset management at KD Group, a Slovene fund manager that invests in south-east Europe. The first change was a decision last year to alter investment strategies at the two state investment funds. Eventually, they will sell their holdings in most Slovene listed companies, moving to more diversified portfolios. 'The funds have started selling their holdings, maximising the prices they are

6

THE ROLE OF GOVERNMENT IN THE ECONOMY (PRIVATISATION)

getting for the companies in a transparent way,' says Mr Groznik, who headed the committee that prepared the plan last March. 'The funds held 25 per cent of many companies, but now their holdings have been reduced to zero in most cases, or reduced substantially in the case of larger companies.'

Bidding is already underway for the largest current privatisation, that of Telekom Slovenije. Submissions are due in early January from bidders interested in buying 49 per cent of the company. The state, which currently holds 74 per cent of the firm, will hold on to 25 per cent.

Under Slovenian companies law, a shareholder who acquires 25 per cent of a company is obliged to bid for all outstanding shares at the same price, meaning that the successful bidder should gain a majority stake by buying the existing free float.

Some observers are sceptical that the transaction will go ahead as advertised.

Mr Marter, the investment banker, thinks the government will cancel the privatisation if the bids received are not close to the existing stock market price. At the same time, he says, Telekom Slovenije is trading at around 10 times earnings, while incumbents tend to be near five times on average.

But Matyaz Jansa, who regulates electronic communications at the economics ministry, argues that the company, with exposure to the fast-growing markets, has potential.

Andrej Bajuk, finance minister, insists that, despite high levels of state ownership, the economy is more open than it looks. Around 30 per cent of bank deposits in Slovenia are held by foreign-owned institutions, he says. 'The steel industry has been privatised, and the second-largest bank is about to go,' he says.

Copyright The Financial Times Limited 2008

Article 10

Financial Times, 11 March 2008

Sweden privatisation scheme faces delays

David Ibison

Sweden's flagship privatisation programme is facing delays as the government grapples with the tumult in global financial markets.

The sell-off is one of the centre-right government's key pledges, made when it was elected 18 months ago.

'We are evaluating timing and price. It is possible that subprime events will have repercussions on our agenda,' Mats Odell, minister for financial markets, who is overseeing the privatisation process, told the Financial Times in an interview.

The government of Fredrik Reinfeldt, prime minister, is in the process of selling stakes in six companies by 2010, including **Nordea**, the banking group, SBAB, a mortgage lender, and **TeliaSonera**, the telecommunications company. The sales mark a break with Sweden's socialist past to allow the free market a greater role in the economy.

But the government faces the prospect of postponing some of the sales until investor sentiment recovers.

Mr Odell said he was confident the government would reach its original goal of raising SKr200bn ($33bn, €21bn, £16bn) by 2010 from the sales but admitted it might not be able to sell all six of the companies as originally planned. So far the government has raised just SKr18bn from the sale of 8 per cent of its 45 per cent stake in TeliaSonera and SKr2.2bn from the sale of its 6.6 per cent stake in **OMX**, a stock market company, to **Nasdaq** and Borse Dubai.

'We are committed to getting the best price [for these privatisations] and we are analysing right now what the right time is to make a deal. There is no deadline,' he said.

Mr Odell said that the government's plans to offload its 100 per cent stake in SBAB might have to be put on hold as 'mortgage lenders are not exactly the top of everyone's list'.

He also acknowledged that current market conditions were not ideal for selling banks. The government is seeking to sell its 19.9 per cent stake in Nordea.

One head of research for a Swedish bank, who asked not to be named, said the privatisation process had 'basically hit a wall' as a result of market conditions.

However, the programme is expected to receive a boost in coming weeks when the government announces the sale of Vin & Sprit, maker of Absolut vodka, for up to $7bn. It is also hoping to sell its 100 per cent stake in Vasakronan, a property company, at a time when the property market is showing early signs of weakening.

■ The analysis

We should start with a little geography and history. Slovenia is in Central-Southern Europe. The country has borders with Hungary in the north, Croatia in the east and finally Italy and Austria in the west. In the early 1990s Slovenia declared independence from Yugoslavia. It has been very much accepted into the international fold, as in 2004 it was granted membership of the European Union and on 1 January 2007 it became a member of the Eurozone.

However, compared to some of the other former Eastern European states it had been a little bit slower to embrace the concept of privatisation. There had been some privatisations in early 2002 with the partial sale of Slovenia's largest bank, Nova Ljubljanska Banka (NLB). However, plans to partially privatise the second leading bank, Nova Kreditna Banka Maribor (NKBM), were put on hold. The first article in this section was published just after NKBM's privatisation had been reactivated.

The Slovenian public were very enthusiastic buyers of shares in this company. The FT article quotes a director of a boutique corporate finance advisory firm in Ljubljana:

'The public have this perception that if the government is selling and people are queuing up, then it must be a good deal.'

This support for the transactions was not surprising given the background of the very strong performance of the Ljubljana stock exchange in recent years. As a result the average price-earnings ratio was in the mid-20s which was almost twice the level of the US stock market. In simple terms this means that investors were rating the Slovenian stock market far more highly than the US market. This high valuation was partly due to their recent entry into the Eurozone. Such a move had done much to reassure investors about the economic policy of the new and emerging country. In addition it removed any currency risk for investors from the Eurozone countries. Finally, as the article suggests, it had encouraged professional fund managers to invest in the Slovenian market. This would have included the so-called tracker funds.

Suppose we have a Eurozone tracker equity fund. This fund must match the performance of the weighted average of the stock markets across the countries of the Eurozone. So when Slovenia joins the Eurozone the fund must go out and buy shares in the Slovenian market. If they do not do this there is a risk that the fund will underperform against the index if the Slovenian stock market surges ahead and they do not have any representation for these shares in their portfolio.

There was one unusual feature of the NKBM privatisation. This was that no extra cash was actually raised by the bank from this share issue. Instead the state was simply selling the three-quarters of the bank's shares that they held to investors through this initial public offer (IPO). The government also committed itself to selling its residual stake in the bank at some stage in the future.

It seems that this latest move back towards privatisations in Slovenia is partly a reflection of a change in attitudes towards the role of state ownership. This has in part been prompted by a change in the investment strategy employed by the state investment fund. In the past they had apparently held most of their funds in Slovenian companies. These were now being sold off as the funds looked to diversify to reduce their risk. This seems to have been part of a more general opening up of the Slovenian economy. The article concludes by saying that 30% of banks' deposits in Slovenia were now owned by foreign-owned institutions. With the privatisation of the steel industry and also the county's second largest bank all was changing in Slovenia.

There is no doubt that a country's political persuasion has a significant impact on attitudes towards privatisation. Sweden offers the perfect example of this. For many years the 'Swedish model' had been firmly based on the government playing a major role in the economy. This included widespread regulation of business practice combined with high levels of taxation that was used to fund generous welfare provision. All this came to an abrupt end when in September 2006 a centre-right coalition swept to power, ousting the Social Democrat government that had dominated Sweden's politics for many years. This caused a seismic shift in economic policy with the new government promising to remove the state from many aspects of business and the economy.

The new Alliance government announced ambitious plans aimed to free business from the burden of official regulation. In addition there were measures designed to get more people into work and various tax-cutting plans to provide greater incentives for the rich.

One immediate area for change in Sweden was that the new government unveiled plans to sell off some $21bn worth of state-owned assets. The Swedish government was planning a new wave of privatisation that would see it getting rid of its holdings in six companies over the next two years. These included a bank, a mortgage lender and a telecom business. The substantial amount of money that would be raised was to be used to reduce the size of national debt despite the fact that it was already just above 40% of gross domestic product. That already made it one of the least debt-ridden countries in Europe. The new political party felt that these companies would perform much better as private-sector businesses rather than in the public sector.

There is no doubt that the major investment banks across the world would be licking their lips at the prospect of the huge fees available to them as they acted as advisers on these transactions. The Swedish government had appointed nine banks to offer advice on obtaining the best price for its portfolio of assets. However, as this article reports, they might have to be a little patient as there would be a delay in the new government's wave of privatisations. They were yet another victim of the global financial market difficulties that arose in the spring of 2008. The government was obviously keen to secure the best possible price and this was impossible at a time when investors had become very risk-averse.

■ Key terms

1. Privatisation (state companies)

This term is generally used where a whole business has its ownership transferred from the government to the private sector. However, it can also cover the introduction of the private sector into some parts of a publicly provided service. For example, the National Health Service might use a private company to undertake services like catering or cleaning.

2. Corporate finance firm (boutique)

This term is normally used to describe a small investment bank that acts as an adviser but does not trade in financial market securities on its own behalf. The advantage of such a firm is that its advice can be seen to be completely impartial.

3. Price–earnings ratio

The P/E ratio is calculated by taking the market share price and dividing it by company's earnings per share. This ratio is often used to compare the current stock market value of a company.

4. Mutual fund (tracker money)

This term is used mainly in the United States for some form of collective investment fund. It can invest a range of assets including shares, bonds and money market securities. When it is organised as a tracker fund this simply means that the fund will attempt to match the performance of some particular financial market index. This could be a stock market index like the FTSE-100. In this case it would have to make sure that its holdings perfectly matched the index. So, if Tesco plc made up 10% of the FTSE-100 the fund would have to hold the same percentage in the fund.

5. Initial public offer (IPO)

An IPO refers to the situation where a company first sells its shares by listing on the stock exchange. This gives it a much wider access to increase its shareholder base. In addition it provides much greater liquidity in terms of the trading of the shares in the company. Companies considering a new IPO will appoint an investment bank to manage the process. The bank will meet the company and be heavily involved in valuing the shares, preparing a prospectus and getting investors interested in the new issue. The investment bank will be very well rewarded for this work with substantial fees often being paid to ensure a successful IPO.

6. Pre-emption rights

This refers to one of the longest-standing principles of corporate law. It gives all shareholders the first right to buy any additional shares being sold by companies. The new shares would be offered to existing holders in direct proportion to their existing holdings. So, if you owned 10% of the existing shares in a company you would be given the right to buy 10% of the new shares being sold via a rights issue. These additional shares are normally sold at a significant discount to the existing market share price to ensure a successful completion of the transaction.

The shareholders involved face three choices:

a) They can exercise their right which means that they agree to buy the additional shares.

b) They can formally renounce the right, which will result in the company selling their rights on their behalf.

c) Finally, they can do nothing. In this case the company will still normally sell the rights on behalf of the shareholder anyway.

7. Minority shareholder

This is where a shareholder has less than fifty per cent of the company.

8. Sub-prime

The sub-prime market refers to the lending of money to much higher risk individuals at a higher rate of interest. When US house prices were rising sharply a number of people were encouraged to take out very large loans (at a very high multiple of their salary) which meant that they had little prospect of ever being able to meet the interest payments let alone any eventual repayment of the outstanding debt. As a result they were forced to default in large numbers.

■ What do you think?

1. What is meant by the term 'privatisation'?

2. What are the arguments in favour and against the privatisation of government owned assets?

3. What are the main economic roles of a government?

4. Is private ownership of companies always better than state ownership?

5. Why have investors around the world been so keen to invest in former state industries as they have been privatised?

6. Explain what is meant by the term 'tracker funds'. Why would they be so keen to purchase shares in the Slovenian stock market at this time?

7. Compare the likely goals of a manager working in the private sector with one working in the public sector.

■ The Web

Go to the European Bank for Reconstruction and Development's website at **www.ebrd.com/index.htm**.
Look at the 'About the EBRD' section.
Now go to 'Countries and Topics'.
Find Slovenia.
Research the 'Factsheet' and the 'Projects' section.
You are now required to prepare a short report on Slovenia and include details of a relevant project supported by the EBRD.

■ Research

Begg, D. and Ward, D., (2007) *Economics for Business*, 2nd edition, Maidenhead: McGraw-Hill. You should look at Chapter 12, page 285.

Begg, D., Fischer, S. and Dornbusch, R., (2008) *Economics*, 9th edition, Maidenhead: McGraw-Hill. You should look at Chapter 18. 'Privatisation in practice' is explained on page 366.

Gillespie, A., (2007) *Foundations of Economics*, 1st edition, Oxford: Oxford University Press. You should focus on Chapter 8, page 111–117 for a very good discussion of privatisation in practice.

Parkin, M., Powell, M. and Mathews, K., (2008) *Economics*, 7th edition, Harlow: Addison Wesley. You should look at chapter 14.

Sloman, J., (2007) *Essentials of Economics*, 4th edition, Harlow: Financial Times Prentice Hall. You should look at Chapter 10.

Sloman, J., (2008) *Economics and the Business Environment*, 2nd edition, Harlow: Financial Times Prentice Hall. The key section is chapter 11, page 332, which looks at the use of privatisation to encourage competition.

 Go to **www.pearsoned.co.uk/boakes** to access Kevin's blog for additional analysis of recent topical news articles and to post your own comments. Download podcasts containing short audio summaries of the main issues relating to each article and check your understanding of in-text questions with the handy hints provided.

Business organisations (from large to small companies)

To some people economics is the science of too many assumptions. If you listen to any good economics lecture it will not be long before you hear the infamous words 'if you make the following assumptions then this outcome is inevitable'. In this topic we discuss the business environment and in particular look at the role that individual companies play in a country's economy. The key assumption made by economists in this subject area is that the goal of any company will be to maximise its profits. Indeed profit maximisation lies at the heart of much of microeconomic theory and practice. However, many people question the extent to which this assumption holds true in the real world. It might seem to be a reasonable assumption when the owner of a company also runs the business; however, in most companies the owners are now diverse groups of shareholders. They provide the bulk of long-term finance to companies. Most of the time they are quite content to leave the managers of a company alone as long as all is well and they are achieving excellent financial returns on their investment. A rich shareholder is a happy shareholder.

In reality the assumption of profit maximisation can be far from the truth, particularly when there is a distinction between the owners and the managers of a business. In the first two articles here we look at one of the most famous companies in the UK, Marks and Spencer (M&S), and we consider the relationship between the company's senior managers and its shareholders. We see what happens when the larger shareholders become unhappy with the performance of the business and the way it is being run. In the third article in this opening section we move on to look at the small business sector. The focus is on the financing problems facing smaller companies in the wake of the prolonged credit crisis.

The following three articles are analysed in this section:

Article 11
Investor fury at M&S role for Rose,
Financial Times, 10 March 2008.

Article 12
M&S tries to placate investors over Rose,
Financial Times, 2 April 2008.

Article 13
Small companies face cash squeeze,
Financial Times, 28 March 2008.

Article 11 Investor fury at M&S role for Rose

These articles address the following issues:

- The role of businesses in the economy
- The economic goal of profit maximisation
- The role of the senior managers in a large company
- The role of shareholders in a company
- What is meant by good corporate governance?
- The financing of companies, short-term and long-term
- The advantages and disadvantages of small companies
- Financial stress for small companies
- Sole proprietorships and start-up companies.

A tale of unhappy shareholders at M&S

If you read the financial pages regularly you will have seen that it is getting more common for large shareholders to criticise the way that a company is being run by its chief executive and the other senior managers. Normally this only starts to happen when the business encounters difficulties and the share price slides. When this is the case the shareholders soon become very agitated. The worry is that when there is a clear split between the owners (the shareholders) and the managers (the board of directors) there is a significant danger that the managers will start to pursue objectives that conflict with the aim of maximising the company's profits and therefore its share price. The directors of a business might target higher pay for themselves or they may opt to take less risk to ensure they stay cocooned in their comfort zone.

The two articles selected here show the unease felt by the major shareholders in Marks and Spencer (M&S). They were very unhappy to see Stuart Rose being promoted from chief executive to executive chairman. This move contravened the fundamental principle of good corporate governance that all companies should split the roles of chairman and chief executive. The shareholders were concerned that they would no longer have an independent voice on the M&S board of directors to protect their interests.

Article 11

Financial Times, 10 March 2008

Investor fury at M&S role for Rose

Kate Burgess, Elizabeth Rigby and Tom Braithwaite

Marks and Spencer was last night facing an investor backlash after it announced plans to elevate Sir Stuart Rose to executive chairman in clear defiance of the UK's corporate governance code.

Legal & General Investment Management, M&S's second largest shareholder, said the announcement was 'unwelcome', as a broader base of leading shareholders voiced their anger at the move, which reflects the problem the retailer has in choosing Sir Stuart's successor.

'As set out in the Combined Code, we believe strongly in the separation of the roles of chairman and chief executive, believing that this provides a much-needed balance in the boardroom and prevents potentially damaging concentration of power,' said Mark Burgess, head of equities at Legal & General Investment Management.

'This is a very retrograde step,' said another investor. The Association of British Insurers said shareholders were pressing for further explanation. Many big investors complained they were informed of the radical changes only yesterday.

M&S said it had taken the decision to promote Sir Stuart to the post of executive chairman, effective from June.

Sir Stuart had always said he would stay on until May 2009, but would never make a further commitment. He will now stay on until 2011 in his new role. Ian

Dyson, finance director, will take on additional responsibilities, while executive directors Kate Bostock and Steven Esom will join the board. Sir David Michels, former chief executive of Hilton Group, will become deputy chairman and senior non-executive director.

Yesterday Sir Stuart defended the move, insisting that just under 30 per cent of the shareholding base contacted by the company were broadly comfortable with the arrangement.

'In the short term in the economic downturn, a change of management is not helpful,' said Sir Stuart. 'This economic blip, I don't believe we are through it and this time next year we will be in deep doobie-land – not just us, but British plc and global plc.'

He argued that he now had '38–40 months' to find a successor, rather than just a year. The change in his role is part of a wider shake-up that will bring a handful of rising stars on to the executive committee. 'I will be fishing below the board and we will see who grows big and strong,' said Sir Stuart.

Lord Burns, the outgoing chairman, said this was the best solution as it kept Sir Stuart on board while creating space for new executives to flex their muscles. 'Stuart has the unique skills to continue the challenge of making M&S a world-class leader, and to develop future leaders for the business,' he said.

But shareholders and analysts yesterday complained the company had failed to manage Sir Stuart's succession effectively.

Article 12   *Financial Times*, 2 April 2008

M&S tries to placate investors over Rose

Elizabeth Rigby, consumer industries editor

Marks and Spencer has drawn up its first serious concessions to shareholders in the row over the promotion of Sir Stuart Rose to the post of executive chairman.

However, several prominent investors told the Financial Times on Wednesday night that they were not fully satisfied with the retailer's proposals and wanted further discussions on a number of issues.

M&S surprised shareholders last month when it announced plans to promote Sir Stuart from chief executive in a move that runs counter to the accepted corporate governance position that the two most powerful jobs in a business should not be held by one person.

The move drew a trenchant response from institutional investors, such as Legal & General and Schroders, which the retailer initially played down. However, the groundswell of dissent has forced M&S to reconsider and a draft letter circulated to leading investors through the Association of British Insurers has now offered a number of concessions.

These included the annual re-election of Sir Stuart; a stipulation he would not receive a pay rise, and the promise of a senior independent director to help check his influence.

One leading shareholder said the concessions did not address its fundamental objection. 'This doesn't get away from the core row, that Rose should not be executive chairman,' he said. 'That is acceptable in the situation of a company under massive distress or in a turnround situation, but this is just wrong.'

Another top 20 institution which had also seen the draft letter said it was also not fully satisfied. 'The glaring admission is why Stuart Rose could not remain as chief executive and the letter is completely silent on this and I think they need to try to say something on it,' he said.

However, Invesco Perpetual, one of M&S's biggest investors, came out in support of Sir Stuart on Wednesday night, arguing that it was important to keep the chief executive on board.

■ The analysis

When M&S poached Stuart Rose from Arcadia in the summer of 2004 it was a case of the return of the prodigal son. This was because he had started his retail career at M&S, joining as a management trainee in the early 1970s. During his initial period at the company he had held a range of different posts, culminating in an appointment as commercial director spearheading their European business. When he left M&S he went on to work for a range of other retail companies and in the process gained the reputation as the person you should call in to revive any struggling retailer. This was certainly his remit at M&S the second time around, as he came back at a time when the company was facing severe difficulties. It had lost a significant amount of market share to the newer kids on the block such as Next and Primark. They had grabbed market share from their older rival and in the process put a severe dent in M&S's bottom line. He soon came up with a radical strategy designed to completely refocus the business. This included buying the women's fashion brand Per Una and selling the company's financial services business. The company was re-focused back on its core business which was women's fashion retailing.

Stuart Rose also reached out to the former lastminute.com entrepreneur Martha Lane Fox to make her a non-executive director. She was called in primarily to help revitalise the company's online retail presence. This was quite a turnaround for a business that in the past had steered clear of any serious internet presence. It was taken as a clear sign that the retailing dinosaur was now waking up and was ready to take on the competition.

Since the low point in 2005 there had been a strong recovery in the business, with the share price hitting an all-time high of £7.50 per share in the summer of 2007. Against this background Stuart Rose was viewed as a messiah-type figure that could do no wrong. Even his decision to turn down a bid from Phillip Green of around £4/share looked like a sound business decision. He could rightly argue that the offer seriously undervalued the business's real worth.

However, in early 2008 this success came to an abrupt halt. The latest trading update revealed that like-for-like sales were down by 2.2%, which resulted in a 20% fall in the company's share price. The stock market did not take kindly to this news, with some investors feeling that they had been rather misled by previous statements. In the wake of this abrupt change in fortunes Stuart Rose could no longer look forward to heading into retirement in the near future with his reputation intact as being 'the man who saved M&S'. He now faced the task of trying to turn around the business a second time.

7

BUSINESS ORGANISATIONS (FROM LARGE TO SMALL COMPANIES)

The first article chosen here was published the day after Stuart Rose announced the plan that would have seen Lord Burns step down as chairman on 1 June 2008 with himself stepping up to become executive chairman. There was immediate unease at the £450,000 pay-off to the former chairman. However, this was a minor irritation to the leading investment management companies such as Legal and General, who were even more concerned about the implications for the independent running of the business in the future. Mark Burgess, their head of equities, is quoted as saying.

'As set out in the combined code, we believe strongly in the separation of the roles of chairman and chief executive believing that this provides a much-needed balance in the boardroom and prevents potentially damaging concentration of power.'

The Association of British Insurers (ABI) was slightly more cautious in their response, merely 'pressing for further explanation'.

In the second article M&S went back to their shareholders to urge them to back the decision to appoint Stuart Rose to his new position. In order to persuade the shareholders they revealed some new measures including:

a) The provision that Stuart Rose would stand for re-election each year in his new role as executive chairman.

b) His annual pay of £1.13 million would remain unchanged.

c) Two new non-executive directors would be appointed to the board. This was seen as providing a counter-balance to the power of Stuart Rose.

d) Finally M&S would go back to having a separate chairman and chief executive from July 2011 when Stuart Rose was stepping down.

Despite these measures many large shareholders still had strong concerns as they felt that they did not deal with the fundamental issue of the importance of maintaining good corporate governance. This would only be achieved if there was a clear separation between the role of chairman and chief executive.

Principal–agent: an interesting aside!

This article is a very good illustration of the principal–agent problem in practice. In large companies there is a clear split between the owners and the managers of the business. The shareholders, are the owners and we refer to them as 'the principals'. In contrast the managers of the company are the agents employed to work on behalf of the owners.

This can cause many problems in reality. This is especially the case when the managers do not appear to be acting in a way that seems to be in the best financial interests of the shareholders, who are generally assumed to want to maximise the value of the shares that they own in the company.

The role of the board of directors (led by the chairman) is to ensure that the managers (the agents) are acting in the best interests of the shareholders (the principals). In practice it is not always clear that this is the case.

■ Key terms

1. Chairman

In most companies the role of chairman is separated from that of chief executive officer. This is to ensure effective corporate governance with the non-executive chairman ensuring that the interests of the shareholders are fully protected.

a) Non-executive chairman

This is supposed to be a person who is independent of the core management team. They will normally be employed on a part-time basis and will chair the main board of directors. In addition the CEO can look to them for advice and guidance.

You will also see the term NED, which stands for non-executive director. Most public companies will employ a number of part-time NEDs to give independent advice on the running of the company's operations.

b) Executive chairman

This refers to a situation where a company has a full-time chairman who also takes the role of chief executive of the business.

2. Corporate governance (code)

This is a general term used to describe the relationship between the owners of a business (the shareholders) and the managers of the business. It covers the various mechanisms by which the shareholders can try to make sure that the managers act in their interest. This should ensure that the managers are open, fair and fully accountable for all their actions.

3. Shareholder

In most companies the shareholders provide the bulk of the long-term finance. This makes them the key stakeholders in the business. They are the owners of the business and the managers must always remember that they are merely acting as agents working on behalf of the shareholders who are the principals. The shareholders range from private investors with small stakes in the business right up to the large financial institutions that often own a significant percentage of the equity of a business.

4. Chief executive (officer)

This is the top person in the company who will have the main responsibility for implementing the policies of the board of directors on a daily basis. Put simply, they are running the business.

5. Association of British Insurers

The ABI (Association of British Insurers) was formed in 1985 and it has the task of giving the view of the UK's insurance industry on a number of issues. The work of the ABI is split into four main departments: General Insurance, Life and Pensions, Financial Regulation and Tax and Investment. The ABI has a membership of around 400 companies and is located in the City of London.

7

BUSINESS ORGANISATIONS (FROM LARGE TO SMALL COMPANIES)

6. **Institutional investors**

   These are the large pension funds and insurance companies that are the key investors in financial markets. They look to invest in long-term assets to match their long-term liabilities (paying out pensions). These investors have flourished in recent years due to the greater wealth of the private sector. In contrast the private clients refer to the individuals who invest on their own behalf.

7. **Financial distress**

   In corporate finance we use the term 'financial distress' to describe a position where a company is failing to meet its commitments to its creditors. This means that it is not making timely interest or redemption payments. More often than not financial distress will result in the bankruptcy of a business.

   In the second article there is a suggestion that it might be acceptable to use the role of executive chairman if a company is facing this kind of financial difficulty.

■ What do you think?

1. How reasonable is it for economists to assume that most firms aim to maximise their profits?

2. How can the owners of a business ensure that the managers of a company do not pursue their own interests rather than that of their shareholders?

3. Select a company of your choice and *briefly* discuss how successful they have been in achieving their corporate goals.

4. What is the role of a non-executive chairman in a company? How does this compare to that of an executive chairman?

5. Why might the major institutional shareholders be concerned about the appointment of Stuart Rose as executive chairman of M&S?

6. In economics what is meant by the concept of the 'principal–agent relationship'?

7. Explain what is meant by the term 'financial distress'?

8. To what extent did the compromise proposals from M&S deal with the concerns of the shareholders who had wanted to see a clear separation made between the roles of chairman and chief executive?

■ Data exercise

You will need the Companies and Market Section of the *Financial Times*. Go to the London Share Price Service. This is normally the two pages inside the back page of the Companies and Markets Section.

   Answer these questions

1. What is the current share price for M&S plc?

2. What is the high and low for this share price in the last 12 months?

3. What is the current P/E ratio for M&S?

4. How does this P/E ratio compare to other similar companies?

5. Finally, get hold of Marks and Spencer's latest Annual Report.

(Hint: you can phone investors relations or download it at their website.)

Based on this information you should now write a short report on the financial performance of the company in the last year. Include some discussion of the share price
performance and volatility.

■ The Web

Go to the official website of the Association of British Insurers.
This can be found at **www.abi.org.uk**.
Go to the 'About us' section.

1. You are required to write a short summary of what it does.

2. Now go to the 'media centre' section and investigate recent press releases and try to
   find its latest report/research into corporate governance. What are its findings?

■ Research

Begg, D. and Ward, D., (2007) *Economics for Business*, 2nd edition, Maidenhead: McGraw-Hill.
You should look at Chapter 8. The principal–agent problem is discussed on pages 169–179. The
role of the Competition Commission in action is well shown on the top of page 148 (Heinz
deal).

Begg, D., Fischer, S. and Dornbusch, R., (2008) *Economics*, 9th edition, Maidenhead: McGraw-
Hill. You should look at Chapter 6. Pages 103–109 include a clear explanation of firms and profit
maximisation.

Gillespie, A., (2007) *Foundations of Economics*, 1st edition, Oxford: Oxford University Press. You
should focus on Chapter 10 for a good discussion of the profit motive. In addition in Chapter
17 you will find a clear explanation of business objectives. The problem of 'the divorce between
ownership and control' is set out on pages 216–218.

Sloman, J. and Hinde, K., (2007) *Economics for Business*, 4th edition, Harlow: Financial Times
Prentice Hall. You should look at Chapter 3.

Small companies held in a bear squeeze

Economists spend a great deal of time analysing the activities of what are termed 'small and medium enterprises' (SMEs). However, the factors that define what exactly an SME is vary according to where you are asking the question, since the factors vary in different countries. In most cases the key criterion is the number of staff that they employ, with other supplementary factors including the firm's turnover and the size of its balance sheet.

For example, the UK's Department for Business, Enterprise and Regulatory Reform (BERR) defines a small enterprise as one with less than 50 employees, and a medium enterprise as one with at least 50 but less than 250 employees. Finally, large enterprises have more than 250 employees.

Whatever the definition of an SME it would be nice to think that many of these companies that start out small each year would have a good chance of developing into much larger businesses employing thousands of people. The reality is that this seldom happens. Indeed an alarmingly large amount will fail within a very short time. However, the small business sector does enjoy a number of important advantages over its larger competitors.

What are the most important of these factors?

1. Small companies tend to be able to offer a much more individual service to their clients. So, unlike larger businesses the owner of a small business might be personally more in touch with all of its customers. The quality of their after-sales service will often be exemplary.

2. Small companies can often be much more innovative with far more scope to enter new markets quickly as they are developing. This is especially the case where high-technology products are involved.

3. Small companies can react much more quickly to changes in a market or to a customer's needs. It is a bit like the advantage that a small boat has compared to a large ocean liner. If there is a problem ahead the boat can turn around easily while the larger vessel might take hours to change direction.

4. Small companies are often able to keep their fixed costs at a minimum. The owners of the smaller business are normally keen to avoid taking on any unnecessary extra costs or financial burdens.

It is obvious that while the small-company sector enjoys some clear competitive advantages there will at the same time be serious disadvantages as well. These include the problem that they may struggle to fund expensive research and development projects. It has long been recognised that the small-company sector finds it much more difficult to raise the finance that is required to make these types of long-term investments. A drawback for small companies is that they may find that some customers will be more reluctant to deal with a small enterprise that is perceived to be less stable and more financially risky. It may take them a number of years to develop the track record that is required to reassure new clients that they are a serious business that will be a reliable trading partner. Finally, most small businesses tend to focus on just one product or service. That leaves them very vulnerable to any fall in demand in this sector. They do not enjoy the diversification that a larger business might have from being involved in a wider range of markets.

I must admit that my own knowledge of the issues that relate to the small-business sector mainly comes from a former football team mate and my current tennis partner. The footballer now runs a highly successful local business designing and fitting luxury kitchens and my tennis partner has a medium-sized company specialising in providing windows and glass roofs for various buildings throughout the UK. Whenever we meet up I always ask them how things are going. Their answers provide an excellent insight into the plight of the small-business sector. During 2008 it became clear that this part of the economy was starting to be adversely impacted by the ongoing credit crisis.

Article 13

Financial Times, 28 March 2008

Small UK companies face cash squeeze

Jeremy Grant and John Willman

A blue leaflet, headlined 'Combating the Crunch', will land in the mailboxes of 20,000 businesses across Britain next week.

Published by the Institute of Credit Management (ICM), which represents people working in company finance departments, it offers four 'top tips' for managing cash flow at this 'crunch time' for businesses.

Tip two advises: 'Make sure your customer's order does not suggest different terms.' Tip four: 'Don't be afraid to ask for payment.'

The ICM says: 'Whether the credit crunch is a reality or a myth, there is no doubt that finance to support business is becoming less readily available.'

As far as the CBI employers' organisation is concerned, perceptions of the global credit turmoil's effect on the UK's 'real economy' has been somewhat overdone. Outside the crisis-hit financial and property sectors, things are 'nothing like as gloomy as you might guess from reading today's headlines', Richard Lambert, the CBI director-general, said this week.

Widening spreads in the corporate bond market – making it more expensive to borrow – are causing some pain for larger UK groups.

But companies are still busy, says Steve Radley, chief economist of the EEF manufacturers' organisation. He says there was some softening of business in the first quarter, but 'exports are holding sales up … There is little tangible evidence that the credit crunch is affecting manufacturers.'

Indeed, some large companies, such as JCB, the Staffordshire-based earth-moving equipment maker, are shielded from the worst.

Matthew Taylor, JCB's chief operating officer, said: 'The credit crunch is definitely having more of an impact. Business confidence has taken a knock generally, and the outlook is worsening. However, [we are] continuing to invest in new products, global production and distribution in order to consolidate market position worldwide.'

As the ICM's leafleting effort shows, however, there are worrying signs of stress lower down the chain – among small and medium-sized businesses. As the top tips suggest, the most serious problem is managing the cash flow seen as crucial to the survival of thousands of businesses that are a pillar of the British economy.

Lynn Willrich runs a Hampshire company with annual turnover of £2m, supplying and installing audio-visual systems to museums and theme parks, as well as the National Trust and English Heritage.

'We're getting hit both ways as a company,' she said. 'We are getting paid later by our customers – they are not paying on time after their invoices are due – and equally we are having to pay our suppliers earlier.'

Meanwhile, bank managers are getting nervous about extending overdrafts and making loans. Some have been asking business owners they have known for years for personal guarantees, such as their homes.

Startups are increasingly being launched as sole proprietorships from home, to avoid having to hire staff, says the Federation of Small Businesses (FSB).

In a survey out this week, the Forum of Private Business (FPB), a similar association, blamed tighter credit conditions for a sharp drop in investment growth by medium-sized companies to 9 per cent in the first quarter of 2008, compared with 27 per cent in the previous three months. It said business confidence in future economic growth had 'weakened considerably since the last quarter'.

Philip Moody, the FPB's senior member services representative, said: 'For a small business, it's all down to cash flow, and if that starts to be restricted it does have a greater impact on a smaller business than a larger one. Small businesses are the lifeblood of the economy and they eventually grow into large businesses.'

Professor Nick Wilson, who holds the ICM chair in credit management at Leeds University Business School, says he has 'definitely' seen signs of stress among smaller companies.

'Smaller companies rely on short-term bank finance, which is the first to go because calling in overdrafts is the easiest thing a bank can do to reduce portfolio risk. That puts them in a very difficult situation because they become very sensitive to the payment behaviour of larger customers,' he said.

Yet there are signs that business could weather the storm better than it did in the recession of the early 1990s. That is because smaller companies are sitting on more cash relative to borrowings than last time. The FSB estimates that small businesses have been borrowing about £40bn a year annually, with savings and deposits with the same banks slightly higher at £44bn.

Stephen Alambritis, its spokesman, said the next year would be 'very tough' but added: 'We think small businesses have learnt the lessons of the early 1990s. They are playing a cleverer game by being not so in hock to the banks.'

Stephen Taylor of Alix Partners, a business turnround firm, said: 'I've been pleasantly surprised at the number of companies taking proactive measures to see them through this period. People are thinking about reducing working capital, asking whether customers can pay them earlier or whether they can reduce inventory.'

But this has not stopped the helplines ringing at bodies such as the FPB. Inquiries about credit and redundancy planning are up.

Peter Matza, of the Association of Corporate Treasurers, said: 'The specialty insolvency practitioners are probably licking their chops over what's coming around the corner. It's impossible to know if that's going to come to pass and, if it does, how widespread it's going to be.'

Copyright The Financial Times Limited 2008

■ The analysis

Sadly it always tends to be the case that whenever there is some major financial market crisis any impact on the small-company sector is the final thing to be considered. This was certainly the case with the credit crunch as it started to bite hard on such businesses in early 2008. First we look at the international financial markets, then the large financial institutions, then the major corporations, and finally the small and medium-sized companies.

This article starts by recognising that 'there is no doubt that finance to support business is becoming less available'. The employers' organisation, the Confederation of British Industry (CBI), believes that the extent of the impact of the credit crunch on the UK's economy has been exaggerated. This is somewhat surprising as the CBI sometimes presents a fairly gloomy assessment, no doubt acting as an effective lobbyist for immediate cuts in the Bank of England's key short-term interest rates.

One definite problem for larger companies has been the impact on the corporate bond market. This is the market that allows companies to raise finance by the issue of debt securities to investors like pension funds and insurance companies. There has been a significant increase in the return demanded from the bonds issued by companies compared to lower-risk issuers like most governments. This difference in relative bond yields is called the 'spread' and it measures the difference between the low-risk bonds (issued by some governments) and the higher-risk bonds (issued by most corporate issuers). This has without doubt made it more expensive for many UK companies to fund their investments through the issue of new bond securities. Another employers' group, the EEF manufacturers' organisation, supports this rosy picture for larger companies, suggesting that 'exports are holding up . . . and there is little tangible evidence that the credit crunch is affecting manufacturers'.

However, there seems little doubt that further down the corporate ladder there were real signs that businesses were being hit. The article quotes the example of a Hampshire-based company that supplies audio-visual equipment to the National Trust and English Heritage. The problem was at both ends of the payment chain. They were being pressurised to pay their suppliers earlier and at the same time they had to wait longer to get paid themselves. Such a situation was clearly damaging their cash flow position. This was potentially critical as maintaining a strong cash flow position is fundamental to ensuring the long-term survival of most small companies.

In these circumstances you might expect such small companies to be approaching their banks for financial support. However, as a result of incredibly tight conditions in the money markets the banks were reluctant to extend overdrafts or make loans to small businesses. If bank finance was forthcoming it was dependent on the provision of personal guarantees often requiring a borrower's equity in their home to be used as collateral. Professor Nick Wilson, of Leeds University Business School, is quoted as saying that he has 'definitely seen signs of stress among smaller companies'. This was in part due to the banks calling in overdrafts as the easiest method of reducing their own risk position.

Against this background there is one set of companies with a growing smile on their faces. These are the insolvency practitioners getting ready to use their skills in coming months as the rate of company failure rises.

■ Key terms

1. Credit crunch

This refers to the crisis that first affected financial markets in the summer of 2007. This was caused by the sub-prime crisis that started in the US. As a result banks became very reluctant to lend to each other and the interbank markets saw their liquidity dry up. In this article the focus is on how the credit crunch impacted on small firms which found it increasingly difficult to obtain bank finance during 2008.

2. Confederation of British Industry (CBI)

The Confederation of British Industry (CBI) is widely described as the employers' organisation. It is a voluntary group made up of around 1500 UK-based manufacturing companies. It carries out a wide range of surveys to gauge its members' views on the current state of economy activity. It provides a useful overview of the state of manufacturing industry.

3. Corporate bond market (widening spreads)

The corporate bond market refers to the issue of debt securities by companies. These bonds represent a debt that must be repaid normally at a set date in the future. Most corporate bonds pay a set interest rate each year, called the 'coupon'. The other key characteristic of a bond is its maturity. This is the date that the bond will be redeemed.

The article refers to 'widening spreads in the corporate bond market'. This is best explained with a simple example. Let us assume that one UK company has close to zero risk of default. As a result their 5-year corporate bond might have a yield of 5.5%. In contrast a 5-year issue from another UK company which has more risk of default might have a yield of 7.5%. This gives us a credit yield spread of 200 basis points (7.5% minus 5.5% is 200 basis points difference). The spread is mainly determined by the bond issuer's relative credit-rating.

4. Engineering and Manufacturing Support and Employment Advice for Business (the EEF manufacturers' organisation)

This is an organisation that offers a range of business services to over 6000 manufacturing, engineering and technology companies. These cover things like advice on health and safety, legal advice, environmental services and current data on pay levels. In addition it represents the interests of this sector at a national and European level. To this end it has offices in London and Brussels.

5. Cash flow

This refers to the amount of cash that a company generates and spends in a set time period. The cash flow available to a business is a crucial measure of liquidity for a company.

6. Start-up

This is a brand new business venture that is at the first stage of development. Such business ventures have a notoriously bad chance of success with very few surviving beyond a year or two.

7. **Sole proprietorship**

This is in many ways the simplest form of business organisation. In this the individual and their company are one single business identity. The big advantage of such a business is that it is easy to set up and is accountable only to the sole proprietor and no one else. The downside is that it does not enjoy limited liability.

8. **Investment (growth)**

This is where a business spends money now in the expectation that it will result in an increase in output or income at some stage in the future.

9. **Short-term bank finance**

Normally in economics we define this as any bank loans that must be repaid within a year. In practice many of these loans will be even shorter-term. The banks can withdraw the finance at very short notice.

■ What do you think?

1. What is meant by the term 'small company'?

2. Explain how the widening spreads in the corporate bond market were adversely impacting on financing costs for larger UK companies?

3. Why were the banks very reluctant to provide financial support to small businesses at this time?

4. Define the term 'short-term bank finance'.

5. How does the UK government provide support to smaller companies?

6. If you have access to information about a local small business, prepare a short outline of how it currently obtains finance.

■ The Web

Go to the government's site for 'Practical Advice in Business',
www.businesslink.gov.uk.
Look at the section on 'Finance and Grants'.
You are now required to provide a short account of the financial advice and help available to small companies in the UK.

■ Research

Begg, D. and Ward, D., (2007) *Economics for Business*, 2nd edition, Maidenhead: McGraw-Hill. You should look at Chapter 8.

Sloman, J., (2008) *Economics and the Business Environment*, 2nd edition, Harlow: Financial Times Prentice Hall. Chapter 6 looks at some of these issues from the viewpoint of small businesses. This section starts on page 185.

Sloman, J. and Hinde, K., (2007) *Economics for Business*, 4th edition, Harlow: Financial Times Prentice Hall. You should look at Chapter 16. This includes a discussion of the role of the small-firm sector.

 Go to **www.pearsoned.co.uk/boakes** to access Kevin's blog for additional analysis of recent topical news articles and to post your own comments. Download podcasts containing short audio summaries of the main issues relating to each article and check your understanding of in-text questions with the handy hints provided.

The economics of the labour market

In the last topic we examined the role of companies in the economy. In order to manufacture their goods companies need to employ labour, which is one of the key factors of production. In the context of the earlier topic 'Costs: in the short and the long run' it should be noted that for a company labour costs can be viewed as being either variable or fixed. In most cases they are more likely to be variable in the sense that labour costs will increase as production levels rise. This will especially be true where the company's labour force is very flexible with large amounts of casual staff and a culture of overtime being worked where required. In contrast most companies will have some core staff that will have to be paid no matter what the level of production might be. In this sense it can be seen that before we label a cost as being either fixed or variable it is necessary to look into a company's particular circumstances.

Economists look at the supply of labour being combined with the provision of capital and the basic raw materials in the production process. The UK labour market is an area that has gone through profound change in recent years. We have seen the role of the trade unions greatly reduced as firstly the Conservatives brought in legislation to restrict their power and then a little later their natural ally, the Labour Party, sought to distance itself from their influence. We have also seen a sharp increase in the level of female participation in the labour market with around 70% of all women now in work. However, it must be recognised that women still earn much less than men. It is likely that this is strongly linked to the increase in part-time work where women tend to be over-represented. In most sectors part-time workers will always be in a weaker bargaining position in terms of winning large pay rises and significant promotions.

One other major development has been the introduction of a national minimum wage in 1999. This policy tends to lead to sharply polarised opinions. Critics argue that a minimum wage results in a rise in unemployment especially among the low-paid. Supporters argue that the minimum wage acts as a vital anti-poverty measure by raising pay levels at the bottom of the earnings scale. In this section we see how wage rates are determined and in particular what the impact of a national minimum wage is on the economy.

The following articles are analysed in this section:

Article 14
Minimum wage increases by 3.8%,
Financial Times, 5 March 2008.

Article 15
German minimum wage ruled illegal,
Financial Times, 7 March 2008.

These articles address the following issues:

- The labour market
- Unemployment
  How is it measured?
  What are the costs of unemployment?
- The supply and demand for labour
- Determination of the equilibrium wage
- What is a minimum wage?
- Price floors – in the labour market
- Impact on wages and unemployment
- View of employers' associations and trade unions
- Low pay and the distribution of income
- Use of the minimum wage as a protectionist measure.

What price a national minimum wage?

If you are fairly young and reading this while studying economics at school or college you probably have some plan in mind of your future career. That is really admirable but I should warn you that the reality often turns out to be very different from our dreams. In my case I had a real passion for labour economics which was inspired by the teaching of Professor Metcalf, my university tutor. He instilled in me a lifelong interest in all aspects of labour economics.

When I worked as a City economist I managed to keep some links to this subject. On one occasion I got invited as one of the main speakers at a conference on 'Britain's Economic Miracle'. I remember with horror when I looked at the audience and saw a who's who of the British Labour movement as well as my mentor Professor Metcalf all waiting to hear my thoughts. I am still not sure how I managed to get through that speech. I felt such a fraud giving my opinions to this esteemed gathering when I knew that their knowledge on the subject was so much greater than mine. A few years later when I left the City to start my lecturing career my original plan was to teach and write about labour economics. However, on my first day my new boss presented me with a corporate finance textbook and told me that I should prepare to teach that course in a few weeks' time. Even after twenty years of lecturing in finance and financial markets at Kingston my interest in labour economics remains strong. For that reason writing this section was always going to be very special to me. So, finally after twenty years, I have a chance to write about labour economics. I am truly a happy man!

Article 14

Financial Times, 6 March 2008

Minimum wage increases by 3.8%

Andrew Taylor, employment correspondent

The UK minimum wage is to rise by 3.8 per cent from October, in line with an increase in average earnings but slightly lower than prevailing retail price inflation, prime minister Gordon Brown announced on Wednesday.

The rise in the adult rate, from £5.52 to £5.73 an hour, was welcomed by business leaders who had warned that increases above inflation would cost jobs in vulnerable areas such as hotels, catering and shops.

The rate for 18- to 21-year-olds will also rise by 3.7 per cent to £4.77 an hour and by 3.8 per cent to £3.53 an hour for 16- to 17-years-olds.

Union leaders, however, accused employers of scare-mongering. They said that the rises would not cover increased food and energy bills, with annual retail price inflation currently running at 4.1 per cent.

The adult minimum wage rate has risen by 59 per cent since it was introduced at £3.60 an hour in April 1999 – more than twice the increase in the retail price index over the same period. A study by Eurostat, the European Union's statistical arm, reported last summer that Britain's minimum wage was the third-highest out of 20 EU nations and almost twice the then US federal level.

Fears expressed by employers when the minimum wage was introduced, that it would cost 1.7m jobs, however, have proved groundless. John Hutton, business secretary, said on Wednesday that the number of jobs in the economy had risen by 2m since 1999.

Paul Myners, chairman of the Low Pay Commission, which recommended the increases to ministers said: 'Despite many predictions to the contrary, job numbers in the industries most affected by the minimum wage have grown, and grown significantly, over the same period.'

Nonetheless, there was relief among employers that the latest rise had not exceeded increases in average earnings, currently running at 3.8 per cent. John Cridland, CBI deputy director-general, said: 'At a time of considerable uncertainty for businesses and with economic growth already slowing, we welcome today's moderate approach.'

The Federation of Small Businesses said it was happy with the outcome while Chris Hannant, head of policy at the British Chambers of Commerce, said it was 'reassuring for employers that the national minimum wage will not increase above average earnings'.

Tony Woodley, joint general secretary of Unite, Britain's biggest union, however, complained: 'At a time when inequality is rising up the political agenda and business leaders are awarding themselves record pay rises, the lowest-paid workers continue to slip back. This can not continue.'

Dave Prentis, general secretary of Unison, the largest public sector union, said the increase 'fell short of its aim to protect the poor from the constant price rises in essentials like fuel, food and housing. A much more realistic figure would be a minimum wage of £6.75.'

Brendan Barber, TUC general secretary, welcomed the rise. He said: 'The truth is that employers will be able to absorb these sensible increases without too much difficulty.'

Article 15

Financial Times, 8 March 2008

German minimum wage ruled illegal

James Wilson and Michael Steen

A German court ruled on Friday that a minimum wage introduced across the country's postal sector was illegal, potentially dealing a significant blow to the Berlin government and supporting efforts by rivals to **Deutsche Post**, the main postal company, to open up the sector to competition.

The minimum wage of €9.80 (£7.50) was widely seen as a protectionist measure in favour of Deutsche Post when it was voted through by the German parliament late last year.

An employers' association backed by Deutsche Post had agreed the salary level with the trade union representing its employees whereas TNT and PIN, two companies seeking to challenge the incumbent, had agreed a lower wage with their own staff. Lower rates apply in eastern Germany.

A court in Berlin noted on Friday night that the German labour ministry had overstepped its legal powers in ruling that the higher wage had to apply to the whole postal sector. It was introduced on January 1.

TNT, the Dutch company, and PIN had brought the legal action together with a trade association.

The minimum wage initiative had been supported by German politicians and may have to be revisited in an embarrassment for the ruling coalition. However, the decision in an administrative court is still likely to be challenged in higher courts.

The German labour ministry said the ruling contradicted other decisions by federal labour courts. It said it was confident the ruling would be thrown out by a higher court.

Verdi, the union, said the court's decision was 'fully incomprehensible' and said it believed it would be struck down.

TNT said the decision was 'good news for us and for our customers and employees in Germany' and was also positive for the country.

'It shows you can do business in Germany because some people had started to doubt that,' said TNT. 'Of course it is not the end, as the German state immediately announced that they will appeal.'

TNT will continue paying its German staff its own minimum wage of €7.50, a rate agreed with unions representing its staff and that it says leaves it with acceptable start-up losses for the German business.

The Dutch group is separately campaigning for an end to value added tax exemptions for Deutsche Post, which it says further skew the postal market.

In December the Dutch government postponed the liberalisation of its postal market, complaining that the German decision to impose a high minimum wage threatened to undermine a level European playing field in the sector. It had planned to open the market to full competition as of January 1, allowing Deutsche Post's Dutch subsidiary, Selekt Mail, to compete fully against TNT.

The Dutch company still has a monopoly at home on letters under 50g, the largest and most lucrative segment of the market.

The court ruling said it left open the question of whether the minimum wage was unconstitutional.

■ The analysis

When we want to assess the current state of the labour market in a particular country we tend to focus on one key measure. This is the percentage of the total labour force that is unemployed. At the time of writing this topic this figure stood at 5.2% in the UK. A separate measure used in the UK is the claimant count which records the number of people claiming 'Jobseeker's Allowance'. This figure stood at 793,000. Unemployment is such a fundamental economic factor because the costs of unemployment are so high. It causes great suffering to those involved particularly when a severe economic downturn results in a sharp rise in the number of those people out of work. The misery inflicted is particularly severe because the incidence of unemployment among individuals and households is very unequal. While some people will go through their entire working life without ever suffering a spell unemployed, others will have to endure regular periods of economic inactivity. The longer someone is unemployed the worse it gets. They are likely to suffer a loss of self-esteem and maybe find themselves eventually cut off from the labour market for ever.

When economists look at the labour market in action they use the demand and supply model. The basics of this approach are set out in the introduction to Topic 2 earlier in the book. In the context of the labour market the employers represent the demand side (they hire people to work for them) and the workers are on the supply side (they offer their services to the employers). Like any other good or service, when labour is cheaper employers will increase their workforce. In contrast the workers will offer more hours of work when higher wages are offered. The level of demand and supply of labour in a particular market will set the equilibrium wage level and also the equilibrium amount of labour to be employed. In most aspects of the labour market both sides face a free market. As an example, if a retailer wants their staff to work extra hours in the evening or at weekends they might have to pay a higher rate of pay to encourage staff to offer more hours. The existence of overtime rates and bonuses shows the competitive labour market in action.

When a country has a national minimum wage in existence all this changes. The crucial economic factor is: at what level is the minimum wage set? If it is set below the existing equilibrium wage it has no economic impact at all because nobody wants to work at or below that wage anyway. However, when the minimum wage is set at a level that is above the equilibrium wage you would expect to see some negative impact on the level of employment in the labour market. This is because it prevents some workers offering themselves to employers at a wage level below this minimum wage. As a result some economists argue that a minimum wage can be unfair in that it can result in those people at the bottom of the earnings scale being even worse off. Instead of working for the low wage that they were happy to accept they instead become unemployed or can find less work than they want.

The first article chosen here shows the UK minimum wage has been increased by 3.8% from October 2008 to £5.74/hour for adults, £4.77 for 18–21-year-olds and £3.53/hour for 16–17-year-olds. Not surprisingly, the employers' groups were pleased that the increase was no higher. They argued that it might have resulted in job losses in certain sectors such as hotels and retail. On the other side, the trade unions, who represent the supply of labour, take a different view. They point to the evidence that the introduction of a minimum wage in the UK had not resulted in a massive increase in unemployment. In fact the business secretary, John Hutton, is quoted as saying that 2m new jobs had been created since 1999. This might not be too surprising as it is often argued by economists that the level of demand for labour is fairly insensitive to pay levels particularly at the lower levels. To use the proper economists' term the demand for labour is fairly 'inelastic', that is demand is not very responsive to price changes. In this case this means the demand for labour is insensitive to the level of wage costs.

The trade unions quoted in the article are, not surprisingly, keen supporters of a minimum wage because it tends to lead to upward pressure on all wage levels. Workers will be keen to see their wage differential maintained. So, if the wages at the bottom all go up there will be strong pressure for other groups of workers on higher pay to seek compensating wage increases.

The second article takes us to Germany where in early 2008 a minimum wage was introduced, but this time just for the postal sector's 220,000 employees. The Federal Government had set the level at €9.80/hour and this had been widely interpreted not as a move to eradicate low pay but rather as a protectionist measure in support of the domestic postal company, Deutsche Post. At this time a number of foreign companies were attempting to break the monopoly position enjoyed by this company in the German postal market. One potential foreign competitor was TNT, the Dutch operator, which had agreed a lower wage level with its own German-based labour force. This article shows that a German court had ruled the introduction of this minimum wage to be illegal. TNT welcomed this decision 'as good news for our customers and employees in Germany'. The move was also likely to lead to the liberalisation of the postal markets in the Netherlands as the Dutch government had postponed the planned opening up of its domestic post market, claiming that the imposition of a minimum wage in Germany hindered the development of a fully open postal market in Europe.

So where does all this leave us as far as the economics of a minimum wage are concerned? Certainly the UK's experience suggests that the scare stories of the catastrophic effects on unemployment from the introduction of a minimum wage were greatly overstated. The reality is that it does not seem to have inhibited the functioning of the labour market for those at the bottom of the earnings league. And at a time of a growing divide between the rich and the poor in society it seems to be more important than ever to set some floor on acceptable wage levels for the low-paid. In a fair society nobody should have to work below this threshold. So if anyone out there wants to hire an ageing labour economist I am free and available to work but make sure you pay me the minimum wage!

■ Key terms

1. Claimant count

This is the key official measure of unemployment used in the UK. It is based on the number of people who are out of work and actually claiming the state benefit currently called 'Jobseeker's Allowance'. During the 1980s the Labour Party used to criticise this figure, claiming that the then government (Conservative) had manipulated the definition of unemployment many times to massage the official unemployment rate. When Labour came to power in 1997 it said it would put a greater emphasis on a broader measure of unemployment which is based on all those people who are looking for work rather than just those claiming benefits. This measure, based on a survey of the labour force, tends to show a much higher level of unemployment than the claimant count.

2. Inelastic and elastic demand

In economics these terms are used to provide a measure of how responsive demand is to any given change in the price level. Certain goods are expected to have a high elasticity of demand, which means that demand for them will fall sharply as their price rises. This might include items like expensive cars and other luxury products. In contrast other goods will have an inelastic demand, which means that their demand will be relatively insensitive to any price change. This could include basic food items and essential heating and light. In the context of this article we have applied these terms to the labour market. The fact that the imposition of a national minimum wage has not had a dramatic impact on UK employment levels suggests that the demand for low-paid labour is fairly inelastic.

3. **Minimum wage**

This is legally the lowest wage that an employer is allowed to pay an employee. It is normally stated as a rate per hour with different bands according to the age of the employee.

4. **Average earnings**

This is the average amount of pay in a particular economy. There is strong interest in this figure as it is seen as a very important factor in determining the level of inflation.

5. **Retail price inflation**

Until 2003 the UK government's target for inflation was set in terms of the percentage annual increase in the average prices of goods and services as measured by the retail price index (RPI). There was some controversy in 2003 when the relevant inflation measure was changed to the consumer price index (CPI) which excludes certain important costs such as council tax and mortgage interest payments.

6. **Low Pay Commission**

From their website: 'The Low Pay Commission (LPC) is an independent statutory non departmental public body set up under the National Minimum Wage Act 1998 to advise the Government about the National Minimum Wage. Our permanent status was confirmed by Government in 2001 and we were given a Terms of Reference for a programme of longer-term research.'

7. **Confederation of British Industry**

The Confederation of British Industry (CBI) is widely described as the employers' organisation. You will see a full discussion of its role in the 'key terms' at the end of the previous topic on Business Organisations.

8. **Federation of Small Businesses**

The FSB is simply a body that represents the interests of small businesses in the UK.

9. **British Chambers of Commerce**

From their website: 'The British Chambers of Commerce is a non-political, non-profit making organisation, owned and directed by its members, democratically accountable to individual businesses of all sizes and sectors throughout the UK.'

10. **Trades Union Congress (TUC)**

This is the trade union umbrella group representing over six and a half million union members based in the UK. They campaign for better working conditions as well as the broader aim of social justice.

11. Monopoly

In economics a pure monopoly exists where only one single supplier exists in the marketplace. This gives them considerable control over the price that is being charged.

■ What do you think?

1. Discuss the various measures of unemployment that are used in the UK. Which is the best measure in your view, and why?

2. According to economists how is the equilibrium wage determined?

3. According to the first article how does the level of minimum wages in the UK compare to other countries?

4. If you were representing small businesses in the UK what arguments would you use for ensuring that future increases in the minimum wage are pegged below the increase in average earnings?

5. What economic arguments could you find to explain the fact that the minimum wage has not adversely affected the employment prospects of the low-paid?

6. Why did the German courts rule the introduction of a minimum wage in Germany to be an illegal act?

7. Do minimum wages cause unemployment?

■ The Web

Go to the website for the Department for Business Enterprise and Regulatory Reform. This body deals with the national minimum wage. Use this link:

www.berr.gov.uk/employment/pay/national-minimum-wage/index.html.

Now answer these questions:

1. What is the current level of the national minimum wage for:

   Workers aged 22 and over?

   Workers aged 16–17?

2. Why do you think the there is this gap between these two minimum wages?

■ Research

Begg, D. and Ward, D., (2007) *Economics for Business*, 2nd edition, Maidenhead: McGraw-Hill. You should look at Chapter 4. The economics of the labour market is set out on pages 87–88.

Begg, D., Fischer, S. and Dornbusch, R., (2008) *Economics*, 9th edition, Maidenhead: McGraw-Hill. You should look at Chapter 10. The minimum wage is discussed on pages 204–205.

Gillespie, A., (2007) *Foundations of Economics*, 1st edition, Oxford: Oxford University Press. You should focus on Chapter 18 to see a clear discussion of the economics of the labour market. The impact of minimum wages is discussed on pages 239–241.

8

THE ECONOMICS OF THE LABOUR MARKET

Parkin, M., Powell, M. and Mathews, K., (2008) *Economics*, 7th edition, Harlow: Addison Wesley. You should go to page 125 to see the minimum wage discussed.

Sloman, J., (2007) *Essentials of Economics*, 4th edition, Harlow: Financial Times Prentice Hall. You should look at pages 176–177.

Sloman, J. and Hinde, K., (2007) *Economics for Business*, 4th edition, Harlow: Financial Times Prentice Hall. You should look at Chapter 18. The analysis of minimum wages is very well explained on pages 381–384.

Go to **www.pearsoned.co.uk/boakes** to access Kevin's blog for additional analysis of recent topical news articles and to post your own comments. Download podcasts containing short audio summaries of the main issues relating to each article and check your understanding of in-text questions with the handy hints provided.

Part B

Macroeconomics

Macroeconomic policy: unemployment, inflation and growth

In the first topic we saw that macroeconomics looks at the economy as a whole and sets out the bigger picture. For this reason it generally concerns governments much more than individuals until the point when the management of the economy runs into severe difficulties, at which stage it affects ordinary people. The various topics that form the basis of macroeconomics dominate the news programmes and the newspapers each day. The performance of the national economy at a macroeconomic level is the principal concern of most governments, which can be illustrated by examining their main economic policy goals:

1. Economic growth

   The level of economic growth is a major focus for governments because this is how the changing level of national income is measured over time. It is generally assumed that it is desirable to target ever-rising levels of income to enable the population to constantly improve their living standards through the purchase of more goods and services.

2. Low inflation

   It is also considered to be important to keep the general level of price inflation at a low and predictable level. This will allow individuals to plan their consumption without the danger of rising prices making goods and services too expensive. The other extreme is deflation when there is a fall in the general level of prices. This is also something that governments try to avoid because consumers stop buying in the expectation that prices will continue to fall in the future. This was the problem faced by the Japanese economy during the 1990s.

3. High employment

   While zero unemployment is not a realistic policy goal governments will want to see as many people as possible in work. This is because the unemployed are seen as a waste of scarce resources as they are not themselves producing goods and services and they are likely to be dependent on the state to provide them with some form of assistance.

To start to cover this topic I have selected three articles which illustrate the global nature of the subject matter. We start with the UK's problems with measuring inflation in practice. In the second article we move to the US and look at the concern that a recession was about to hit the US following the release of the latest employment data. Finally we examine the economic problems affecting China with inflation rising to high levels and the government showing concern for the political consequences of this data.

The following articles are analysed in this section:

Article 16
Inflation jumps to 9-month high on data move,
Financial Times, 19 March 2008.

Article 17
Overview: recession fears rise after US employment fall,
Financial Times, 7 March 2008.

Article 18
Are rising prices in China driven by the supply of meat or money?
Economist, 13 March 2008.

These articles address the following issues:

- Measuring inflation

  Consumer price index

  CPI, CPIX and RPI
- Energy tariffs
- Policy of Central Banks
- Inflation versus real economy
- Inflation targets and interest rates
- Inflationary expectations
- US employment release
- Recession
- Term auction facility
- Commodity prices
- Causes of inflation
- Cost-push, demand-pull
- People's Bank of China
- Money supply measures.

Inflation: easy to define but harder to measure

What is the annual rate of inflation? One might think that this should be a simple question for an economist to answer. Surely there should be one definitive figure rather like the return on share investments in the first half of 2008 or the amount of money that the Fed lent to the US money markets in January 2008. In reality while it is easy to provide a definition of inflation, this important economic concept is rather harder to measure. It is like many other things: the answer often depends on who is asking the question.

So what are the main measures of inflation in the UK?

a) The consumer price index (CPI) – the Bank of England's target measure.

   In 2003 this became the official measure of inflation that the Bank of England is required to keep at an annual rate of 2%.

b) The consumer price index excluding food and energy prices – the Government's preferred measure, at least when it is lower.

   This is the measure that excludes the most volatile elements of inflation like seasonal food and energy prices.

c) The retail price index (RPI) – used by wage bargainers especially when it is higher.

   This is the oldest available UK measure of inflation and is used to determine the annual increase in certain state payments like pensions and benefits. It is a wider measure than the CPI as it includes housing costs such as council tax and mortgage interest payments.

Article 16

Financial Times, 19 March 2008

Inflation jumps to 9-month high on data move

Delphine Strauss

Consumer price inflation jumped to a nine-month high in February as statisticians changed the way they accounted for higher gas and electricity tariffs, official data showed yesterday.

The Office for National Statistics said the consumer prices index rose 2.5 per cent in the year to February, in line with expectations but above January's 2.2 per cent reading and further above the Bank of England's 2 per cent target.

The change is largely because the ONS has begun recording increases in gas and electricity prices in full at the time they are introduced, rather than phasing in changes over four months as it did previously.

Yet the reading underlines the challenge facing policymakers who must reconcile continuing market turmoil and the risk of a sharp economic downturn with rising inflationary pressures.

Although markets have been betting since Friday that the monetary policy committee will cut interest rates at its next meeting in April, most economists think the Bank will wait until May, wanting more evidence that demand is slowing enough to bring inflation back to target.

Yesterday's data gave some comfort in the form of lower core inflation – excluding food and energy prices – which slowed to 1.2 per cent. There was also some let-up in overall food price inflation, although a 17.6 per cent annual increase in milk, cheese and egg prices was the biggest in a decade.

Ross Walker, economist at the Royal Bank of Scotland, said that unless inflation jumped sharply in March, it looked likely to undershoot the MPC's central projection for the first quarter of the year.

Malcolm Barr, economist at JPMorgan, said the data supported the case for an early rate cut and suggested the MPC could focus more on the renewed problems in financial markets. 'The ongoing deterioration in global financial con-

ditions is clearly a downward influence on growth and the inflation outlook,' he said.

However, analysts expect higher oil and food prices and a weaker pound to force inflation above 3 per cent by the summer. Policymakers will also be worried that rising inflation expectations and higher prices charged by producers could make it harder to return inflation to target over time.

'For core-goods inflation to remain at current rates, retailers' margins would have to take an absolute hammering,' said Jonthan Loynes, at Capital Economics.

Ben Broadbent, economist at Goldman Sachs, said weaker demand growth would limit companies' ability to pass on higher costs, but added: 'In some areas – energy and food stand out – demand is sufficiently price-insensitive to allow a reasonable rate of pass through.'

Inflation on the retail prices index was unchanged at 4.1 per cent, held in check by house depreciation and by smaller rises in mortgage interest payments.

■ The analysis

At the time of the publication of this article there was much comment about the relative inertia of the Bank of England in response to the growing crisis in the world's financial markets. It was being compared rather unfavourably to the US central bank, the Federal Reserve, which had been very proactive with regular injections of billions of dollars into the money markets and aggressive cuts in interest rates during the first quarter of 2008. While the Fed was clearly attempting to throw every available resource into attempting to ward off a recession the Bank of England's attention seemed to be elsewhere. This article shows the problem being faced by the Bank of England. It has a far narrower mandate than the Fed. Put simply, the Bank of England has only one economic target and that is to keep the annual rate of CPI at 2%. Despite the growing economic crisis inflation in the UK the annual rate of CPI remained well above the Bank's target. This explained the majority decision (seven for no change and two for an immediate cut) of the Bank's Monetary Policy Committee to leave interest rates unchanged at their meeting in the first week of March 2008.

The Office for National Statistics (ONS) blamed the rise in CPI on higher energy bills. This was partly due to a change in the way that the ONS incorporated changes in gas and electricity prices. In the past it had phased in any rises over a four-month period recognising that consumers would not actually pay the higher bills until they had consumed the energy and had their meters read by the energy suppliers. In 2008 the price rises were incorporated into the CPI in one hit in this February figure. Indeed, if this effect were ignored, the ONS argued that the annual inflation rate would have remained unchanged at 2.2%.

A good way of examining changes in inflation is to focus on core inflation which excludes the especially volatile prices such as energy and food prices. Using this measure the annual rate of inflation actually fell back from 1.3% to 1.2% in February 2008. Exhibit 9.1 shows the annual price rise in the main twelve categories of goods and services included in the CPI for this month. It shows the wide variations in inflation with sharp falls in the prices of clothing and footwear, communication, and recreation and culture more than offset by sharp price rises in the prices of education, food and non-alcoholic beverages and transport.

What are the implications of the inflation data? Firstly, it was now expected that in the coming months the CPI would go above 3.1%, which means that the Bank would miss its inflation target by a full percentage point. This would trigger the need for the Governor of the Bank of England to write a letter of explanation to the Chancellor of the Exchequer. So the 'Dear Gordon' letter of a year or so ago would now be followed by a 'Dear Alistair' letter in the next few months. Indeed, this happened just a few months later in June 2008. Against this background the Bank of England would have to remain cautious in terms of further easing in monetary policy. Unless the government changed the Bank's mandate from its sole focus on inflation, the UK central bank would be unable to make any dramatic changes in interest rates to stimulate economic activity.

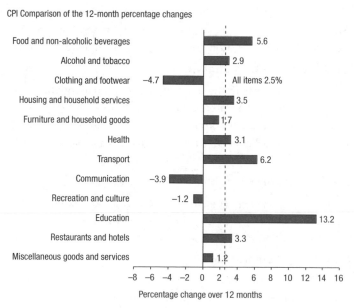

CPI Comparison of the 12-month percentage changes

Percentage change over 12 months

Exhibit 9.1

(Source: First release of Consumer price index, ONS website March 2008)

■ Key terms

1. **Consumer price inflation**

   Until 2003 the UK government's target for inflation was set in terms of the percentage annual increase in the average prices of goods and services as measured by the retail price index (RPI). There was some controversy in 2003 when the relevant inflation measure was changed to the consumer price index (CPI) which excludes certain important costs such as council tax and mortgage interest payments.

2. **Tariffs (gas and electricity)**

   In economics the term 'tariff' is normally associated with some form of government tax or duty imposed on imported products. In recent years the move towards free trade has seen the elimination of most tariffs. However, this term can also refer to a certain system of prices. In this context 'gas and electricity tariff' simply means the charges for these products from the various energy supply companies in the UK.

3. **Office for National Statistics (ONS)**

   The Office for National Statistics (ONS) is a department of the government that has the function of producing official data on the UK as a country and as an economy. The remit of the ONS is wide-ranging as it publishes statistics on so many areas, from births to deaths and everything in between, including marriages, divorces and travel to the UK as well as the standard economic data like inflation and unemployment.

4. **Bank of England**

   This is the UK's central bank. It was made independent from the UK government in 1997. Since then it has been in charge of setting short-term interest rates in the UK money markets. The key part of the Bank of England is the Monetary Policy Committee which meets monthly to set the level of short-term interest rates.

5. **Inflation target (Bank of England's)**

   When the government made the Bank of England independent (free to set interest rates without any political interference) in May 1997 it also gave it a target for controlling inflation. This target is currently 2% and is set in terms of the CPI. It is argued that maintaining low inflation is essential in order to achieve sustainable long-term economic growth.

6. **Economic downturn**

   This is simply any slowdown in economic activity. In an extreme case this can result in a recession (defined as two or more successive quarters of negative economic growth) or even a depression (a severe economic downturn that lasts several years).

7. **Monetary Policy Committee**

   The Bank of England's Monetary Policy Committee (MPC) is in charge of setting UK interest rates. It is made up of nine members: the Governor of the Bank of England, two Deputy-Governors, two Bank of England and two non-executive Directors and four independent members. The MPC is required by the government to ensure that

the UK economy enjoys price stability. This is defined by the government's set inflation target of 2%.

8. Interest rates

When an individual or a company borrows money there is a cost that they have to
pay in order to obtain the funds. If it is a short-term loan (up to one year) this is normally referred to as an 'interest rate'. So we might take out a one month bank loan
with an annual interest rate of say 8.5%. This is the interest rate, or the cost of
obtaining the funds.

9. Core inflation

This simply refers to the annual rate of CPI excluding certain especially volatile prices
including seasonal food and energy. It is also sometimes called the 'underlying' rate
of inflation.

10. Global financial conditions

This refers to the current state of financial markets. If they are relatively stable they
might be deemed to be 'favourable'. In contrast, financial markets can be said to be
'in turmoil' when financial institutions are themselves facing funding difficulties. This
was the case with Northern Rock (in the UK) in late 2007 and Bear Stearns (in the US)
in March 2008.

11. Economic growth

This can be defined as an increase in the general level of production of goods and
services in a country. We normally measure this each quarter, although most attention will be focused on the annual data because the quarterly data are too volatile.

12. Weaker pound

This refers to a fall in the value of the pound sterling. For example, as measured in
pounds per dollar, the exchange rate might fall from $2.10/£1 to $1.90/£1 which
means customers will get fewer dollars for their pound.

13. Inflationary expectations

This is a key concept in economics; it attempts to measure what people believe will
happen to inflation in the foreseeable future. The significance of inflationary expectations is that they will influence everybody's decisions. This might include the level of
wage demands or any investment decisions.

14. Retailers' margins

This is simply the difference between the price that a retailer pays for a product and
the price that is charged to the customer in the shop. When the economy is very
active retailers will try to increase these margins to enhance their profitability.

15. Price-insensitive

As we saw in Topic 3 the elasticity of demand is an important concept for economists.
This measures how sensitive demand is to a given price change. There are some products where demand is highly inelastic. For example, a consumer will be reluctant to
stop buying basic food or heating for their home no matter how high these prices

become. In contrast the demand for more luxury products will generally be more price-sensitive.

16. **House depreciation**

The term 'depreciation' is used to measure the declining value of an asset over time. For example, a company can claim the annual reduction in value of a piece of industrial machinery as a legitimate business expense. For most periods in the UK housing market we have tended to think more of appreciation rather than depreciation. However, if there is no annual capital growth in house prices then depreciation in house values become a more relevant concept. It measures the decline in the value of a house as certain fittings become outdated or wear out.

17. **Mortgage interest payments (MIPs)**

These are the monthly payments made by house owners to service their outstanding mortgage debt. The amount of the MIPs will depend on the size of the mortgage and the level of mortgage interest rates.

■ What do you think?

1. What is inflation? How is it usually measured in the UK?

2. What exactly is meant by the term 'consumer price index'?

3. It is often argued that inflation is only a problem when it is unpredicted. Do you agree with this viewpoint? Outline why you agree or disagree.

4. Explain what is meant by the term 'deflation'.

5. With reference to the *Financial Times* article why do the latest CPI data suggest that the Bank of England will find it difficult to make further cuts in interest rates in coming months?

6. What is meant by the term 'core inflation'?

7. Take a look at the Federal Reserve's website (**www.federalreserve.gov**) and then explain how the primary objective of the US central bank differs from that of the Bank of England.

8. It has become normal for central banks to set an inflation target. What are the arguments in favour of this development?

9. How might the weakness of the pound in foreign exchange markets affect the inflation rate?

■ Data exercise

Go to the Office for National Statistics official website **www.statistics.gov.uk**
Find the latest consumer price index first release.
Now answer these questions.

1. What is the annual rate of the three main measures of inflation: CPI, RPI and RPIX?

2. Find the chart that shows a comparison of the 12-monthly percentage changes in the twelve main categories of the CPI (Food and non-alcoholic beverages to Miscellaneous goods and services). Write a short report on the current pattern of annual price inflation across these categories.

3. Using the Internet compare the annual rate of UK inflation with other major economies'?

■ The Web

Go to the Bank of England's website at **www.bankofengland.co.uk**.
Now go to the Monetary Policy section.
Select the Latest Inflation Report.
Based on this Report, you are required to prepare a short PowerPoint presentation:

Slide 1: Provide a short overview of the Bank's inflation outlook.

Slide 2: What are the current trends in money and asset prices?

Slide 3: What are the current data showing in terms of the level of demand in the real economy?

Slide 4: Discuss output and supply pressures.

Slide 5: Set out the outlook for costs and prices.

Slide 6: Give an overview of prospects for inflation.

Slide 7: Based on this Report what are the prospects for short-term interest rates in the next year?

■ Research

Begg, D. and Ward, D., (2007) *Economics for Business*, 2nd edition, Maidenhead: McGraw-Hill. You should look at Chapter 9 and 10. The costs of inflation are set out on page 226

Begg, D., Fischer, S. and Dornbusch, R., (2008) *Economics*, 9th edition, Maidenhead: McGraw-Hill. You should look at Chapters 25 and 26. You will see the macroeconomic models of inflation.

Gillespie, A., (2007) *Foundations of Economics*, 1st edition, Oxford: Oxford University Press. You should focus on Chapter 29. On page 385 you will see a good section entitled 'Why does inflation matter?'

Sloman, J., (2007) *Essentials of Economics*, 4th edition, Harlow: Financial Times Prentice Hall. You should look at Chapter 9.

Sloman, J., (2008) *Economics and the Business Environment*, 2nd edition, Harlow: Financial Times Prentice Hall. This topic is covered on page 10.

Sloman, J. and Hinde, K., (2007) *Economics for Business*, 4th edition, Harlow: Financial Times Prentice Hall. You should look at Chapter 26, pages 585–592. The concept of deflation is discussed on pages 590–591 (see Box 26.3).

9

MACROECONOMIC POLICY: UNEMPLOYMENT, INFLATION AND GROWTH

US economy heading into recession!

Economists who work in the financial markets spend much of their time analysing the various economic statistics published by governments across the world. There is one particular economic release that is always the most eagerly awaited. That is the monthly US 'Employment Situation Report'. This can in just a few seconds transform the market's perception of where the US economy is heading. When these data hit the screens huge fortunes are made and lost in a few seconds. The skill of a City economist lies in being able to provide an instant assessment of the significance of this new release. The headlines on the news screen services are just the highlights from the full press release from the Bureau of Labor published at the same time. Economists must speed-read the full report and be able to pick out the full highlights to brief their traders, sales staff and clients. This is a skill that is highly valued and explains why City economists can command such massive financial rewards.

Article 17

Financial Times, 7 March 2008

Overview: recession fears rise after US employment fall

Dave Shellock

Escalating fears of a US recession and growing concerns about credit markets drove global equities sharply lower this week and kept the dollar under pressure, which in turn sent commodity prices to fresh records.

A week of increasingly gloomy news culminated on Friday with the worst US employment report for nearly five years and moves by the Federal Reserve to increase liquidity in the banking system.

Non-farm payrolls fell by 63,000 last month, the biggest monthly drop since March 2003. In particular, analysts noted that private sector payrolls shrank by 101,000, compared with a 26,000 drop in January.

'A decline of that magnitude screams recession,' said Paul Ashworth at Capital Economics.

The futures market moved to fully price in a 75 basis point cut in the Fed funds rate to 2.25 per cent at the US central bank's next policy meeting on March 18 – and raised the odds of a full percentage point easing to about 34 per cent.

The jobs data came hard on the heels of news that the Fed had increased 28-day funding under the bi-monthly Term Auction Facility from $60bn to $100bn, plus additional 28-day repos totalling up to a further $100bn.

'The scale of the emergency liquidity funding is without precedent in modern times,' said John Kemp, analyst at Sempra Metals.

Lena Komileva, economist at Tullet Prebon, said: 'Rising tensions in the euro and sterling term money markets increase pressures on the European monetary authorities to follow in the Fed's footsteps and step up efforts to inject liquidity in domestic markets.'

Signs of stress in the money markets were evident as three-month sterling and euro interbank lending rates spent much of the week at levels not seen since January.

Credit spreads ballooned and equity markets sank as uncertainty about bond insurers, forced selling and margin calls at hedge funds, and record US mortgage delinquencies heightened concerns about further problems in the financial sector.

Ben Bernanke, Fed chairman, urged banks to write down more mortgage principal to help borrowers.

Larry Hatheway, chief economist at UBS, said he believed the changing tenor of US policy discussions marked an important third stage in the evolution of the financial crisis.

'Specifically, policy may now have to move beyond liquidity provision and rate cuts to minimise the risk of market failure,' he said.

Investment-grade credit indices in the US, Europe and Japan hit record levels, while in equity markets the S&P 500 touched its lowest level since September 2006.

Over the week, the US benchmark fell 2.8 per cent, the pan-European FTSE Eurofirst 300 shed 3.5 per cent and the Nikkei 225 in Tokyo tumbled 6 per cent.

Government bonds had a volatile week as the spread between the two- and 10-year US Treasury yields, watched as a measure of risk aversion, touched its highest level since June 2004.

The spread between 30-year agency mortgage bonds and 10-year Treasuries widened to more than 200bp this week, the highest since 1986.

Divergent interest rate expectations between the US and eurozone meant that the two-year US Treasury yield fell 12bp to 1.52 per cent but the two-year Schatz yield rose 12bp to 3.26 per cent.

In the currency markets, all eyes were on the dollar as speculation of aggressive Fed easing and expectations that eurozone rates would be on hold for some time paved the way for the greenback's slide to record lows against the euro. Jean-Claude Trichet, the European Central Bank president, adopted a hawkish tone after eurozone interest rates were left on hold on Thursday.

Sterling regained the $2 level as the Bank of England opted to hold rates steady.

Commodity prices continued to climb as the dollar sank, with oil, gold and copper all hitting record highs.

April West Texas Intermediate, the US crude benchmark, hit $106.54 a barrel, with additional support coming from Opec's decision not to increase supplies. Gold rose as high as $991.90 an ounce and copper touched $8,820 a tonne.

■ The analysis

This FT article reported on the latest US Labor Report for February, published on Friday 7 March 2008 at 1.30p.m. London time. The news wires across Wall Street confirmed the financial market's worst fears. The employment data showed a 63,000 fall in non-farm payrolls which was particularly worrying as it was the biggest monthly decline for five years. The detail behind the headlines was just as gloomy. There was a particularly sharp fall of 101,000 in private-sector payrolls. This was not that surprising as the private sector tends to be the first to react to lower spending by reducing its labour force. The public-sector job cuts would be expected to follow in coming months. These data led an analyst at Capital Economics to conclude that 'a decline of that magnitude screams recession'.

9

MACROECONOMIC POLICY: UNEMPLOYMENT, INFLATION AND GROWTH

Financial markets reacted instantly to the data. The US money markets took an immediate bet that the Fed would reduce it key short-term interest rate, the Fed Funds Rate, to 2.25% at its next meeting on 18 March. This prediction proved to be correct just a few days later. The Fed was also clearly concerned about the vulnerability of the US banking system as it announced plans to increase two key injections of liquidity in the money markets. The 28-day term auction facility was raised to $100bn and the normal repo operations increased to a further $100bn. When the large US investment bank Bear Stearns was forced into a dramatic rescue by JPMorgan a few days later it could hardly blame the Fed for a lack of intervention. The US central bank was doing all it could to save the financial institutions and mitigate the worst effects of the economic downturn.

Not surprisingly the US equity markets reacted very badly to the data. The S&P 500 stock market index fell nearly 3% to its lowest level since September 2006. There were also sharp falls in European and Japanese share prices. The weaker-than-expected economic data was terrible news for equity prices as any slowdown would translate into lower corporate profits, lower dividends and lower share values. The stock market would remain in the doldrums until it could start to see the first signs of economic recovery in the distant future.

The banks were also desperate to secure some additional liquidity from the money markets. This resulted in a sharp rise in the 3-month interbank rates in both the US and European markets. The bonds markets were not immune to these pressures either. The article notes that 'credit spreads ballooned'. This means the relative yield on more risky bonds increased sharply. In times of uncertainty it is always to be expected that there will be a 'flight to quality' with bond investors preferring the relative safety of high quality including US, German and UK government bonds rather than the more risky alternatives.

The unease in financial markets also caused major problems for the beleaguered hedge funds. They were reliant on massive loans taken out from the banks to enable them to take huge trading positions. When the banks started to recall these loans the hedge funds did not have enough available cash so they had to liquidate their investments, often incurring massive losses. Some hedge funds had taken huge gambles and this time they lost. One such casualty was the private equity giant The Carlyle Group which saw its hedge fund fail in mid-March 2008.

The article ends with an intriguing final paragraph; this refers to the spread between the two-year Treasury note yield and the 10-year US Treasury bond yield. It has long been recognised by bond and stock market traders that this spread (the difference in yield between the 2-year US Treasury notes and the 10-year Treasury bonds) was a crucial indicator of the financial market's expectations about future moves in the Fed's interest rate policy and inflationary expectations in the economy. The steepening in this spread at this time was caused by the strong expectation of further cuts in the Fed Funds Rate. This cut caused the decrease in 2-year yields and at the same time the continued risk of inflation produced the increase in 10-year bond yields, because the risk of higher inflation caused investors to demand a higher rate of return on bonds. This especially applies to long-term investors as the uncertainty of their purchasing power is even greater.

■ Key terms

1. Recession

A severe economic slowdown normally defined as two or more successive quarters of negative economic growth.

2. Credit markets

This refers to the financial markets where debt securities are first issued (the primary market) and then traded (the secondary market). The issuers of these debt instruments will be mainly companies and governments and the investors will be pension funds and insurance companies.

3. Unemployment and non-farm payroll employment release

This economic release is made up of three parts. The first figure is the percentage rate of unemployment which is based on a random survey of people. The second part tells us the change in thousands each month in the number of people on companies' payrolls. It excludes various special categories such as farm workers (hence the 'non-farm'), the self-employed, unpaid family workers and the armed forces. The final measure looks at the current trends in employee wage costs. It can provide early evidence of any rising cost-push inflation.

4. Federal Reserve

The Federal Reserve is the central bank of the United States. The key part of the Fed is the Federal Open Market Committee (FOMC) which decides on changes in US monetary policy. It is made up of twelve individuals. The core seven come from the Central Federal Reserve Bank (based in Washington) and the other five represent the various Federal District Reserve Banks. One of these, New York, has a permanent place on the FOMC. The other eleven banks share the remainder of the votes on a complex rotation system. The FOMC reviews the outlook for the economy before deciding on the next move in interest rates.

5. Liquidity (banking system)

In financial markets this normally refers to how easily an asset can be converted into cash. Therefore notes and coins are the most liquid financial asset. In general the more liquid an asset the lower is its return.

6. Term auction facility

This was an emergency facility used by the Federal Reserve to inject large amounts of liquidity (cash) into the US money markets during the period of the credit crunch.

7. Futures market

In the money markets there is a well established futures market that allows banks to deal at a set interest rate for a transaction on a specified future date. For example, a bank could arrange to lend £10m to another bank at a set interest rate on a specific date in the future. The attraction of this deal is that both parties know now what the interest rate is going to be. There is no uncertainty as this transaction will not be affected by any subsequent rise or fall in money market interest rates.

8. **Fed Funds Rate**

   This is the most important short-term interest rate in the United States. It refers to the overnight interbank lending that takes places in the United States money markets. The money that one bank lends to another comes from any excess reserves held at the Fed. A target level for the official Fed Funds Rate is set by the Federal Open Market Committee.

9. **Euro and sterling term money markets**

   This is where the banks that have too much money lend cash to the banks which lack funds. The main financial market product traded in the money markets is the London Interbank Offered Rate (Libor) which is the rate used for loans made to low-risk banks in the London money markets. You can get a Libor rate for a wide range of money market maturities. It starts with overnight money and then goes to one month, three months, six months and one year.

10. **Credit spreads**

    This is a measure of the relative cost of issuing more risky bonds. It is best seen with an example. Let us assume that the United States government has close to zero risk of default. As a result a 10-year US Treasury bond might have a yield of 4.5%. In contrast a 10-year issue from Ford Motor Company which has significantly more risk of default might have a yield of 6.5%. This gives us a credit yield spread of 6.5% minus 4.5% which is 200 basis points difference. In this case investors were selling lots of the higher yielding (more risky) bonds which caused 'credit spreads to balloon' as the relative cost of these bonds rose.

11. **Bond insurers**

    These are financial institutions (called 'monolines') that use their high credit ratings to provide insurance on debt issues by relatively risky borrowers. As a result a borrower rated at just a single A might be able to issue some bonds rated at triple A. The advantage to the borrower is that they will save an enormous amount of interest on their bond issues.

12. **Margin calls (at hedge funds)**

    A margin call refers to the request, normally from a brokerage house, that a particular investor must supply additional cash to their account. In this case this is where the bank has lent large amounts of cash to the hedge funds. This particularly extreme form of fund manager will employ a range of different investment tools in an attempt to maximise the returns or try to make gains even in a falling market. The funds are highly dependent on large amounts of borrowing from the banks. If the banks now start to 'call' this money back the hedge funds will be in financial trouble and they will be forced to make immediate sales of financial assets, often incurring serious losses as a result.

13. **Mortgage principal**

    This is the total amount of mortgage debt that is owed by an individual. The mortgage interest payments service this debt.

14. Credit indices

We need to start with the idea of a credit default swap. This is a financial market instrument that is designed to offer a bond investor complete protection against the risk of default. Essentially, the seller of the swap takes over the risk of default on the bond issuer for a one-off payment. So, in the event of any default the seller of the swap will be fully liable to pay the par value of the bond and any due interest payments to the credit swap buyer. A credit index is created to allow investors to trade credit market risk without having to buy and sell individual credits. Instead they trade one of the credit default indices based in the US, Europe or one of the emerging markets.

15. Hedge fund

This refers to a particular type of investment management where the fund manager will employ a range of different investment tools in an attempt to maximise the returns or try to make gains even in a falling market. The fund will rely on large amounts of borrowing and will use derivative markets and short selling to achieve these aims.

16. Government bonds

The United States has the world's largest government bond market. The Treasury market is backed by the US government and as a result is seen as having no default risk. It sets the standard for all other dollar-denominated bonds. As a result other dollar issues will see their yields set in relation to the equivalent US Treasury issue. The market can be split into three divisions:

a) Treasury bills:

This covers three months to one year maturity issues.

b) Treasury notes:

This covers 2–10-year maturity and coupon bonds.

c) Treasury bonds:

This covers bonds with a maturity of 10 years plus.

17. Standard and Poor's (S&P) 500

The S&P 500 composite index is based on the market movements of 500 companies that are listed on the New York Stock Exchange. This index is one of the most widely used measures of US equity performance.

18. Nikkei 225

This is the most-closely followed index of Japanese share prices. The index is quite broad as it is based on Japan's top 225 blue-chip companies quoted on the Tokyo Stock Exchange.

19. FTSE Eurofirst 300

This is one of the FT's more recently created stock market indices. It attempts to track the performance of the leading European stock markets. It is shown on the front of the FT each day in the World Market's Data section.

9

MACROECONOMIC POLICY: UNEMPLOYMENT, INFLATION AND GROWTH

20. **Risk aversion**

   This is the natural desire for an investor to avoid taking any unnecessary risks unless the amount of return that is on offer fully compensates for the additional risk. So, in times of financial market uncertainty it is normal to see a 'flight to quality' with investors in bonds preferring to buy high-quality issues.

■ What do you think?

1. What is the difference between a recession and a slight economic downturn?

2. What action did the Fed take in response to the latest employment data discussed in this article?

3. How did the major financial markets react to the publication of the employment data discussed in this article? Explain in particular why stock markets fell sharply in response to these data.

4. Explain the significance of the spread between 2-year US Treasury Notes and 10-year US Treasury Bonds. How do financial markets use this spread as a guide to the future trend in short-term interest rates and longer-term inflationary expectations?

■ Data exercise

You will need the *Financial Times*.
Go to the Companies and Markets Section.
Now locate the 'Benchmark Government Bond Table' in the Market Data page.
Look at the four bonds in the US section.
   Answer these questions:

1. What is the yield on a 2-year US Treasury Note?

2. What is the yield on a 10-year US Treasury Bond?

3. What is the difference (spread) between these two yields?

4. How has this changed in the last day, week, month and year?

5. Try to explain the significance of this data.

■ The Web

Go the Bureau of Labor's official website (**www.bls.gov/ces**).
Go to the Economics News Releases.
Read the Employment situation summary.
Take some notes for future reference.
   You are now required to write a short essay on the latest report from the Bureau of Labor. This should be approximately 300 words.

■ Research

Begg, D., and Ward, D., (2007) *Economics for Business*, 2nd edition, Maidenhead: McGraw-Hill. You should look at Chapter 10. Unemployment is covered on pages 227–231.

Begg, D., Fischer, S. and Dornbusch, R., (2008) *Economics*, 7th edition, Maidenhead: McGraw-Hill. You should look at Chapter 27.

Gillespie, A., (2007) *Foundations of Economics*, 1st edition, Oxford: Oxford University Press. You should focus on Chapter 27. The causes of unemployment are set out on page 348. In addition the concept of an economic recession is well explained on pages 290–291.

Sloman, J., (2007) *Essentials of Economics*, 4th edition, Harlow: Financial Times Prentice Hall. You should look at Chapter 9.

Sloman, J. and Hinde, K., (2007) *Economics for Business*, 4th edition, Harlow: Financial Times Prentice Hall. You should look at Chapter 27, pages 580–585 to see a discussion of unemployment. You will also see the impact of a recession on unemployment discussed on page 658.

9

MACROECONOMIC POLICY: UNEMPLOYMENT, INFLATION AND GROWTH

The rise and rise of Chinese inflation

In my first year studying at university I took a course called 'The problems of the British economy'. As this was sometime in the late 1970s there was lots of scope. At that time the British economy had many problems. As it is a long time ago I cannot remember all the detail from the course but I do know that we spent quite a few weeks on inflation and in particular the causes of inflation. This article from *The Economist* does much the same thing but this time with reference to China where inflation had just hit a 12-year high. There were worries that there could be a further sharp rise in inflation in the near future.

Article 18   *Economist*, 13 March 2008

Are rising prices in China driven by the supply of meat or money?

In a country where bouts of inflation have triggered social unrest, the jump in China's inflation rate to a 12-year high of 8.7% in February is cause for concern. But economists are sharply divided on the cause of this inflation and the degree to which policy needs to be tightened.

The People's Bank of China (PBOC) is expected soon to lift interest rates and banks' reserve requirements once again. Some people fear a repeat of 1987–88 or 1993–94 when high inflation forced the government to tighten monetary policy sharply, causing a hard economic landing.

One difference between today and previous surges in inflation is that the increase over the past year has been caused mainly by food prices, which jumped by 23%. Vegetable prices are 46% higher than a year ago, pork is 63% dearer. The impact of various supply shocks, notably blue-ear disease which killed thousands of pigs, were aggravated last month by the worst snowstorms for 50 years, damaging crops and disrupting transport. Non-food prices rose by only

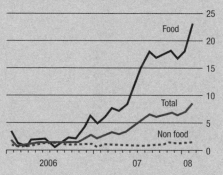

Hot food
China's annual consumer-price inflation, %

Source: National Bureau of Statistics

1.6% over the past year. In 1994, by contrast, non-food inflation hit 20%.

To the extent that food prices have been pushed up by one-off supply factors, they should flatten later this year, causing inflation to fall. If so, it is argued, there is no need to slam on the brakes. Moreover, higher interest rates would do little to curb food prices. Some policy makers also worry that if China raised interest rates sharply at the same time as America is cutting them, this would attract bigger capital inflows and the extra liquidity could actually worsen inflationary pressures.

Indeed, some economists believe that excess money is already partly to blame for rising inflation. In the past there has been a tight correlation between China's inflation and money-supply growth. Monetary growth surged before both bouts of inflation in 1987–88 and 1993–94. In 1993 the annual rate of growth of the M2 measure of money hit 40%.

Today it is less clear that the money supply is out of control. Over the past year M2 rose by 17.5%, not much faster than the average during 1998–2003 when prices were flat or falling. But Hong Liang, an economist at Goldman Sachs, reckons that the M2 measure of money understates the amount of liquidity sloshing around in China. She prefers M3, a broader measure, which includes deposits in non-bank financial institutions and securities issued by financial institutions. According to her calculations, M3 growth has risen sharply since 2005, from around 15% to 23%. This suggests that higher inflation could prove to be more persistent and spread from food to other goods and services, requiring the PBOC to tighten by much more.

But another difference between today and previous bouts of inflation is that in the past rising inflation went hand-in-hand with a widening current-account deficit – a classic symptom of overheating. Today China has a huge surplus. This offers another tool to fight inflation: a more rapid appreciation in the yuan alongside a modest interest-rate rise could curb imported inflation and cause less harm to domestic demand. Indeed, this is something that most economists can agree on: regardless of what is driving inflation up, a stronger yuan would help to pull it down.

■ The analysis

For a number of years there had been a tendency to forget about the problems of inflation as it had remained subdued, at least in most developed nations. However, in the early part of 2007 we began to see a resurgence in inflationary worries caused mainly by higher worldwide commodity prices. The commentators who had thought that inflation was dead were now forced to think again. In China inflation had just risen to an annual rate of 8.7%.

Why is rising inflation so feared by policy-makers? The first problem is that it causes shops and other businesses to have to change prices regularly. This means that there are financial costs involved in companies having to physically change their price list as inflation impacts on their costs base. To be honest this is normally fairly trivial until inflation starts to get totally out of control and causes them to have to update prices on a monthly, weekly, or even daily basis. A much more serious problem with inflation is that it can result in an unwanted and quite unfair redistribution of income. This applies where certain groups in society become clear losers. They do not enjoy the economic power that will enable them to demand a significant increase in their wages to offset the price rises that they face. This could apply to pensioners on a fixed income or families dependent on the state for their incomes. It could explain why past 'bouts of inflation have triggered social unrest' in China.

9

MACROECONOMIC POLICY: UNEMPLOYMENT, INFLATION AND GROWTH

127

The article suggests that economists did not agree on the causes of this latest inflation rise in China. What are the normal causes of inflation?

We normally identify two main factors behind inflationary pressures:

a) Excessive demand causing demand-pull inflation.

This can often be attributed to both monetary and fiscal policy being too lax. This means that interest rates are too low (lax monetary policy) or there is an over-generous balance between the level of taxation and government expenditure (lax fiscal policy). Both of these can cause too much consumption which results in rising prices.

b) Rising cost pressures causing cost-push inflation.

This is associated mainly with rising labour costs (wages per unit of output) or raw material prices (commodities). A company is likely to respond to any increase in its costs by looking to pass this on to consumers through higher prices. This will be dependent on the strength of demand at the time. If demand is too weak the market will not stand any significant price rise. In this case the company will have to take a hit in the form of reduced profit margins.

How do these explanations of inflation fit the evidence in China?

There was strong support for the viewpoint that much of the increase in Chinese inflation was the result of higher costs. The article clearly shows the marked increase in food prices with the price of vegetables and pork up by 46% and 64% respectively in the last year. In sharp contrast, non-food prices were only up by 1.6% in the last year. It was argued that these inflationary pressures would be temporary and so it would be inappropriate in these circumstances for the Chinese authorities to aggressively tighten monetary policy at this stage. Such action might also attract large capital inflows from overseas and this surge in liquidity flowing into the Chinese economy might actually result in even higher inflation.

Indeed, the article suggests that economists believe that there was already strong evidence to support the view that in the past there has been a strong link between China's inflation and money-supply growth. The article makes reference to the past two periods of significant increases in price inflation (1987–88 and 1993–94) which in both cases was accompanied by a surge in the rate of growth of one particular measure of money supply called M2. At the time of the article there seemed to be less concern about this measure of money supply which was growing at a more modest level. However, an economist at Goldman Sachs was quoted as saying that her preferred measure of money supply, M3, had seen a sharp acceleration in its growth rate. If this was true this was more worrying as it suggested that inflation would soon become more widespread within China and not just confined to a few food products. This would require the People's Bank of China (PBOC) to aggressively tighten monetary policy to curb the inflationary threat.

The PBOC had another weapon in its armoury to counter the inflationary threat. China was enjoying an ever-growing level of current account surplus. This suggested that they could allow their currency (the yuan)* to appreciate in value. Such a measure would be useful in acting as a counter to the imported inflation and due to the record current account surplus they could ignore any resulting loss of competiveness. This would reduce the need for the PBOC to act too severely in trying to curb domestic demand with higher interest rates. If this all worked out there will be no need for me to start a new course called 'The problems of the Chinese economy' in the near future!

*You should note that China's official currency is called the renminbi (meaning the 'People's money'). However, when it is traded internationally it is called the yuan.

■ Key terms

1. **Inflation**

   As we have seen earlier (Topic 1) this is normally defined as any sustained increase in the general level of prices for goods and services. It is normally measured by a consumer price index that records the monthly changes in a basket of goods and services reflecting typical spending patterns across different time periods and in different countries. This means that the basket used in China will be poles apart from that used in the UK.

2. **Tightening (monetary policy)**

   When you see the term 'monetary policy' in the context of central banks it refers to interest rate policy. Central banks tighten monetary policy when they raise interest rates.

3. **People's Bank of China (PBOC)**

   This is the central bank of China which was created in 1948. The PBOC is in charge of monetary policy within China as it has the responsibility of maintaining financial stability.

4. **Interest rates**

   When an individual or a company borrows money there is a cost that they have to pay in order to obtain the funds. If it is a short-term loan (up to one year) this is normally referred to as an 'interest rate'. So we might take out a one-month bank loan with an annual interest rate of say 8.5%. This is the interest rate, or the cost of obtaining the funds.

5. **Reserve requirements**

   This is where the commercial banks are forced to hold deposits with the central bank. The amount that they are required to hold is normally a percentage of eligible liabilities. What are the eligible liabilities? These are simply the value of the deposits held in their accounts in a certain period. The larger a bank's deposits, the more reserves it will have to hold.

6. **Hard economic landing**

   This is where economic activity comes to an abrupt halt. The result is severe economic disruption with many companies failing and widespread unemployment.

7. **Supply factors**

   In economics, supply and demand are the fundamental factors that are important in determining price changes. If there is a fall in supply of a particular good or service economists would predict that the resulting scarcity would result in a price rise. In this case there has been a sharp fall in the supply of mainly food products such as pork caused by factors like 'blue-ear disease'. This has caused a 63% increase in pork prices.

8. **Capital inflows**

These are the inflows of capital that are recorded in a country's balance of payments. These can be borrowing from overseas, sales of overseas assets or foreign investment into the country.

9. **Liquidity (extra)**

In economics this normally refers to how much money is flowing around in the economy. The more liquidity that is in existence the more the risk of rising inflation as excess demand forces prices up.

10. **Correlation (tight)**

This is defined as a measure of the strength of the relationship between two economic variables. In this case the article claims that there is a strong relationship between China's inflation and the rate of growth of certain money supply measures.

11. **Money supply growth**

This is defined as the total amount of money that is in circulation in a particular country's economy at a set time. In practice there is no single definition of money supply. Instead we have various measures depending on how widely we define the concept of money.

12. **Money suplly definitions**

There are many different measures of money supply that are used by most countries. In the UK we start with a narrow definition such as M0 which includes only cash deposits held at the central bank plus all the liquid cash circulating in the economy. This measure is often referred to as 'narrow money'.

M2 is a broader definition of money. It includes M0 plus all retail sight deposits held at banks and building societies. Sight deposits can be withdrawn with no notice (current accounts).

M4 is wider still as it equals M0 plus all sterling deposits held with the banks and building societies. This will include various time deposits that are tied up for a fixed period.

13. **Non-bank financial institutions**

This covers any financial institutions that are not officially defined as banks. It will include building societies, most insurance companies and investment banks.

14. **Current account deficit**

The current account records trade in goods (the visible balance) and the other side made up of services, transfers and interest, profits and dividends (the invisible balance). If it is in deficit a country is earning less income from its exports than it is spending on its imports.

■ What do you think?

1. Explain what is meant by the terms 'reserve requirements' and 'tightening monetary policy' in the context of a central bank's economic policy instruments.

2. What does the article say were the main causes of the sharp rise in Chinese inflation?

3. Explain the difference between a narrow and a broad measure of money supply.

4. How can the Chinese authorities use a strong currency to counter these inflationary pressures?

5. It is possible that this rise in inflation in China could result in a significant redistribution in income within the country. Explain why this might be a serious problem.

6. Would you describe this rise in Chinese inflation as being more of a 'demand-pull' or 'cost-push' phenomenon?

■ Data exercise

You will need to go to *The Economist*'s website, **www.economist.com**.
Now go to the Country Briefings and locate China.
Using this source find out the following information for the current year:

1. Real GDP growth.

2. Consumer price inflation.

3. Current Account Balance (as a % of GDP).

4. Commercial Bank Prime Rate.

5. The current exchange rate: renminbi:US$.

■ The Web

Go the People's Bank of China's official website
www.pbc.gov.cn/english.
Go to the section on Monetary Policy.
Now answer these questions:

1. What is the objective of monetary policy?

2. What are the monetary policy instruments?

3. Look at the latest monetary policy committee report and summarise the details.

■ Research

Begg, D. and Ward, D., (2007) *Economics for Business*, 2nd edition, Maidenhead: McGraw-Hill. You should look at Chapter 12. China's growth rate is discussed on pages 288–290.

Begg, D., Fischer, S. and Dornbusch, R., (2008) *Economics*, 9th edition, Maidenhead: McGraw-Hill. You should look at Chapter 26.

9

MACROECONOMIC POLICY: UNEMPLOYMENT, INFLATION AND GROWTH

Article 18 Are rising prices in China driven by the supply of meat or money?

Gillespie, A., (2007) *Foundations of Economics*, 1st edition, Oxford: Oxford University Press. You should focus on Chapter 29.

Sloman, J., (2007) *Essentials of Economics*, 4th edition, Harlow: Financial Times Prentice Hall. You should look at Chapter 9.

Sloman, J. and Hinde, K., (2007) *Economics for Business*, 4th edition, Harlow: Financial Times Prentice Hall. You should look at Chapter 26 pages 585–592 in particular for a clear explanation of inflation and its causes (cost-push and demand-pull).

PODCAST

Go to **www.pearsoned.co.uk/boakes** to access Kevin's blog for additional analysis of recent topical news articles and to post your own comments. Download podcasts containing short audio summaries of the main issues relating to each article and check your understanding of in-text questions with the handy hints provided.

Money and interest rates

The concepts of money and interest rates are important to most people. We all tend to think that we never have enough money to spend and that the level of interest rates that we face is always too high. Before we get into the analysis of the article in this section let us take a brief look at the concepts of money and interest rates.

To economists money is important because it has a number of key functions. Most obviously it can be used as a medium of exchange. In simple terms this means to buy goods and services. This covers cash and all the money that we keep in banks and building societies to enable us to make payments. These days this is mainly through credit and debit cards rather than the use of cheques which are becoming less common. The second function of money is as a measure of value. This means that we can assess the relative value of a particular item or service. As a result a painting by an unknown artist might be worth £100 while a new work by Damien Hirst could sell for £5m. Finally, economists point to the use of money as a way of storing financial wealth so that it can be used in the future. This enables individuals to save some of their current earnings to provide a nest egg for their future well-being.

Economists also see interest rates as playing a vital role in the economy. Their level is determined principally by the demand for loans from individuals and companies and the supply of loans from the banks and other financial institutions. This causes a set of interest rates to be established in the money markets with a range of time periods all the way from overnight money to one-year borrowing. The demand for loans from companies is particularly important and this is driven by the rates of return they think they can expect to earn on these funds. In good times there are opportunities for high profits which make companies keen to borrow more money at high interest rates. In contrast in bad times these opportunities diminish so that companies become less willing to borrow money at high interest rates.

In this section we examine how these two concepts relate to the economic problems being faced by one particular country during the first half of 2008. The country is Iceland and it was pushed on to the front page of every broadsheet when its central bank was forced to raise interest rates to 15% in an attempt to bring some order back to the economy and to defend its currency that was depreciating on the foreign exchange markets. At the core of the problem was an increasing lack of confidence in the entire banking system. The major Icelandic banks had borrowed heavily to help fund some major overseas corporate acquisitions. This example illustrates the role that banks play in the economy. You will find a detailed analysis of the process of financial intermediation as we examine the way that banks facilitate the transfer of funds from lenders to borrowers. There are also explanations of a number of key financial ratios that are used to assess the financial health of banks.

The following article is analysed in this section:

Article 19
Concern grows for Iceland as rates hit 15%,
Financial Times, 26 March 2008.

This article addresses the following issues:

- The role of banks in the economic system
- What is meant by the term 'financial market intermediation'?
- Maturity transformation
- Risk transformation
- Banks' skill and expertise
- The importance of confidence in the banking system
- How can we test the financial safety of the banks?
- Deposit ratios
- Capital adequacy
- Liquidity ratio
- The role of central banks
- Signs of an overheating economy
- Falling currency
- Current account deficit
- Rapid economic growth
- A sovereign credit-rating downgrade.

Iceland coming out of the winter darkness and into the chaos of spring

In recent years financially astute UK savers began to see a number of newer banks starting to top the 'best buys' tables in the money pages of the weekend papers. These banks offered investment products under the brand names Kaupthing Edge and icesave. What these banks have in common is that they are all owned by Icelandic banks: Kaupthing Bank offers the Kaupthing Edge brand while Landsbanki offers the icesave products in the UK.

However, in the first half of 2008 fears grew about the state of Iceland's financial services companies as the country became an unlikely victim of the world's growing economic crisis. To an extent this was a problem that had been waiting to happen. The economy had been living on borrowed time with the banks raising record amounts of international debt to finance the country's ambitious overseas spending spree. As credit conditions tightened concerns grew about the viability of the entire banking system and as a result confidence in the economy was severely damaged. This prompted one of the leading credit rating agencies to downgrade the financial outlook for Kaupthing, Landsbanki and other Icelandic banks. Against this background UK savers began to fear that one of the Icelandic banks might soon become the next Northern Rock.

Article 19　　　　　　　　　　　　　*Financial Times*, 26 March 2008

Concern grows for Iceland as rates hit 15%

David Ibison in Stockholm

Fears that Iceland could be the first country to fall victim of the global financial turmoil grew yesterday when its central bank abruptly increased interest rates 1.25 percentage points to 15 per cent in an attempt to restore confidence in its struggling currency and stave off a full-blown economic crisis.

The bank said 'deteriorating financial conditions in global markets' had contributed to the emergency move. Confidence in the krona, Iceland's currency, has been shattered this year because of perceived imbalances in the economy and fears the banking sector is in danger of collapse. The krona has weakened by 22 per cent against the euro so far this year.

The rapid weakening of the currency prompted the central bank to adopt unusually blunt language yesterday, warning if the decline was not reversed Iceland faced 'spiralling increases in prices, wages and the price of foreign exchange'.

'Only time will tell if this works,' Ingimundur Fridriksson, governor of the central bank, told the FT. 'We are a small open economy and we are obviously

→

affected by moves in the international economy.'

Yesterday's move saw the krona gain as much as 6.3 per cent against the dollar, while the country's benchmark index of the 15-most traded stocks had its biggest gain in more than 15 years, rising 6.2 per cent.

The bank last raised rates in November 2007 and said then it would leave them unchanged until the middle of this year, but was prepared to take extraordinary action if the krona depreciated severely. Inflation was 6.8 per cent in February and has outpaced the central bank's target of 2.5 per cent since 2004.

'It will be necessary to continue to pursue a very tight monetary policy in order to bring inflation and inflation expectations under control, and increase confidence in the krona," the central bank said. Thor Herbertsson, co-author of an influential report in 2006 on Iceland's economy with Fredric Mishkin, a member of the US Federal Reserve board, said Iceland could be thrust into crisis as a result of the global economic situation. 'Let's say Iceland is not in more danger than some Wall Street banks,' he said.

But at the same time as international investor confidence in Iceland has fallen sharply, policymakers and economists have tried to reassure markets by drawing attention to the country's economic fundamentals and the underlying strength of the banks.

Richard Portes, president of the Centre for Economic Policy Research, and the author of a respected report on Iceland's economy last year, has urged investors to pay more attention to the data.

He points out overheating is being tackled, with economic growth slowing, hitting 2.9 per cent in 2007 and zero this year.

He adds that Iceland's current account deficit – the source of many of the concerns about the economy – has narrowed from 26 per cent of GDP in 2006 to 16 per cent in 2007.

He has also made clear that Iceland's banks are sound by international standards, with deposit ratios in line with international norms, high capital adequacy ratios by European standards and credible funding profiles.

Finnur Oddsson, managing director of the Icelandic Chamber of Commerce, said: 'The global turmoil is certainly hurting the financial sector, but the danger of things toppling over here is greatly exaggerated.'

Copyright The Financial Times Limited 2008

■ The analysis

This article highlights the key role played by the banks in any country's economy. In many ways they provide the fuel that drives economic activity. We rely on them to ensure the most efficient allocation of capital resources, ensuring that the best investment opportunities are adequately funded.

Economists use the term 'financial intermediation' to describe the key function of the banking system. What does this mean in practice? Essentially this is where the banks act as middlemen between one set of players in the economy (the lenders) and the others (the borrowers). The lenders are the financial institutions and individuals with money that they want to invest. Their aim is to deposit this money as safely as possible but at the same time to earn as high as possible a rate of return. In contrast, the borrowers are made up of companies, government and individuals without enough income to fund their spending needs. They want to borrow the money for as long as they need it and at the lowest possible rate of interest. The banks are very skilled at operating between these two sides and normally making large amount of money in the process, although they have to juggle the apparently incompatible objectives of the two groups.

I want us to take a quick look inside the banks' daily operations to see how it all works in practice. In particular let us examine how banks enable this transfer of funds to take place.

a) Maturity transformation

The first major problem that banks face is that the lenders and borrowers have very different requirements in terms of the length of time that they want the funds for. On the one hand the lenders are often reluctant to tie up their money for long periods of time while on the other hand the borrowers might be looking for very long-term funding for new investment projects. The banks can manage this process relatively easily. They are quite willing to lend to borrowers for long time periods while taking their customers' money for potentially much shorter periods. This apparent imbalance is solved for them through having a very large pool of depositors' cash that they can use to their advantage.

The banks work on the principle that the depositors are very unlikely to all be looking to access their funds at the same time. Indeed, many of them leave their money in their bank accounts for year after year. This loyalty allows the banks to make long-term loans to their borrowing customers (mortgages or corporate loans) while allowing their lending customers to make short-term deposits (these may be instant-access current accounts or longer-term time deposits). This vital role played by the banks is maturity transformation in action. It works as long as savers have absolute confidence in the financial security of the bank. Take this way and the whole system can collapse in seconds. Remember the queues that formed outside Northern Rock as frantic savers sought to rescue their funds until the government stepped in with its guarantee.

b) Risk transformation

If a bank depositor could be a fly on the wall and see the destination of their hard-earned cash they might get quite a shock. They might for example see the cash being lent to an individual or a company with a very bad credit history. In this situation the depositor might want to intervene and ask for their deposit money back. Luckily for our peace of mind, once we hand over our money to the bank we usually imagine it being very prudently invested. The reality is that if this were always the case we would not get much interest on our money. The bank has to make it work on our behalf. So they lend it to a wide range of individuals and companies. Again, by spreading the cash around a wide group of borrowers they can spread their risk. So, for every one case of a customer defaulting there will be many more borrowers who make timely interest payments and repay the principal on the due date.

c) Expertise and knowledge

Finally, banks have an expert knowledge of financial markets and institutions. Over a period of time they have developed a number of different financial products that encourage the transfer of funds from the lenders to the borrowers. It is of course true that banks can sometimes get things wrong. They can become over-dependent on the money markets to fund their loans to customers. And when these markets virtually shut down the bank ends up in trouble, just like Northern Rock. Other financial institutions can invest too much in certain financial products that later turn out to be worth much less than they paid for them, as Bear Stearns did. Such cases can damage the confidence of savers in the banking system and reduce the flow of funds to potential borrowers.

In this article from the *Financial Times* we are not looking at the problem of one bank but rather the pressure that has developed on the entire banking system in Iceland. In the spring of 2008 it suffered an almost total loss of confidence and as a result risked leaving the entire Icelandic economy in crisis. At the heart of the problem was the ambitious growth of a number of their major banks, including Kaupthing, Glitnir and Landsbanki. These banks had been transformed from boring domestic institutions to become major deal-makers on a global scale. They had helped finance the invasion of Icelandic invest-ment overseas which gave them a major presence, for example, on the UK high street. One Icelandic investment company, Baugur, owned outright or had a major stake in household names like House of Fraser, Principles, Debenhams, Karen Millen, Oasis and Coast, while the banking group Kaupthing had financed the entrepreneur Robert Tchenguiz, who had built up massive investments in the likes of Somerfield, Sainsbury and Mitchells and Butler. Finally, Landsbanki ran the online savings bank icesave, which had used very attractive interest rates to attract large amounts of cash from UK savers. The net result of all this investment activity largely financed by foreign currency loans was that Iceland built up a level of external debt that amounted to almost three times the total size of its economy.

While this was just about manageable in the boom times when credit was cheap and freely available it became a serious problem in the global turmoil following the collapse of Northern Rock and the demise of Bear Stearns. These developments not surprisingly focused attention on the perceived risk attached to the overstretched banks in Iceland where the financial markets saw a risk of imminent default. The economic miracle that this country had enjoyed in recent years was rapidly turning into an economic nightmare.

One clear symptom of these problems was the collapse in confidence in the krona, which had depreciated sharply particularly against the euro as international investors saw the risk of Iceland facing an economic hard landing. This resulted in the central bank warning that if this slide was not halted the economy faced 'Spiralling increases in prices, wages and the price of foreign exchange'.

With the annual rate of inflation hitting 8% the central bank was forced to take dra-matic action. It raised official interest rates by 1.25 percentage points to 15% in a desperate move to restore some confidence back into the sliding currency and to head off economic meltdown.

A somewhat more optimistic assessment of the Icelandic economy was offered by Richard Portes, Head of the Centre for Economic Policy Research. In his report on the economy he highlighted that economic activity was already coming back under control. He pointed to data showing that economic growth slowed to less than 3% in 2007 and was forecast to be flat in the current year. Even more importantly he argued that the

Icelandic banking system was secure by international standards. His assessment was based on the following measures:

a) The deposit ratios were in line with normal international levels. This means that the amount of the banks' loans compared to their deposits. For example, one bank might have loans amounting to £100m compared to total deposits of £800m. This gives them a deposit ratio of 12.5%. If they increase their loans to £150m with the same amount of deposits the ratio increases to 18.75%. The higher the level of this ratio the more dependent the banks are on borrowed funds. So in times of financial crisis banks will be trying to keep this ratio as low as possible.

b) The banks' capital adequacy ratios were high by European standards. This is a very important measure of risk for any bank. It is normally measured as a ratio of a bank's capital to its assets. The Bank for International Settlements (based in Basel) stipulates that banks must operate with a capital adequacy ratio no lower than 8%.

One sign of growing investor unease was the decision of the major credit-ratings agencies to downgrade their outlook for Iceland's sovereign credit rating from the top rating of triple A to negative. These measures were in part a reflection of the concern that the Icelandic government would be forced to offer large amounts of financial support to the banking system to head off the financial crisis. It was clear that Iceland's economic miracle was fading fast.

■ Key terms

1. **Central Bank of Iceland**

   This is an independent central bank which has the task of operating monetary policy with the aim of maintaining price stability. Like most central banks it is required to support the other economic objectives (reasonable economic growth and high employment) as long as they do not conflict with its primary target.

2. **Interest rates (Iceland)**

   All central banks have one major interest rate that is used to signal changes in their monetary policy. In Iceland this rate is called the 'policy rate'. This was raised to 15% in response to the economic crisis experienced in March 2008.

3. **Krona**

   Iceland uses the term 'krona' (meaning 'crown') for its national currency. This is also true in most of the other Nordic states (including Sweden, Denmark and Norway).

4. **Open economy**

   This term is used to describe an economy that is largely free of any barriers to free trade. As a result it is an economy that is highly dependent on foreign trade in terms of its economic growth prospects.

5. **ICEX Benchmark stock market index**

   This is the main measure of the performance of the stock market in Iceland. It is based on the performance of 15 leading companies.

6. **Inflation**

   This is normally defined as any sustained increase in the general level of prices for goods and services. In Iceland, as in most other countries, it is measured by a consumer price index that records the monthly changes in a basket of goods and services reflecting typical spending patterns within the country.

7. **Monetary policy**

   When you see the term 'monetary policy' in the context of central banks it refers to interest rate policy. A central bank tightens monetary policy when it raises interest rates. A central bank eases monetary policy when it cuts interest rates.

8. **Inflation expectations**

   This refers to the situation where people within a country start to take account of inflation in their decisions. For example, wage negotiators will start to build in a certain level of price inflation before agreeing to a new wage settlement.

9. **Current account (deficit)**

   The current account records a country's trade in goods (the visible balance) and the other side made up of services, transfers and interest, profits and dividends (the invisible balance).

10. **Deposit ratios**

    Deposit ratios are simply the ratio of the amount of the banks' loans to their deposits. The higher the level of this ratio the more dependent the banks are on borrowed funds. So, in times of financial crisis banks will be trying to keep this ratio low.

    Economists often refer to a similar measure of security in a bank's balance sheet. This is called the 'liquidity ratio' and is simply the amount of a bank's assets held in a liquid form. For example, one bank might have £900m of assets. Out of this there might be only £90m held in liquid form (for example, in cash). This means that their liquidity ratio would be 10%. The higher the ratio the safer it will be if it faces a sudden increase in the demand from its customers to get access to their deposits. However, this argument in favour of high liquidity ratios must be balanced with the acceptance that it will generally result in lower bank profits. The greater proportion of the bank's assets held in cash the lower the return it will generally achieve.

11. **Capital adequacy ratios**

    This is a very important measure of risk for any bank. It is normally measured as a ratio of a bank's capital to its assets made up of its loans and investments. The Bank for International Settlements (based in Basel) stipulates that banks must operate with a capital adequacy ratio no lower than 8%.

■ What do you think?

1. What are the functions of money?

2. What do economists mean by the term 'financial intermediation'?

3. What is meant by the term 'tiger economy'?

4. What evidence can you find in the article to support the hypothesis that the Icelandic economy had been overheating in the few years leading up to 2008?

5. How do you expect the increase in official interest rates to impact on the Icelandic banking system and its economy?

6. In the context of the Icelandic banking system explain what is meant by the terms 'deposit ratio' and 'capital adequacy ratios'?

7. What is meant by the term 'bank's liquidity ratio'? What are the arguments in favour of and against a bank wanting to operate with a low liquidity ratio?

8. What are the main functions of a central bank? How did the Central Bank of Iceland act to try to prevent the slide in the national currency?

9. An article in the FT on 25 March 2008 stated:

   'The transformation has seen Iceland's GDP per capita rise to about $40,000 (€25,600, £19,900) – the sixth highest in the OECD, the club of the world's rich nations. But this transformation has come at a cost. Rapid growth has created imbalances in Iceland's economy and the global credit crisis has exacerbated fears that the rapid expansion of the economy and the banking system may be a house of cards poised to topple.'

   You are required to comment on this viewpoint. In particular, discuss whether the ambitious policies of the banking sector had been beneficial to the long-term economic health of Iceland's economy.

10. What does it mean when a credit-rating agency downgrades a country's rating to negative? What were the reasons that this happened to Iceland at this time?

10

MONEY AND INTEREST RATES

■ Data exercise

'Best Buys'*
Savings

Instant Access (top five)

	Gross Rate (%)	Min Deposit (£)
Bradford and Bingley	5.5	2000
Halifax	5.25	2500
Northern Rock	4.90	2500
West Bromwich BS	4.75	500
Stroud and Swindon BS	4.70	3000

Monthly Interest

		Gross Rate (%)	Min Deposit (£)
Birmingham Midshires		6.32	1
Kaupthing Edge		6.31	100
Chelsea BS 90-day term		6.31	250
SAGA		6.23	1
Chelsea BS 50-day term		6.13	250

Fixed Rate Bonds

		Gross Rate (%)	Min Deposit (£)
FirstSave	1 year	7.10	1000
First Save	2 year	7.10	1000
FirstSave	3 year	7.10	1000
icesave	1 year	7.01	1000
Halifax	1 year	6.85	1

*This table is based on the 'Best Buys' column published in the Saturday Money *Guardian* each week.

Questions:

1. If you invested £3000 in an instant access account:

   What is the difference between the highest and the lowest amount of total interest you would receive in the first year? (assume the interest rate remains the same for this period).

2. If you invested £1000 in the best monthly interest account:

   What would your first month's interest be? (assume the interest rate remains constant in this month).

3. If you invested £5000 in a 3-year fixed rate bond with FirstSave:

   How much money would you have in your bond at the end of the three years?

■ The Web

Go to the official website of Central Bank of Iceland.
This can be found at **www.sedlabanki.is**.

1. What is the central bank's inflation target?

2. What is the current level of the following Icelandic interest rates?

   a) Policy Rate

   b) Overnight rate

   c) Current account rate

■ Research

Begg, D. and Ward, D., (2007) *Economics for Business*, 2nd edition, Maidenhead: McGraw-Hill. You should look at Chapter 9.

Begg,. D, Fischer, S. and Dornbusch, R., (2008) *Economics*, 9th edition, Maidenhead: McGraw-Hill. You should look at Chapters 22 and 23.

Gillespie, A., (2008) *Foundations of Economics*, 1st edition, Oxford: Oxford University Press. You should focus on Chapter 28. On page 364 you will see a good discussion of the relationship between interest rates and asset prices.

Sloman, J., (2007) *Essentials of Economics*, 4th edition, Harlow: Prentice Hall. The most important section is chapter 8.

Sloman, J., (2008) *Economics and the Business Environment*, 2nd edition, Harlow: Prentice Hall. This topic is covered in chapter 10.

Sloman, J. and Hinde, K., (2007) *Economics for Business*, 4th edition, Harlow: Prentice Hall. You should look at Chapter 28.

PODCAST

Go to **www.pearsoned.co.uk/boakes** to access Kevin's blog for additional analysis of recent topical news articles and to post your own comments. Download podcasts containing short audio summaries of the main issues relating to each article and check your understanding of in-text questions with the handy hints provided.

10

MONEY AND INTEREST RATES

Fiscal policy

Economists normally refer to two instruments of macroeconomic policy. The first is monetary policy and this is normally controlled by the nation's central bank. We saw in the previous topic that interest rates are an important weapon in any country's economic policy-making. When economic activity is perceived to be too strong the central banks will look to tighten monetary policy by raising the level of short-term interest rates. In contrast, when there is a significant economic downturn they will ease monetary policy by reducing the level of short-term interest rates.

The other economic policy instrument is fiscal policy. This can be defined broadly to cover any decision made by the government in relation to public spending or taxation. Just like monetary policy it too can be used to influence the level of economic activity with the aim of keeping unemployment at a low level while at the same time ensuring that there is no significant risk of excessive inflation. However, in recent years there has been an attempt in the UK to operate fiscal policy much more in line with longer-term economic objectives. This leaves the Bank of England to use monetary policy to alter the level of demand in order to keep the economy growing at the correct rate. Economists sometimes call this activity fine tuning.

This can be contrasted with the experience of the United States where in 2008 the authorities used a combination of both monetary and fiscal policy measures to head off an imminent recession caused by the ongoing credit crunch. The US Federal Reserve cut short-term interest rates several times and the US government came up with an emergency package of tax cuts amounting to some $145bn. This was a good example of a very aggressive fiscal policy in action.

What are the key economic aspects of fiscal policy?

1. Government spending:

   Each year the government conducts a detailed spending review which outlines its plans for the next three years. We can usefully split this spending into central government and local government spending. Central government funds a range of public services covering areas like education, health and defence. In contrast, local government focuses on housing and environmental and leisure services.

2. Taxation:

   This comes in two main forms. Direct taxes are based on an individual's incomes and a company's profits. They include income tax, national insurance and corporation tax. In contrast, indirect taxes are paid when money is spent. They include value added tax and excise duties which are levied on particular goods and services like tobacco and alcohol.

3. Budget deficit and surplus:

   A budget deficit is where the government spends more than it receives in tax revenue. The reverse is a budget surplus where tax receipts exceed government spending.

4. The type of tax system in use:

Economists like to differentiate between the two main types of tax system that can be used. The first is called 'progressive' and here the individual pays a higher average amount of tax as their income increases. For example, in the UK the taxable income rates were as follows in 2007/08:

A basic rate of income tax of 22% on income from £2231 to £34,600.

A higher rate of 40% on any income over £34,600.

A regressive system of tax would see the average amount of tax fall as an individual's income rises. A good example of this would be VAT. A person will pay the same £50 VAT that is chargeable on a particular good whether they earn £10,000 per year or £10m per year.

In the article featured here we see the problems that faced the then Chancellor of the Exchequer in the autumn of 2006. The latest figures showed a sharp rise in public borrowing. This threatened to put at risk the government's promise that over the economic cycle the government would only borrow to invest and not to cover current spending.

Article 20
Brown's golden rule threatened by red ink,
Guardian, 20 October 2006.

This article addresses the following issues:

- Fiscal policy defined
- Public finances
- Budgets
- Public-sector net borrowing
- Corporation tax.

Say goodbye to prudence as the public debt spirals!

You sometimes read these really sad stories of an old lady dying and leaving her final estate of £200,000 to help the Chancellor pay off the National Debt. Sadly this generous gift to the government will not make much of a dent in the outstanding figure, which has grown to alarming proportions in recent years. Back in 1960 the National Debt stood at just £30bn. By 1980 this had grown to almost £100bn. And today it stands at something like £500bn. So my advice is not to even consider leaving any money to help the government's finances. Spend it while you can!

Article 20 — Guardian, 20 October 2006

Brown's golden rule threatened by red ink

Ashley Seager

Gordon Brown ran into criticism yesterday after new figures showed the public finances suffered their biggest September shortfall on record, confounding his attempts to shrink it.

The main culprit for the worsening deficit was a more rapid increase in spending than planned in the budget. Central government spending is running 7.6% higher than last year, compared with a Budget forecast in March of 4.7%.

The budget swung to a deficit of £5bn last month, £1.8bn worse than September last year. That meant that for the first half of the 2006/07 fiscal year there was a deficit of more than £13bn, similar to last year's figure despite Mr Brown's Budget pledge to narrow it by around £8bn this year from 2005/06's £15bn.

Public sector net borrowing, which includes capital spending, widened to a September record of £7bn from £5bn last year. For the fiscal year to date, PSNB came in at £25.4bn, £4bn worse than last year.

'Today's record public-borrowing figures are further proof that Gordon Brown has made a mess of the public finances,' said shadow chancellor George Osborne.

Statisticians cautioned, however, that some one-off factors such as earlier than usual transfers of grants from central to local government may have skewed the figures. The booming City is also likely to pay very strong income and corporation tax revenues to the Treasury over the coming months.

'It remains possible, as we have seen in some previous years, that the Treasury will rein in all or most of this potential spending overshoot before the end of the financial year,' said John Hawksworth, head of macroeconomics at PricewaterhouseCoopers.

■ The analysis

Every month the government releases a whole series of economic statistics. You can get a good summary of these at the UK statistics authority's website (see the Web exercise at the end of this article for the full link). One piece of data that seldom hits the headlines is the latest monthly estimate of the public-sector net borrowing (PSNB). This is the difference between the level of government spending and the taxation revenue that is supposed to fund it. This used to be called the 'public-sector borrowing requirement' (PSBR). I think that the rebranding of this figure has caused its meaning to be lost. The old definition was perfect because it stated the obvious. If a government does not raise enough tax revenue to cover its spending it must borrow the difference. 'Borrowing requirement' sounds more serious than 'net borrowing'.

The data in this article refer to September 2006 when the PSNB widened to a record £7bn compared to £5bn in the same month in the previous year. For the fiscal year 2006/07 to this date the total level of PSNB came in at £25.4bn, which was £4bn, higher than the previous year.

Not surprisingly, the opposition parties were not impressed with the data. The shadow Chancellor, George Osborne, argued that the data underlined what a mess the government's finances were in. Perhaps a more balanced view was offered by the head of macroeconomics at PricewaterhouseCoopers. He is quoted as saying:

'It remains possible, we have seen in some previous years, that the Treasury will rein in all or most of this potential spending overshoot before the end of the financial year.'

Despite this there is little doubt that the figures would have been embarrassing for the Chancellor. This is particularly true since he had established his so-called 'golden rule' for public finances. The essence of this was that the government may only borrow to invest over the course of a full economic cycle. This means that while borrowing for investment in, for example, new schools or hospitals is fine, borrowing to fund current spending is not permissible. With the start of the credit crunch just a few months away it was clear that the economic climate and the state of public finances were worsening fast. It looked as if it would soon be a good time for a Prime Minister to hand the baton on to his Chancellor.

■ Key terms

1. **Central government spending**

   This covers all the spending made by central as opposed to local government. It will cover areas like defence, health and education.

2. **Budget (forecast)**

   This is an annual event where the Chancellor sets out the government's spending and tax plans for the next few years.

3. **Capital spending**

   There is a very important distinction made between two types of government spending. The first is current spending which covers spending on items that will have a short life. For example, this could be the purchase of stationery items for a school. In contrast, capital expenditure is going on assets that will have a long life. This could include new school buildings, transport systems or hospitals.

4. **Public-sector net borrowing (PSNB)**

This is one way of measuring the difference between the government's spending and revenue. It is the difference between the revenue the government receives each month and its spending on schools, prisons, defence, etc.

5. **Corporation tax**

This is a tax that companies must pay based on the profits that they earn.

■ What do you think?

1. What is meant by the term 'fiscal policy'?
2. Explain the difference between direct and indirect taxes.
3. What is meant by a progressive tax system?
4. Explain in your own words what was meant by the Labour government's golden rule in relation to public-sector borrowing.
5. What are the main reasons that fiscal policy can be difficult to use to fine-tune the economy?

■ Data exercise

Examine the following breakdown of UK government revenue and spending for 2007/08:

Revenue

Corporation Tax	£24bn
Income Tax	£154bn
Business Rates	£22bn
VAT	£81bn
Corporation Tax	£47bn
Excise Duties	£41bn
National Insurance	£97bn
Other	£85bn
Total	£551bn

Spending

Social Protection	£159bn
Personal Social Services	£26bn
Health	£105bn
Other	£62bn
Housing	£22bn
Public Order	£33bn
Industry, Agriculture etc.	£21bn
Debt Interest	£31bn

11

FISCAL POLICY

Education	£78bn
Transport	£20bn
Defence	£32bn
Total	£589bn

You must now answer the following questions:

1. What percentage of total UK tax revenue comes from income tax?

2. What percentage of total UK tax revenue comes from VAT and excise duties?
    Why should we be particularly concerned about this figure?
    Hint: see above for the definition of a regressive form of taxation.

3. What percentage of total government spending goes on debt interest?

■ The Web

Go to the UK Statistics Authority website at: **www.statistics.gov.uk**.
Go to the section on the UK economy.
Find the latest figures for the PSNB.
This should be:

a) Public-sector net debt as a percentage of GDP.

b) Public-sector net borrowing (£ billions).

■ Research

Begg, D. and Ward, D., (2007) *Economics for Business*, 2nd edition, Maidenhead: McGraw-Hill.
You should look at Chapter 11. Fiscal policy is fully explained on pages 248–255.

Begg, D., Fischer, S. and Dornbusch, R., (2008) *Economics*, 9th edition, Maidenhead: McGraw-Hill. You should look at Chapter 21. The government budget is explained well on pages 418–419.

Gillespie, A., (2007) *Foundations of Economics*, 1st edition, Oxford: Oxford University Press. You should focus on Chapter 26.

Sloman, J., (2007) *Essentials of Economics*, 4th edition, Harlow: Prentice Hall. You should look at Chapter 10, pages 356–364.

Sloman, J. and Hinde, K., (2007) *Economics for Business*, 4th edition, Harlow: Prentice Hall. You should look at Chapter 30.

Go to **www.pearsoned.co.uk/boakes** to access Kevin's blog for additional analysis of recent topical news articles and to post your own comments. Download podcasts containing short audio summaries of the main issues relating to each article and check your understanding of in-text questions with the handy hints provided.

International Economics – balance of payments and exchange rates

In the introduction to Topic 10 we discussed some of the main economic policy goals on which governments focus. We can now add to these the desire to avoid any serious balance of payments problems. The balance of payments is a statistical record of all the economic transactions between residents of one country and the residents of the rest of the world. It looks at the balance between the money that countries earn from their export of goods and services abroad and the money they spent on goods and services that have to be bought in from abroad. It is important for a country not to be spending much more on imports than it is earning from its exports. As a result governments will examine these flows carefully and target an appropriate balance of international trade flows.

In the economics training courses that I have run for investment banks I usually spend a significant amount of time explaining the workings of the balance of payments. A clear knowledge of this economic concept is vital in allowing us to fully understand many of the problems of the world economy. In the first article selected here we examine the problems caused to the US economy by the existence of an almost permanent current account deficit. While at the same time we see that the position of Japan, which normally has a current account surplus, is far from perfect. In the second article we continue to look at Japan as we discuss the link between the balance of payments and the exchange rate.

The following articles are analysed in this section:

Article 21
Why the US current account deficit is a cause for concern
Financial Times, 26 August 2004.

Article 22
How far can the dollar fall before Japan feels the need to intervene?
Economist, 19 March 2008.

These articles address the following issues:

- The balance of payments

  current account

  capital account

  financial account
- Fiscal deficit or surplus
- Private-sector investment and the savings ratio
- The role of international capital flows
- Link between the balance of payments and the exchange rates

Article 21 Why the US current account deficit is a cause for concern

- The impact of appreciation and depreciation in currencies
- Foreign exchange reserves and currency intervention
- Real exchange rates
- What are cash and carry trades?

Current account deficits and surpluses: a tale of two brothers

My first job in the City after graduating from LSE was with a UK government bond market-maker called W. Greenwell. It was 1984 but it might just as well have been 1884. This was a very old-fashioned City institution run by a small number of very rich partners supported by a willing staff that included ex-royal butlers and tea ladies who would come around every morning and afternoon to serve drinks in fine china cups. It was a world that was soon to be swept away in the wake of the 'big-bang' reforms that came into effect in October 1986.

I was an economist at W. Greenwell. My job was to sit among the senior partners and try to give advice on the issues of the day. I can still remember the first question that I was asked by one of the senior partners as he smoked his cigar. It was 'Should we worry about the US current account deficit?' And here we are nearly a quarter of a century on from then and I am still not sure what the correct answer is. In this article one of the FT's feature writers, Martin Wolf, gives his answer.

Article 21

Financial Times, 25 August 2004

Why the US current account deficit is a cause for concern

Martin Wolf

Do current account deficits matter? I have argued that they can, most recently last week. The view that I am wrong has been advanced both in letters published in the Financial Times and in private e-mails. Since the high and rising US current account deficit is one of the most remarkable features of the world economy, deciding whether it matters is of some significance.

The argument that deficits are unimportant goes back to Adam Smith's assault on mercantilism in *The Wealth of Nations*. The aim of economic activity is consumption, he insisted, not the accumulation of treasure. Trade deficits permit a country to consume more than it produces. This then is a good thing.

More technically, with a lower cost of capital than it would have without the capital inflow, the US can enjoy higher living standards. The standard of living of the rest of the world will also be higher, provided the returns on its investments in the US are greater, at the margin, than the returns on spending at home. The export of capital to the US from the rest of the world is, therefore, a win–win proposition.

This argument is correct, so far as it goes. But it does not go quite far enough. There are three different reasons why one might still be concerned about deficits: US savings may fall too low; the rest of the world may be wasting its capital; and reversals of capital inflows may destabilise the world economy.

→

Lawrence Summers, president of Harvard and former US treasury secretary, emphasised the first of these points in his Niarchos lecture to the Washington-based Institute for International Economics.* US savings have reached all-time lows, he noted, as a share of gross and net national product. Net national savings (that is, after allowance for depreciation) are running at about 2 per cent of net national product. In effect, foreigners are now funding close to three-quarters of US net investment.

Why should these low savings matter to the US if the rest of the world is willing to fill the gap? The answer is that the return on foreign savings does not belong to Americans, even if the sums are invested in the US. Americans own only the return on their own exiguous savings. These low savings impose a constraint on future increases in their standards of living.

This would not have been the case if the rising capital inflow had raised the overall rate of investment. But the counterpart of the higher capital inflows has been higher public and private consumption and so lower savings, not a sustained rise in net (or gross) investment.

Why have US savings fallen so low? Two trends are at work: first, a long-run decline in the share of private savings in gross and net national income; and second, big swings in government savings, most recently into huge deficit. Since the current account deficit exceeds the fiscal deficit, the US is currently enjoying both guns and butter.

The second point is quite different. The rest of the world is offering the US more than one-tenth of its gross savings. A transfer of savings on this scale to the world's richest country from what are often much poorer countries looks perverse. It suggests gross inefficiencies in capital markets, domestic policies or both.

The third point is the risk of destabilising reversals of capital flows. One danger does not exist. Since the dollar is the world's key currency and principal reserve asset, US financial liabilities are either denominated in the national currency or are claims on real assets whose prices are flexible. The US cannot suffer from the currency mismatches that have proved so devastating to other countries. That is why the US is the world's borrower of last resort.

Yet the fact that the US offers no hedge against depreciation of the currency exacerbates risks to creditors. They may also conclude that the US would need a sizeable depreciation in the real exchange rate if it had to live with significantly lower capital inflows. It may well need a sizeable depreciation merely to stabilise the current account deficit, as a share of gross domestic product, given the prospective deterioration in net investment income. US exports would now need to rise by 50 per cent if they were to equal imports. If the relative prices of exports were to fall as well (that is, the terms of trade were to deteriorate), the increase in the volume of exports needed to balance trade would be still larger.

Aware of this, private creditors may wonder whether the prospective returns on US assets cover the risks of a rising exposure. Just as happened in emerging markets, fear of withdrawal of money by others could precipitate a self-reinforcing run on the currency. Without the massive foreign currency intervention by foreign governments in recent years that would probably have happened already.

So do the deficits matter? The world does need the US to run a large current account deficit to balance excess savings elsewhere. Moreover, the country may be able to run a sizeable deficit perhaps one as large as today's forever. In the short run, the huge fiscal deficit has also been a great help. Without it, sustaining US demand after the implosion of the stock-market bubble would have required dramatic monetary loosening, possibly zero interest rates. That might have had destabilising effects on the dollar's value against other floating currencies.

Yet there are also good reasons to be concerned, not just over the scale of the US current account deficit but also over its persistent tendency to rise as a share of GDP. Americans should be concerned about the impact on them of rising external deficits that are financing consumption more than investment. The rest of the world should worry about its failure to use its own savings more productively.

It should also think about the potential for much greater US protectionism. Both sides should worry about the potential for destabilising reversals in capital flows.

The steady rise in US deficits has proved better than the plausible alternative of a world slump. But the fact that the alternative to the unacceptable is the unsustainable should worry any prudent observer of the world economy.

*The United States and the Global Adjustment Process, March 23 2004, www.iie.com

Copyright The Financial Times Limited 2008

■ The analysis

There has been a long-standing debate about the significance or otherwise of a country running a persistent current account deficit. After all, the US has been in almost permanent deficit for many years and yet the economy has performed well throughout most of this period. Before we begin to analyse this article we need to make sure that we are clear about what is meant by the term 'balance of payments'. To keep it simple let us reduce the world to just two countries: the US and Japan. The US has a current account deficit whereas Japan has a current account surplus.

The balance of payments position for the US and Japan is shown in Exhibit 12.1.

Exhibit 12.1

USA

It has a current account deficit:
This means it is spending more on imports than it is receiving in income from exports.
It has a capital account surplus to fund this deficit.
This means that it is borrowing money from overseas.
It is increasing its stock of overseas liabilities.

So where is the deficit within the US?
Can we blame the government? The answer is, partly, yes.
The government runs a public-sector deficit.
Its spending is more than its revenue (mainly from taxes).
Can we blame the private sector? The answer is yes, again.
Domestic household savings are insufficient to fund company investment.

JAPAN

It has a current account surplus:
This means it is earning more income from exports than it is spending on imports.
It has a capital account deficit as this surplus is used.
This means it is investing money overseas.
It is increasing its stock of overseas assets.

So where is the surplus within Japan?
Can we find it in the government sector? The answer is no.
The government runs a public-sector deficit.
Its spending is more than its revenue (mainly from taxes).
So it must be in the private sector . . .
Domestic household savings are far higher than company investment.

*In most economics textbooks you will see the capital account broken down into a capital account (for capital transactions) and a financing account (for financing transactions). To keep things simple here I have adopted the common approach of just using the capital account to include both capital and financing transactions.

The US situation

As the exhibit shows, the US has a very large current account deficit. This means that it spends far more on imports than it earns from exports (both of these relate to goods and services). To finance this deficit it runs a capital account surplus. This means that it is living beyond its means and must borrow money from overseas to fund its consumption. As a result it increases its financial liabilities to the overseas sector. Who can we blame for this deficit? Well we can start with the private sector (everything apart from the government) which is in deficit. The exhibit shows that company investment exceeds the available domestic savings. What about the government? Yes, the government is also to blame as it runs a large fiscal deficit with government spending outstripping tax revenue.

So in the US both the private and the public sector are borrowing vast amounts of capital from overseas to fund their consumer demand. For this reason I call the US Mr Party!

The Japanese situation

Japan has a very large current account surplus. This means that it receives far more income from its exports than it spends on imports (both relate again to goods and services). In order to achieve some financial return on this money it has to be invested overseas and this is shown by the capital account deficit. This increases Japan's financial assets held overseas.

What causes this surplus? This is not down to the government which like the US actually runs a fiscal deficit with government spending outstripping tax revenue. The surplus comes entirely from the private sector. The level of household saving far exceeds the needs of Japan's companies looking for investment funds. So unlike the US, the Japanese population seems to enjoy saving rather more than consuming. For that reason I call Japan Mr Prudent!

Two brothers

So if we pretend that Mr Party (the US) and Mr Prudent (Japan) are two brothers living in adjacent houses what we are saying is that Mr Party can go out all the time and have a fun time because his prudent brother finances his excess spending. The question is whether this position is sustainable in the long term.

The FT article starts with the arguments in favour of the viewpoint that the current account deficit does not really matter. The arguments that support this view begin with the simple statement that if the economic aim in life is to maximise consumption then the current account deficit is a positive factor as it allows a country to consume more than it earns. The second factor in favour of a current account deficit is that by encouraging large capital inflows from overseas a country can actually achieve lower financing costs for companies than would exist without these inflows of foreign capital looking for investment opportunities in the US.

So, what are the three arguments against this view? In other words, why does the US current account deficit matter?

1. US savings are too low

    The first counter-argument is that it has allowed US savings to fall to dangerously low levels. The article quotes the figure for US net savings running at 2% of national income. This means that the 'savings shortfall' must be financed by foreigners who are 'funding close to three quarters of US net investment. So why have US savings fallen to such a low level? If you refer back to Chart 1 you will see that the US current account deficit is matched by a deficit in the government as well as the private sector. So the foreign savings are being used to fund increased consumption by both ordinary individuals and the government in the US.

    The problem with this situation is that the income on these savings goes to the foreigners that provide the finance. This is a permanent drain on the US economy. Returning our two brothers analogy, Mr Party has to pay substantial interest each year to Mr Prudent. This just makes his financial position even worse.

2. The world's capital markets are inefficient

    The article's second concern is that the rest of the world is transferring a tenth of their gross savings to the US. What is the economic sense in the mostly poorer countries making these huge transfers to the richer country?

3. The risk of a sudden and destabilising reversal in these capital flows

    Perhaps the strongest argument in favour of the deficit being a problem is the risk that at some stage foreign investors will start to worry about the currency risks involved in holding a substantial part of their investments in the US dollar. If investors decide that the actual returns on US financial assets do not justify these risks they could decide to withdraw their funds from the US. This could make the US economy very vulnerable.

To conclude, the sheer scale of the US current account deficit means that it cannot be ignored. It has to be worrying that these large inflows of capital are merely being used to finance US consumption rather than investment. In addition there must be a danger that at some stage in the future pressure will grow in the US which will force US politicians to resort to more protectionist policies. This could involve direct action to curb the level of imports coming into the US. The days of free trade might be over.

In many ways Mr Prudent has been financing his fun-loving brother for too long. It is about time he started to have a bit more fun himself. It's time for him to party!

■ Key terms

1. **Current account deficit (part of the balance of payments)**

   The balance of payments is a crucial economic indicator for any country. It is normal to break this down into two sides: the current account and the capital account. The current account is much the easier to understand. It records trade in goods (the visible balance) and the invisible side made up of services, transfers and interest, profits and dividends. Strictly speaking, we have to balance the current account with a matching but opposite figure on the capital account.

   What does the balance of payments look like overall?

   The current account – this focuses on physical goods and services, any flows of income and transfers.

   The capital account – this focuses on the flow of funds in and out of the country due to the buying or selling of fixed assets (capital goods). It also includes the payment of grants by the government to pay for overseas projects and any money received from the European Union for large capital projects.

   The financial account – this records purchases and sale of assets.

   It includes all cross-border transactions involving financial assets like shares, bank deposits and government bonds.

   We also take account of any official financing which records the change in the stock of foreign exchange reserves held by the country in question.

   Finally, we take account of all the many errors and omissions. A few years back someone combined the current account data from all countries in the world. This must by definition sum to zero as one country's import must be another country's export. It actually showed a deficit of some $100m. Maybe someone is trading with little green men from far away!

2. **Mercantilism**

   An economic policy that dates back to the time of the famous economist Adam Smith (1770s) that argues for a more interventionist policy from governments as they try to increase the level of exports and minimise the level of imports. This viewpoint sees any one country only making gains at another's expense. In other words, to have a winner you must have as loser.

3. **Consumption**

   Put simply, this is something most of us enjoy doing – spending money. Economists make a distinction between consumption by the private sector (you and me) and the public sector (the government).

4. Cost of capital

This is simply the cost of finance for a company looking to make a new investment. It is normal to break this down into the cost of equity finance and the cost of debt finance.

5. Standard of living

A key economic goal for most countries is to raise the standard of living of their population. This equates to the average spending per person. It is usually measured by looking at total gross domestic income per person. One drawback of this measure is that it does not show how the total income is actually distributed. It is widely thought that the UK economy is becoming more and more financially divided with the rise of the super-rich taking an increasing share of national income at the expense of the poor.

6. Savings

All the income we do not consume we save. We often measure the level of savings in an economy by looking at the country's savings ratio. For example, the UK savings ratio is defined as the proportion of gross disposable income households save rather than spend. It was around 6% at the time of the article.

7. US Treasury Secretary

This is the Head of the US Department of Treasury. It is the part of the US Administration that deals with financial and economic policy-making.

8. Depreciation

This represents the reduction in the value of long-term assets due to wear and tear etc.

9. Net national product

This is GDP *minus* Capital Consumption. You will see GDP defined in the key terms for Topic 5.

10. Net investment

This can be defined as investment net of any depreciation.

11. Fiscal deficit

This is where a government is spending more than it is receiving in tax revenue. We normally measure this as a percentage of a country's total income.

12. Capital markets

This refers to the financial markets where companies can access additional finance to fund new investment projects.

13. Financial liabilities

This is where one party (the debtor) is required to make some kind of financial payments to another party (the creditor).

14. **Real exchange rate**

    This is the nominal exchange rate adjusted for relative price change between countries involved.

15. **Currency intervention**

    This is where a government, or more often its central bank, engages in foreign exchange trading in order to influence the value of its currency on the international currency markets. In simple terms, they will sell their currency and buy some foreign currency in order to bring about a fall in the value of the domestic currency. In contrast, they will buy their currency and sell some foreign currency in order to bring about a rise in the value of their currency.

16. **Stock market bubble**

    This term is used to describe any situation where the price of financial assets rises to a level far above any realistic value based on fundamental values like dividends or a company's earnings.

17. **Floating currencies**

    This describes the process of allowing a currency to float freely on the foreign exchange markets without any official foreign exchange intervention.

■ What do you think?

1. What do we mean by the current account of the balance of payments?
2. What do we mean by the capital account of the balance of payments?
3. The article gives two reasons that suggest that the current account deficit does not matter. Briefly explain them both.
4. The article gives three main reasons that the US current deficit does matter. Briefly explain each one of these.
5. What is meant by the term 'savings ratio'? Why was it so low in the US?
6. Why do countries sometimes intervene in the foreign exchange markets to influence the value of their currency?

■ The Web

Find the Bureau of Economic Analysis official website (**www.bea.gov**).
Go to the 'US Economy at a glance' section.
Now go to the data on the US Current Account.
Write a short report (one page of A4) on the latest data.

■ Research

Begg, D. and Ward, D., (2007) *Economics for Business*, 2nd edition, Maidenhead: McGraw-Hill. You should look at Chapter 13. The balance of payments is discussed on pages 302–305.

Begg, D., Fischer, S. and Dornbusch, R., (2008) *Economics*, 9th edition, Maidenhead: McGraw-Hill. You should look at Chapter 28. This has an excellent section on the exchange rate and the balance of payments.

Gillespie, A., (2007) *Foundations of Economics*, 1st edition, Oxford: Oxford University Press. You should focus on Chapter 31, pages 417–421 for a good discussion of the balance of payments.

Sloman, J., (2007) *Essentials of Economics*, 4th edition, Harlow: Financial Times Prentice Hall. You should look at Chapter 12.

Sloman, J. and Hinde, K., (2007) *Economics for Business*, 4th edition, Harlow: Financial Times Prentice Hall. You should look especially at Chapter 27. You will see the current account and capital account explained on page 608.

12

INTERNATIONAL ECONOMICS – BALANCE OF PAYMENTS AND EXCHANGE RATES

The end of the 'cash and carry' trades

If you can recall from your childhood the story of Goldilocks and the Three Bears you will remember that is important when serving porridge to make sure that it is just right. Serve it too hot or too cold and nobody will eat it. Interestingly, the same principles apply in the currency markets. No country likes its currency to be too strong or too weak. It wants it to be perfectly valued. Sadly in the real world the actual value of currencies seldom meets this requirement.

At the time of this article there was a great deal of concern about the relative performance of the leading currencies. On the one hand the euro and the yen were rising to record highs, causing concerns to companies trying to export out of these economic areas. On the other hand, sterling and the dollar were both extremely weak. Indeed, at one stage on the world's foreign exchange markets selling the dollar became close to a 'one-way' bet with traders very reluctant to hold a currency in such free fall. Concern was growing about the state of the US financial system and as a result the dollar had fallen to below ¥100 and above $1.55 against the euro. In the past such volatility would very likely have prompted the Fed, the European Central Bank, the Bank of England and the Japanese Ministry of Finance to launch a coordinated intervention on the foreign exchange markets to defend the dollar. However, there was a widespread acceptance that such actions had failed in the recent past and it was best just to let the markets decide the dollar's fate.

Article 22

Economist, 19 March 2008

How far can the dollar fall before Japan feels the need to intervene?

In recent years the yen has been a profitable carry-trade currency, used by investors to borrow cheaply in order to splurge on risky assets around the world. If the carry trade is now part of a bygone era, so is the weakness of the yen. It has soared almost 30% against the dollar since June and on March 17th it hit a 12-year high of ¥95.76. After the Federal Reserve cut interest rates on March 18th, the dollar remained under pressure.

The yen's strength causes little jubilation in Japan. A strong yen squeezes company profits since Japan is heavily dependent on exports. Toyota, for example, bases its earnings on an exchange rate of ¥105: every 1 appreciation against the dollar costs the firm ¥35 billion ($350m) in annual operating profit. That, in turn, hurts the Nikkei 225, which has tumbled even faster than the yen climbs; it has shed more than 20% since the start of the year. Almost 60% of the companies on the exchange's main market are trading at less than their book value. Moreover, a strong yen cuts into economic growth.

Even without a governor for the Bank of

Japan, the market is starting to price in a quarter-point rate cut at the bank's next meeting in early April. At the same time, the rising yen is becoming a political issue. Fukushiro Nukaga, the finance minister, called its appreciation "excessive" and worrisome. In the past, the finance ministry has moved fast to prevent the yen from becoming too strong. As recently as 2003-04 it sold ¥35 trillion to prevent a rise in the currency that might derail its nascent economic recovery.

Japan has several reasons to hold fire, however. Although a strong yen hurts exporters, it helps hold down the prices of imports, for such things as oil and food. It is not considered overvalued on a trade-weighted basis or against other currencies. In inflation-adjusted terms, a rate of ¥100 to the dollar is equivalent to ¥125-130 a decade ago, according to Eisuke Sakakibara of Waseda University (who was known as "Mr Yen" for managing Japan's currency interventions from 1997 to 1999 at the Ministry of Finance). Even if it were to sell yen, America may be an unwilling buyer; its carmakers say the appropriate exchange rate is ¥90-100 to the dollar, notes Yasunari Ueno of Mizuho. He believes the Japanese government won't consider intervening until the rate goes at least to ¥90.

Today it is not even certain how effective intervention might be. Globally, daily foreign-exchange transactions exceed $3.2 trillion, more than twice the value in 2003. For intervention to work, Japan would need to recruit other central banks to the cause. But the dollar may not be weak enough for that—even against the yen.

■ The analysis

In currency markets governments always seem to be in search of the 'holy grail' which is a currency that is neither too strong nor too weak. They want it to be at a fair value. At the time of this article there was much concern in Washington as the dollar had been falling against the euro and most other currencies since 2002. US politicians were alarmed at the weakness of the dollar which was viewed as a clear sign of the economic decline of the country. In practical terms it was also making it more expensive for Americans to travel overseas or to import goods. In this article we see the flip side. What happens when a currency appreciates sharply in value?

The article starts by describing the yen as being a profitable 'carry-trade currency'. What does this term mean? This was a very popular foreign exchange trading technique driven by the existence of significant interest rate differentials between countries. In this strategy an investor will sell a currency from a low-interest-rate country and then invest the funds in another currency from a higher-interest-rate country. The investor uses this technique to exploit the difference between interest rates in these two countries.

Let us make up a very simple example:

a) A foreign exchange trader with XYZ Bank obtains a loan of ¥10,000 from Japanese Bank at a rate of interest of just 0.5%.

b) He then goes into the foreign exchange market and converts the yen into US dollars.

c) He uses the proceeds to purchase a US Treasury Bond with a yield of 5.5%.

d) This gives him an annual profit in terms of income of 5% (5.5%–0.5%).

This is, however, a far from risk-free transaction. The major risk for the foreign exchange trader is that the US dollar might fall in value against the yen. Do not forget that the trader will (at some stage) have to repay their loan taken out in yen. If the dollar falls in value against the yen the trader will have to repay substantially more US dollars to obtain the necessary amount of yen.

For example, it could be that $1 was equal to ¥100 when the loan was taken out in the first place. If the dollar has fallen sharply the trader might now have to give up $1.50 to obtain ¥100. As a result, when the trader needs to repay the ¥10,000 loan they will need to find $150 compared to the $100 they invested in US Treasury Bonds. This shows us that any profit in terms of higher interest can easily be wiped out by currency losses.

Going back to the article, there is a suggestion that the era of carry trades and a weak yen was now firmly in the past. The interest rate differential between the US and Japan had fallen back due to sharp reduction in US interest rates in the wake of the global credit crisis. As a result the yen hit a 12-year high of ¥95.76. Despite this there was little sense of celebration in Japan to mark this rebound in the currency. It is important to remember that the Japanese economy had been in the doldrums since the boom of the late 1980s had come to an abrupt end. Any economic recoveries since then have been rather anaemic and very short-lived.

The one economic success story has been in the exporting companies that have been highly successful in selling their products particularly into the US markets. The strength of the yen now threatened this one 'green shoot' of recovery, which risked pushing Japan back into serious recession. The danger to corporate Japan is well illustrated by the data from Toyota, the Japanese car maker. The article says that it 'bases its earnings on an exchange rate of ¥105, every ¥1 appreciation against the dollar costs the firm ¥35bn ($350m) in annual profit'.

At a more macro level this vulnerability of Japanese companies to the rise in the yen is shown in the performance of the main Japanese stock market index, the Nikkei 225. This had seen a decline of 20% since the start of 2008. It is clear that the market's concern was that the yen's appreciation would damage economic growth in Japan and seriously undermine the recovery in company profits.

The article made it clear that this issue was starting to have an impact on a political as well as an economic level. The Japanese Finance Minister is quoted as saying that the appreciation was 'excessive and worrisome'. In these circumstances one might expect the Bank of Japan and the Finance Ministry to be taking some form of coordinated action to stem the yen's advance. With interest rates still close to zero the Bank of Japan could hardly cut interest rates. However, the Japanese Finance Ministry might take more direct action in the foreign exchange markets with some form of direct intervention. As recently as the fiscal year 2003/04 it had sold ¥35 trillion to prevent a rise in the currency which might have damaged the economic recovery.

The situation in 2008 was very different for three reasons. Firstly, the rise in the yen was having one major beneficial economic effect. It was acting to constrain the rise in the prices of imported goods such as oil and some food products. Secondly, it was argued after adjusting for relative inflation that the yen was not actually considered to be fundamentally overvalued against the US dollar. Finally, it was far from clear that any official intervention would be that effective. The foreign exchange markets had a daily turnover of some $3.2 trillion. It was unlikely that Japan acting on its own could really significantly change the value of its currency. To be effective such intervention would require concerted intervention involving many other willing countries, which was unlikely to happen.

■ Key terms

1. **Carry trade**

   This was a very popular foreign exchange trading technique which is possible due to the existence of significant interest rate differentials between different countries. In this strategy an investor will sell a currency from the low-interest-rate zone and then invest the funds to buy another currency in a high-interest-rate zone. The investor is using this technique to exploit the difference between interest rates in these two zones. This strategy is far from risk-free as there is a chance that an adverse movement in the currency markets can more than offset any income gains.

2. **Weak yen**

   This is where the yen can only be exchanged for smaller amounts of foreign currency. As a result it will require larger amounts of yen to purchase goods or services from overseas. At the same time it will be cheaper for other countries to import Japanese goods and services.

3. **Strong yen**

   This is the reverse of a weak yen. It occurs when the yen can be exchanged for larger amounts of foreign currency. As a result it will require less yen to purchase goods or services from overseas. At the same time it will be more expensive for other countries to import Japanese goods and services.

4. **Nikkei 225**

   This is the most-closely followed index of Japanese share prices. The index is quite broad as it is based on Japan's top 225 blue-chip companies quoted on the Tokyo Stock Exchange.

5. **Book value**

   Put simply, this is what a company would be worth if it went out of business immediately. It is normally calculated as total assets minus any liabilities and intangible assets such as goodwill. At the time of this article it was argued that 60% of companies on the Japanese main stock market were trading a share price that was below their book value.

6. **Economic growth**

   This is where a country increases the level of production of goods and services during a set time period (usually a quarter or a year). It can be measured by national income, gross domestic product or gross national product. This is discussed in the key terms for Topic 5.

7. **Bank of Japan's Governor**

   This is the head of the Bank of Japan. At the time of the article there was a significant problem for the government in trying to appoint a successor to Toshihiko Fukui who stepped down on 19 March 2008. The Prime Minister, Mr Fukuda, was prevented from naming a new Central Bank Governor by the opposition party.

8. **Japan's Finance Minister**

This is the head of the Japanese Ministry of Finance and a key member of the Cabinet. At the time of the article the position was held by Fukushiro Nukaga.

9. **Appreciation (of the currency)**

This is simply where we see an increase in the value of one currency relative to another currency.

10. **Foreign reserves (intervention)**

These are the reserves of foreign currency that are normally held by a country's central bank. It sometimes uses these reserves to intervene in the foreign exchange markets in order to have an impact on currency values. It can sell these reserves of foreign currency and buy domestic currency to try to strengthen its own currency. Or it can buy more reserves of foreign currency by selling its own currency to try to cause depreciation in its domestic currency.

■ What do you think?

1. What is meant by the term 'carry trade' in the context of the foreign exchange markets?

2. Why does a strong yen impact adversely on Japanese corporate profitability?

3. Find four examples of real Japanese companies whose earnings are especially vulnerable to a sharp appreciation in the yen. (Hint: they will be companies that are highly dependent on exporting their goods, so they are well known even in the UK.)

4. At the time of this article the Japanese government produced estimates that a 10% appreciation in the yen versus the dollar exchange rate would reduce total export growth by the equivalent of 0.8% of gross domestic product (GDP). Use this figure to estimate the adverse impact on Japanese GDP growth caused by the 8% rise in the yen against the dollar in the first quarter of 2008.

5. What reasons are given for the reluctance of the Japanese authorities to intervene to halt the rise in the yen through official intervention?

6. What is meant by a trade-weighted currency index? Find the current value of the sterling and dollar index. (Hint: look at the front of the FT in the World Market data.)

■ Data exercise

You will need the *Financial Times*.
Go to the Companies and Markets Section.
Now locate the 'Benchmark Government Bond Table' in the Market Data page.
Look at the four bonds in the US section.
Look at the four bonds in the Japanese section.

Based on these data discuss the possibility of a making a profitable 'carry trade' involving these two currencies. What is the main risk in such a transaction?

■ The Web

Go the Bank of Japan's official website **www.boj.or.jp**/en.
Go to the section on Monetary Policy.
Now locate the latest minutes of the Monetary Policy Meetings.
Read the section on 'Recent developments in financial markets'.
You are now required to write a short summary of this section.
What impact did this have on the outcome of the meeting?

■ Research

Begg, D. and Ward, D., (2007) *Economics for Business*, 2nd edition, Maidenhead: McGraw-Hill. You should look at Chapter 13. Exchange rate policy is set out on pages 305–307.

Begg, D., Fischer, S. and Dornbusch, R., (2008) *Economics*, 9th edition, Maidenhead: McGraw-Hill. You should look at Chapter 28. Various exchange rate regimes are set out on pages 544–545.

Gillespie, A., (2007) *Foundations of Economics*, 1st edition, Oxford: Oxford University Press. You should focus on Chapter 30. A fixed-exchange-rate regime is covered on pages 400-402.

Sloman, J., (2007) *Essentials of Economics*, 4th edition, Harlow: Financial Times Prentice Hall. You should look at Chapter 12.

Sloman, J. and Hinde, K., (2007) *Economics for Business*, 4th edition, Harlow: Financial Times Prentice Hall. You should look at Chapter 27, pages 606–625 to see a detailed explanation of the interaction between the balance of payment and the exchange rate.

Go to **www.pearsoned.co.uk/boakes** to access Kevin's blog for additional analysis of recent topical news articles and to post your own comments. Download podcasts containing short audio summaries of the main issues relating to each article and check your understanding of in-text questions with the handy hints provided.

12

INTERNATIONAL ECONOMICS – BALANCE OF PAYMENTS AND EXCHANGE RATES

The international business environment

The increasing globalisation of businesses and the financial markets that serve them is one of the most important changes in economics in the last couple of decades. When I was studying at university the main textbooks focused almost exclusively on the UK economy. There were occasional references to leading research from US economists but that was about as international as most of the teaching was at that time. If that was a reasonable approach then it most certainly is not now. The increasing emphasis on free trade and the existence of a worldwide system of financial markets means that all countries are now interdependent on each other for their economic success. It used to be said that if the US sneezes the UK catches a cold. These days the UK economy is vulnerable to changes in economic activity in most countries worldwide.

At the forefront of this move towards globalisation has been the growth of the multi-national companies. What is the key characteristic that distinguishes them from other companies?

At the simplest level they are any type of business that either directly owns or at least has control over subsidiaries in more than one country. This is in contrast to a simple domestic company where the entire business is located in just one territory. It might well trade with many other countries but the domestic ownership is what separates it from these multinational enterprises.

The multinational company structure varies widely. We can split them into three broad forms based on the organisation of their production process:

1. Vertically integrated multinational enterprises:

    These will be engaged in different stages of the production process across many coun-tries. For example, they might own oil exploration assets in one country, an oil refinery in another and some retail petrol sites in another.

2. Horizontally integrated multinational enterprises:

    These produce the same or similar products in different countries. For example, such an enterprise might be a large international pharmaceutical company that produces and sells a range of prescription drugs across many different international markets.

3. Diversified multinational enterprises:

    These involve themselves in the production of a wide range of goods or services in many different countries.

In the article chosen for this section we see how the world is shrinking fast such that corporate transactions take place that would have been totally unthinkable maybe even a decade ago. The car giant Ford was selling its luxury brands Jaguar and Land Rover and the buyer was a highly diversified Indian multinational company called Tata. The location of economic power across the world was changing fast and this case shows that perfectly.

The following article is analysed in this section:

Article 23
Tata's bid promise to keep UK car plants open won over unions
Financial Times, 27 March 2008.

This article addresses the following issues:

- The globalisation of economies
- The role of conglomerates
- International mergers and acquisitions
- Multinational businesses
- Business plans
- The impact of globalisation on trade unions and the labour force.

UK car industry goes up the junction as Jaguar and Land Rover are bought by Indian company

At the time of writing this case the big sports story dominating the news was the creation of the Indian premier cricket league. It was recognised that this was going to have a profound impact on international cricket. Indeed, when the new 2008 *Wisden* was reviewed in the *Guardian* its writer, Martin Kettle wrote,

'the impact of the officially sanctioned Indian Premier League and its rival, the Indian Cricket League, is of a different order. They are starting to draw in the best players from across the world for three-hour matches between Indian city franchises tailored to a global television audience centred on the Indian market.'

Against this threat he doubted if English county cricket would exist in five years. As a cricket fanatic and somewhat of a traditionalist I have to admit that possibility made me very sad. In contrast, as something of a philistine in relation to cars, personally I shed few tears for the loss of two of the most iconic UK car brands to the Indian industrial conglomerate. We are living in a new world where most successful businesses are now powerful multinational enterprises.

Article 23

Financial Times, 27 March 2008

Tata's bid promise to keep UK car plants open won over unions

Jonathan Guthrie, Joseph Leahy and John Reed

Tata Motors has promised to keep Jaguar and Land Rover's three UK plants and two product engineering sites open until at least 2011 as part of its winning bid to buy the two carmakers, it emerged yesterday.

The Indian group's pledge appears to have played a decisive role in securing unions' endorsement of its $2.3bn (£1.44bn) bid for the two brands, which will see Ford Motor continue to supply them with engines, components and technology, and its credit arm to provide vehicle financing for up to a year.

The purchase marks a new peak for global acquisitions by India's expansive companies, led by the Tata group, one of its oldest and biggest conglomerates.

Bankers believe there will be many more such deals as cash-rich emerging market companies take advantage of the downturn in the west and a slump in activity by private equity firms to buy up some of their better established but struggling rivals.

Tata's pledge – at a meeting with unions in London in November – was welcomed in Britain's West Midlands region as giving breathing space to Jaguar and Land Rover factories that have been regularly tipped for closure. In a cost-conscious industry where rationalisation and relocation to lower-cost countries are common, the plants produce only about 300,000 vehicles. Jaguar is losing money but Land Rover is profitable.

Unions succeeded in pressing Tata to pledge broad support for the carmakers' existing five-year business plan. Dave Osborne, national secretary for the car industry in Britain's Unite union said: 'Tata has confirmed there will be no changes to the manufacturing and product development footprint under the business plan, which runs up to 2011.'

Tata said: 'It is true, as per the business plan agreed between the management of Jaguar and Land Rover and the unions, and it is based on assumptions made in that business plan.'

Aniket Mhadre, analyst with Centrum Broking in Mumbai, said: 'In the short term, it's very negative for Tata Motors, primarily because Jaguar is lossmaking.'

Tata is said to have made no specific commitment to maintain the two brands' staffing at its current level.

Copyright The Financial Times Limited 2008

■ The analysis

The nature of the business world is changing fast. In the past most large multinational companies were based in the US or Western Europe. They might have located their production sites in developing countries to take advantage of lower wage costs. However, the more skilled operations would have been reserved for the highly developed economies. The fact that this was now changing was in part a reflection of the wide pool of well-educated and better-trained employees available in countries like China, India and the emerging Eastern European states. The economic benefits of these developments are obvious. Companies can produce at a much lower cost and savings are passed on to the consumer in the form of lower prices. The losers are the workers in the more developed nations that become priced out of the labour market. This article focuses on a relatively new trend. This is the rapid growth of large multinational companies now based in what were formally seen as the poorer developing parts of the world.

We should start by setting out the background to this corporate deal that hit the headlines in the spring of 2008. Just under a year before, Ford had announced its intention to combine the two brands, Jaguar and Land Rover, and to try to find a buyer for them. The deal was motivated by Ford's desire to focus on its core business, and these two brands were proving to be a distraction in the UK. It had originally paid over $4bn for them and although Land Rover remained profitable Jaguar had been loss-making from the start. Ford appointed the accountancy firm KPMG to help them find a buyer for the businesses.

After nearly a year the deal was made to sell them to the Indian company Tata. This is a powerful multinational conglomerate with a market capitalisation of some $70bn. It has business interests in over 70 countries and employs almost 300,000 people worldwide. Its significance to the Indian economy could hardly be overstated. The revenues it generated each year amounted to 3% of the total GDP of the country. This particular multinational corporation (MNC) was the leading car manufacturer in India but it also had commercial links to car companies in other parts of the world, including MG Rover and Fiat.

So how would the deal impact on the UK's economy? The concern in these cases is normally that the new owner will embark on a wide-scale rationalisation of the business with severe job losses resulting in the domestic market. There might well be a pressing business case to relocate jobs to the much lower-cost locations available around the world. This was certainly the concern of the UK trade unions. The FT article quotes apparently reassuring words from the national secretary of the car workers union, Unite:

'Tata has confirmed there will be no changes to the manufacturing and product development footprint under the business plan, which runs up to 2011.'

Despite this commitment it seemed unlikely that the 16,000 staff that worked at the UK car plants in Merseyside and the West Midlands would be secure. There is no doubt that Tata would have to make changes and in particular reduce the costs of manufacturing these cars in the UK. As the banking analyst is quoted as saying, 'In the short term, it's very negative for Tata Motors, primarily because Jaguar is loss-making.'

A successful business like Tata will in the medium term make sure that its new acquisitions are profitable. With this in mind some kind of rationalisation of the business was inevitable. So, just as the first match in the Indian Premier League was about to change English cricket for ever, UK car buyers would have to get used to their Jaguars being made thousands of miles away. Everything was changing as globalisation swept across the world.

■ Key terms

1. **Winning bid**

   When a company is put up for sale or is the subject of a takeover approach the winning bid is the one that secures the company. It should be noted that sometimes the bidder can end up paying more than the business is worth. Economists call this phenomenon the 'winner's curse'.

2. **Conglomerate**

   This refers to a company that is made up of several different businesses. The attraction of this type of set-up is that it provides a diversification of risk. This means that if one part of the company hits any financial problems this might be offset by the performance of the others. In addition a multinational conglomerate has the advantage of having markets in a range of countries. This can again allow the company to diversify its risk.

3. **Global acquisitions**

   An acquisition is where one company buys a controlling interest in another company. When it is global it simply means that the acquiring company is buying a business in another country. It becomes a cross-border deal.

4. Rationalisation

In a business context this refers to a major reorganisation of a company. This will normally aim to improve the efficiency and profitability of a business. In this case it is likely to result in job cuts in the UK as the new owners look to find cheaper costs of production elsewhere.

5. Business plan

This is a document that is written by a company's senior managers to give details of the future course of the business. It is frequently prepared by a company in preparation for a new or a first issue of capital. It will usually include a detailed financial forecast showing plans for several years in the future.

■ The Web

Go to the website of the Tata Group at **www.tata.com**.
Look at the company's 'Profile' and 'Our Companies' section.
Based on this information prepare a short PowerPoint presentation of no more than six slides. This should explain the organisation of the business and give details of their global reach.

■ What do you think?

1. What are the main economic and political reasons for the increased globalisation seen in certain industries?

2. There are three main types of multinational enterprise. Briefly explain the difference between them.

3. What is meant by the term 'industrial conglomerate'?

4. What are the main advantages and disadvantages for a country that faces a large amount of inward investment from multinational corporations?

5. How can multinational companies use foreign production to their advantage?

6. How would you expect the car workers' union Unite to react to news of this deal?

7. What are the implications for consumers from the increased trend towards globalisation?

■ Research

Begg, D. and Ward, D., (2007) *Economics for Business*, 2nd edition, Maidenhead: McGraw-Hill. You should look at Chapter 14. The best section is titled 'To what extent are markets becoming global?' on pages 334–339.

Begg, D., Fischer, S. and Dornbusch, R., (2008) *Economics*, 9th edition, Maidenhead: McGraw-Hill. You should look at Chapter 36. There is a good discussion of globalisation and multinationals which starts on page 705.

Gillespie, A., (2007) *Foundations of Economics*, 1st edition, Oxford: Oxford University Press. You should focus on Chapter 34. The impact of globalisation is very well explained.

Sloman, J., (2007) *Essentials of Economics*, 4th edition, Harlow: Financial Times Prentice Hall. You should look at Chapter 11. There is a good discussion of multinationals and developing countries on pages 424–425.

Sloman, J., (2008) *Economics and the Business Environment*, 2nd edition, Harlow: Financial Times Prentice Hall. The most important section is Chapter 7 on multinational corporations.

Sloman, J., and Hinde, K, (2007) *Economics for Business*, 4th edition, Harlow: Financial Times Prentice Hall. You should look at Chapter 23.

Go to **www.pearsoned.co.uk/boakes** to access Kevin's blog for additional analysis of recent topical news articles and to post your own comments. Download podcasts containing short audio summaries of the main issues relating to each article and check your understanding of in-text questions with the handy hints provided.

13

THE INTERNATIONAL BUSINESS ENVIRONMENT

Part **C**

Financial markets and institutions

Financial markets

Financial markets exist to facilitate the transfer of funds from people who have excess funds (the lenders) to those who have a deficit of funds (the borrowers). The lenders include individuals, banks, pension funds and insurance companies. The borrowers include individuals, companies and governments. If we examine the individuals the concepts of excess and deficit funds should become much clearer. If you are at the stage of being at university it is very likely that you have a financial deficit. Your spending will be greater than your earnings. This is only to be expected. You are investing time and money partly in the hope of securing a well-paid job after graduation. When this happens you can start to repay your loans and eventually when your income rises you might even get into a position of having a financial surplus. At this stage you will invest this money in a bank or in some shares. This cash will find its way to one of the individual or corporate lenders probably via a financial intermediary like a bank.

The way that cash moves from lenders to borrowers is normally through one of the financial markets that have been created for this purpose. The various financial markets are there to meet the specific requirements of its participants. We can see this by briefly introducing each of the major markets that exist:

1. The money market

    This allows the banks with surplus cash to lend these funds to the banks with a financial deficit. The key characteristic of this market is its short-term nature. Money market securities are defined to have a maturity of anything up to one year. The key interest rate that is traded in this market is called the 'London Interbank Offered Rate' (Libor). This is the rate used for loans made to low-risk banks in the London money markets. You can get a Libor rate for a wide range of money market maturities. It starts with overnight money and then goes to one month, three months, six months and one year. This is the market that saw a sharp reduction in liquidity in the wake of the credit crunch.

2. The bond markets

    Many of the borrowers need to obtain funding for much more than one year. These will include governments, companies and banks that can all access the bond markets to issue longer-term securities.

3. The equity markets

    These allows the lenders to contribute risk capital to a range of different businesses. They lend their money to these companies without a guarantee of any capital repayment or dividend income in the future. This makes it a risky form of investment but with the possibility of securing very high rates of return at some stage in the future.

4. The foreign exchange markets

   These allow people to convert one currency into another. For example, a Japanese investor can exchange their yen for US dollars and use the proceeds to buy some government bonds issued by the United States Treasury. You will see this discussed in detail in Topic 12 which covers international economics.

5. The derivative markets

   These are the financial instruments which have been developed to allow investors to manage and exploit risk. The name 'derivative' is used because they derive from the fundamental financial products outlined above. The most common examples are futures, options and swaps.

It is likely that as you study economics you will start to develop a keen interest in the trading and performance of these financial markets. I often find that my own students become keen to try their hand at real trading by forming small investment clubs. This is a good way to start to establish a feel for the factors that drive the prices of financial market securities. My advice would be to at least start by not playing with real money but rather just create fictional portfolios and then measure your performance over time. You will quickly see whether you have the right skills needed to become a successful market guru.

The first article featured here looks at the importance of good timing in terms of trading in financial markets. In the second article we will look at the important role of monolines which act as insurers of risk in the bond markets. The following articles are analysed in this section:

Article 24
Time to go shopping?
Economist, 23 March 2008.

Article 25
A monoline meltdown?
Economist, 26 July 2007.

These articles address the following issues:

- Bull and bear markets
- Pension funds and insurance companies
- Equity market valuations
- Dividend yields
- Investment grade bonds
- Spreads
- Corporate debt
- Hedge funds
- Monolines
- Collaterised debt obligations.

Wise investors buy at the bottom, not at the top

After writing my first book *Reading and Understanding the Financial Times* many friends and even vague acquaintances thought it might be worth asking me for some investment advice. One of the things that struck me was that most people were looking to sell their shares immediately after a sharp fall in their value and add to their portfolio when the markets had been rising strongly. While this was perfectly understandable it is the wrong thing to do. A wise investor always looks to buy cheap and sell at the very top of the market. This article from *The Economist* suggests that there might have been just such a buying opportunity for investors in the spring of 2008.

Article 24

Economist, 23 March 2008

Time to go shopping?

The best opportunities happen when the clouds are darkest

Buy when the barbarians are at the gates. That philosophy is easy to spout in theory, difficult to execute in practice. But might this be the right moment?

Bear-market bottoms usually require three things. First, they require the existence of forced sellers, to have driven prices down rapidly. Secondly, they offer some clear appeal on valuation grounds. Third, they need a catalyst, an event which, while gloomy, might conceivably mark the worst moment of the crisis.

All the requirements were in place in early 2003. Pension funds and insurance companies had become forced sellers of equities for solvency reasons. The dividend yield had risen sharply from its pitiful level during the dotcom boom; in

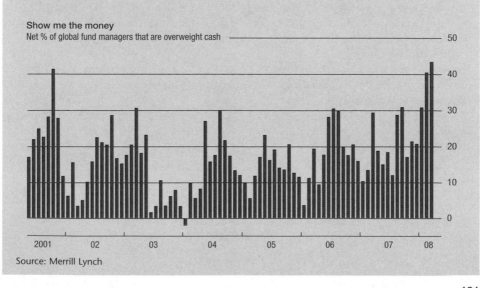

Show me the money
Net % of global fund managers that are overweight cash

Source: Merrill Lynch

the UK, it was higher than the yield on government bonds for the first time since the late 1950s. Finally, the onset of the Iraq war proved the catalyst, perhaps due to the sheer relief that all the uncertainty was out of the way. Equities duly rallied, sharply.

And there is a plausible case for saying all three elements are in place this time. Not, however, for equities but for investment-grade corporate debt. First, there have been forced sellers; notably hedge funds and specialist vehicles like conduits. Second, spreads over government bonds seem to offer a return that compensates for a very high level of defaults. Third, the collapse of Bear Stearns could conceivably mark the worst moment of the crisis.

Sentiment is also pretty gloomy at the moment, usually a bullish sign. According to Merrill Lynch's monthly poll of fund managers, a net 42% of asset allocators are overweight cash, a record level. Since slightly more are underweight equities than bonds, that might suggest the stockmarket is a better bet. However, it is hard to argue that there have been forced sellers of equities; shares have held up rather better than corporate bonds. And equity valuations are only decent by historical standards, rather than compelling, even if one discounts the fact that profits are high relative to GDP.

The problem for corporate debt is the balance of short-term supply and demand. There may still be forced sellers, as banks tighten credit to hedge funds and other counterparties – and, because credit is tight, there may not be many investors with the firepower to buy.

But it is possible to argue that the odds of a recovery are improving. The rapid rate cuts and frequent money-market interventions of the Federal Reserve indicate the American central bank will do anything to revive the market. If things get worse, it might even resort to buying assets outright.

In addition, bond prices have fallen so far and for so long that people are starting to talk about a buying opportunity. The fund management group T. Rowe Price has argued that this is the time to buy floating-rate bank loans which have drifted to big discounts to par value. Barclays Capital argues that AAA-rated commercial mortgage-backed securities look attractive because they have been oversold. Peter Oppenheimer of Goldman Sachs argues that 'we still believe that equity markets and credit markets will recouple, but it is more likely that credit spreads tighten rather than equity sells off sharply.' And, as evidence for these views, the premiums to ensure against default of investment-grade bonds fell 17% between March 13th and March 19th, according to JPMorgan Chase.

Oppenheimer says that, at the current level of investment-grade spreads, the implied default rate over the next five years is 9%. That is 4.5 times higher than the maximum default rate for investment-grade bonds. Even in a distressed market, that leaves plenty of margin for error.

It will take strong nerves and the ability to discern corporate survivors from likely victims to start buying corporate debt now. There are plenty of defaults to come, particularly in the high-yield sector. But the best buying opportunities are most likely to occur when all seems gloomy.

■ The analysis

When I worked as an economist at W. Greenwell I was fortunate to see one of the most brilliant financial market traders in action. What is more this was an example of somebody who successfully changed his role in mid-career. He went from being a fairly good bond market salesman to become an outstanding bond market trader. I sat close by him for a few years trying to interpret the new economic data releases to improve his trading strategy. During this period the most valuable thing he taught me was that successful investing is all about getting the timing just right. It always comes back to two important questions.

Question 1) When should you buy?

Question 2) When should you sell?

This article starts by defining the conditions that are necessary for establishing what they call 'a bear-market bottom'. In financial markets this is the lowest point that you need to hit before a recovery can start. It is also the perfect buying time. So, what conditions must be present to enable us to identify this point?

Condition 1: You must have forced sellers:

These are simply investors who for whatever reason must sell part of or even their entire portfolio. They might be a bank needing to improve its cash position or a fund manager who has to return some investment funds back to investors.

Condition 2: Financial markets must be fairly valued:

There must be real evidence that the price of the financial market securities in question have now fallen to such a low level that they are now clearly worth buying.

Condition 3: Some external catalyst exists and this points to the turning point in the market's fortunes:

A really important event has just taken place. This somehow signals that the bottom of the market has been reached.

We certainly had this at the start of 2003 . . .

■ Insurance companies became forced sellers of equities . . .

During the long bear market which lasted from 2000 to 2003 the London stock market was one of the worst-hit centres, with share prices losing half their value. As a result of this there were great concerns about the financial health of the UK pension funds. This forced these large fund management companies to take significant remedial action. In the short term they sold large amounts of equities to ensure that they had enough cash to cover the payouts required on their policies. In the longer term many of these financial institutions made a significant shift in their investment strategy in order to further strengthen their balance sheets. They decided to sell large amounts of the more-risky equities and replace them with some safer bond market instruments.

■ Rising level of dividend yields suggested equities were good value . . .

The sharp fall in share prices was, unusually, not matched by an equivalent fall in company dividends. This may be because the market overreacted and anticipated an even greater deterioration in the financial position of companies, which did not materialise. As a result there was a significant rise in the average level of dividend yields. This meant that you could get blue-chip company stocks with yields that were actually higher than the available yield on government bonds. This sort of opportunity is extremely rare in financial markets and many investment gurus argue that all bull markets are associated with the presence of high dividend yields.

How did the increase in dividend yields come about?

The yield on government bonds might be 4%

The dividend yield on a particular share might be 3%

This could be based on:

A dividend = 3p for a share valued at 100p

This gives us a dividend yield of 3%

If the dividend stays at 3p but *now* the same share is valued at just 50p this gives us a higher dividend yield of 6%.

So, the company's dividend yield now exceeds that available on government bonds!

Back in 2003 this actually happened in reality for the first time in half a century. There were some particularly extreme examples. These included the banking sector with Lloyds TSB showing a dividend yield of nearly 9% at one stage. It should be stated, however, that chasing the highest yields can be a risky strategy for an investor. The danger is that the share price might fall even lower, which means that the resulting capital loss will wipe out any attractive flow of dividend income.

■ There was a very clear external catalyst for the rebound . . .

Financial market confidence is often undermined by the risk of some terrible event taking place. However, strangely, once it actually happens there can be an immense sense of relief. Somehow the markets seem to prefer to see the reality of the event rather than face many more months of uncertainty. This was certainly the case with the second Iraq war which finally started in March 2003.

The important question at the time of this article was whether five years on we now had another example of a bear market bottom? So were the three necessary conditions back in place? The answer was yes, but this time the rebound might be in the corporate bond market rather than the stock market.

■ We had forced sellers again . . .

There had certainly been lots of forced sellers. The hedge funds had reacted to their deteriorating financial state by selling large amounts of bonds.

■ The bond markets were good value . . .

The available yield spread between corporate bonds and government bonds had reached a level that seemed to more than compensate for any genuine risk of default. As a result the bond markets were sensibly pricing the risk of default.

■ There was one pivotal market event . . .

Finally, the collapse of Bear Stearns might eventually be seen to represent the nadir of this particular weak market and was therefore the moment when recovery could start.

■ Other evidence supporting a rebound in the corporate bond market . . .

There were a number of other factors that supported this optimistic view. For one thing the sentiment of the fund managers was very downbeat. The article quotes a survey of fund managers conducted by Merrill Lynch that showed 'a net 42% of asset allocators are over-weight cash'. This meant that the fund managers were being highly defensive in loading up their portfolios with lots of cash. At some stage they would be looking to go back into the financial markets with plenty of this money likely to be invested in the bond markets.

■ What types of bonds might recover first?

The article identifies a number of possible types of bonds that could be the ones that recover first, including floating-rate bank loans and mortgage backed securities. Both of these products had seen particularly sharp falls in the wake of the credit crisis and the concerns about the financial safety of the banking sector.

It always takes a few brave investors to go back into the market and start buying. However, as we said earlier, the sensible investor is always the one who buys cheap. So maybe the time was indeed right to start to buy corporate bonds again.

■ Key terms

1. **Bear market (bottom)**

    This refers to a sustained period in which the prices of financial securities (especially shares) have been falling. This creates a very pessimistic financial market mood with most investors unable to see when there will be a recovery in prices. This situation is normally associated with an economic recession. The period in the 1930s in the US is a perfect example of a prolonged bear market.

2. Pension funds and insurance companies

These are the large financial institutions that are the key investors in financial markets. They look to invest in long-term assets to match their long-term liabilities (paying out pensions). These investors have flourished in recent years due to the greater wealth of the private sector.

3. Corporate debt (investment grade)

The corporate bond market refers to the issue of debt securities by companies. These bonds represent a debt that must be repaid normally at a set date in the future. Most corporate bonds pay a set interest rate each year, called 'the coupon'. The other key characteristic of a bond is its maturity. This is the date on which the bond will be redeemed.

4. Hedge fund

This refers to a particular type of investment management where the fund manager will employ a range of different investment tools in an attempt to maximise the returns or try to make gains, even in a falling market. The fund will rely on large amounts of borrowing and will use derivative markets and short selling to achieve these aims.

5. Bullish (sign)

This refers to the opposite of a bear market. It is a sustained period in which the prices of financial securities (especially shares) have been rising. This creates a very optimistic financial market mood with most investors unable to see when there will be any downturn in prices. This situation is normally associated with an economic boom. The period in the mid to late 1990s in the US is a perfect example of a bull market.

6. Liquidity valuation

There are a number of financial techniques that are used by economists to correctly value a company's share price. One of the most common is the dividend valuation model. With this we take the future cash flows which will be earned by a company and multiply them by an appropriate discount factor to get their present value.

7. Money market

This is the financial market where short-term securities are traded. They include repos, commercial paper and short-term interbank loans (Libor). The main players in this market are the banks looking to make up a temporary shortfall in their cash position. Other banks with a surplus of cash can lend money to them.

8. Floating rate (bank loans)

With these loans the interest rate that is charged will not be fixed in advance. It will instead be set in terms of some benchmark market or official interest rate with a fixed additional spread. The benchmark might be an official central bank interest rate (like the Fed Funds Rate) or a money market rate (like Libor).

For example, the floating-rate bank loan might have an interest rate set at Libor plus 25 basis points. So, if Libor is 6.75% when the interest rate is next set, the interest rate for the loan will be set at 6.75% plus 25 basis points, that is 7%.

9. **Mortgage-backed securities**

A mortgage-backed security is created where a large pool of mortgages are collected together and traded between various large investors.

10. **Default**

This is where a borrower takes out a loan but fails to keep to the original agreed schedule of interest payments and final capital repayments. A bond issued by the United States or United Kingdom government is generally regarded to be free of default risk. In contrast, a bond issued by a company might well have significant risk of default. For example, a company might not be able to keep up with the interest payments on the loan as a result of a downturn in its profitability. The concept of default is analysed further in the next article.

■ What do you think?

1. What is meant by the term a bear-market bottom?

2. The article states there are three factors which must exist to establish the existence of a bear-market bottom. What are they?

3. In the context of financial markets what is meant by the term 'forced seller'? Explain why UK pension funds were forced to sell large amounts of equities in 2003.

4. What is the danger of buying shares in a particular company purely because they have a history of paying high dividends?

5. The article quotes a survey of fund managers conducted by Merrill Lynch that showed 'a net 42% of asset allocators are overweight cash'. What does this mean?

6. What are floating-rate bank loans? In what circumstances should a borrower prefer them to normal conventional loan agreement?

■ Data exercise

You will need a copy of the *Financial Times*.

Go to the Companies and Markets section.

Now find the London Share Price Service (normally just four pages inside the back page). Next select any five companies from the different equity sectors shown. For example,

Food and Beverages

Financial General

Travel and Leisure etc.

You are required to set up an Excel spreadsheet and enter the relevant financial data each day for one semester (say eight weeks). This will enable you to follow their major financial developments.

At the end of the period write a short report on what has happened to your companies. You should highlight any sharp changes in share prices, earnings per share, yields and PE ratios.

In addition, give some investment advice to somebody who might be looking to invest in this portfolio of shares.

■ The Web

Go to the FT's website at **http://FT.com**.
Now go Market Data.
Select Bonds and Rates.
Find the Global Investment Grade table.
Select a day of your choice.

Now examine the Table (Global Investment Grade Bonds). You should now discuss the relative risk of any five major corporate bond issues in comparison to the relative Benchmark Government Bond. You should calculate the spread on these bonds and relate this to their credit rating.

■ Research

For a good understanding of the financial markets there is no short cut. You need to read the *Financial Times* regularly, particularly after days when there have been significant movements in the main financial markets. Read the articles carefully (look at the Lex column as well) and you will soon get a feel for what drives the financial markets.

Bailey, R., (2005) *The Economics of Financial Markets*, 1st edition, Cambridge: Cambridge University Press.

Begg, D. and Ward, D., (2007) *Economics for Business*, 2nd edition, Maidenhead: McGraw-Hill. You should look at Chapter 5. The topic of financial markets is discussed on pages 100–101.

Begg, D., Fischer, S. and Dornbusch, R., (2008) *Economics*, 9th edition, Maidenhead: McGraw-Hill. You should look at Chapter 22. The financial markets are introduced on pages 438–439.

Boakes, K., (2008) *Reading and Understanding the Financial Times*, Harlow: Financial Times Prentice Hall. You should read Topic 3 for more information on financial markets.

Sloman, J. and Hinde, K., *Economics for Business*, 4th edition, Harlow: Financial Times Prentice Hall. You should look at Chapter 19. Financial markets are discussed on pages 407–413.

Los endos for the monolines

To understand the workings of financial markets one must appreciate that there is a significant interaction between them all. This is sometimes described as 'the domino effect' as the collapse in one market impacts on another and then that impacts on another etc. At the time of this article this relatively obscure financial institution was coming into prominence and having a major impact on the world's financial markets. They get their unusual name from the fact that they operate in a single business area. They provide insurance against the risk of default by lower-rated (high-risk) debt issuers, ranging from US state bonds to various other securities that are backed by mortgages, credit card loans and other similar assets. In the early days of the sub-prime crisis there were concerns that these companies were themselves now at severe risk of financial meltdown. The problem of the sub-prime market in the US had impacted on the collaterised debt obligation markets, which in turn had impacted on the monolines, and their demise could now impact on the US municipal bond market which could finally damage the entire banking system. This shows the domino principle in action.

Article 25   *Economist*, 26 June 2007

A monoline meltdown?

A hedge fund stalks sub-prime's next potential victim

As America's subprime-mortgage tempest spreads, Wall Street's latest parlour game is to bet on who will be next to get caught in the storm. A fair few have placed their chips on the so-called monoline insurers, an obscure but important bunch who guarantee the timely repayment of bond principal and interest when the issuer defaults.

The two largest monolines, MBIA and Ambac, both started out in the 1970s as insurers of municipal bonds. In recent years, much of their growth has come in structured products, such as asset-backed bonds and the now infamous collateralised debt obligations (CDOs). The total outstanding amount of paper insured by monolines reached $3.3 trillion last year.

André Cappon of CBM Group, a financial consultancy, describes monolines as 'rating agencies that put their money where their mouth is.' Arguably the keenest of credit-market observers, they extend their gold-plated credit ratings to paper they deem worthy of their protection, in return for a premium.

The monolines' share prices have tumbled this year as the depth of the sub-prime crisis has sunk in (see chart). The cost of insuring against their own default has shot up, prompting talk of a 'monoline meltdown'. This week Ambac's second-quarter profit missed forecasts due to a $57m write-down on credit derivatives.

The industry's tormentor-in-chief is William Ackman, who runs Pershing Square, a hedge fund. Mr Ackman has spent the last five years, no less, telling anyone who will listen that the monolines are doomed, with MBIA particularly vulnerable. He points to their massive leverage: outstanding guarantees amount

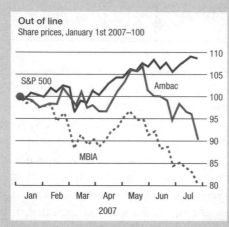

Out of line
Share prices, January 1st 2007—100

S&P 500

Ambac

MBIA

Jan Feb Mar Apr May Jun Jul
2007

110
105
100
95
90
85
80

Source: Thomson Datastream

Rob Haines of CreditSights points out, they are highly conservative in other ways. They model each transaction under a variety of high-stress situations and only accept those that show no losses in all scenarios. This may explain why they had little exposure to New Century, the biggest mortgage lender to go bust so far. Subprime makes up only 1–3% of their direct exposure.

To wipe out the monolines' capital cushion, it would take a loss twenty times bigger than the hit they took last year. Even in today's febrile markets that is hard to imagine, especially since the insurers are at the back of the queue when it comes to taking losses on CDOs. So, though losses may run into the hundreds of millions, they are unlikely to be big enough to deprive the biggest monolines of their cherished triple-A rating.

The monolines may lose business as investors turn their back on CDOs and other structured products. But MBIA's finance chief, Chuck Chaplin, thinks the general confusion over credit risk may even help them, as more debt issuers seek comfort in guarantees. It remains to be seen if that optimism is, like Mr Ackman's pessimism, somewhat overdone.

to 150 times capital. He also questions MBIA's 'aggressive' accounting techniques. Earlier this year the company paid $75m to settle allegations that it used reinsurance contracts to conceal losses.

Amid the market's jitters, other hedge funds are readily buying into this message. That may be all Mr Ackman, who holds a short (bearish) position in MBIA shares, wants. But most analysts think his analysis is based on a misunderstanding.

Monolines may be highly geared compared with traditional insurers. But, as

■ The analysis

The background to this article was provided by the spectre of sharply falling share prices with investors actively betting on which group of companies would be next to be hit. Some people had pointed to the monoline companies as likely candidates. To begin with, what are monolines? They are financial institutions that provide insurance against default by one of the higher-risk bond issuers. The issuer pays a premium to a monoline which then guarantees investors that there will be no default on their bonds. This is a great benefit to the issuer as the lower risk means that the returns that they have to offer on the bonds are much lower. The key is to price the default risk correctly so that the premiums charged more than cover the risks, allowing the monolines to make a good financial return. This acts to reduce their funding costs and seems to be a win–win situation for all parties involved.

1. The bond issuers:

   Get to issue debt securities at a much lower cost than they would otherwise.

2. The bond investors:

   Get insured against the risk of default on these bonds.

3. The monolines:

   Get paid fees for providing this service.

This all looks rather good, so what had gone wrong? The problem was that at this time the monolines had moved away from just insuring rather dull financial market products. They had diversified into the much more risky structured investment products like collaterised debt obligations (CDOs). You will find a detailed explanation of CDOs in the next topic, which examines their role in the demise of Bear Stearns. These products had become rather toxic, with multiple defaults triggered by the credit crunch. Against this background the largest monoline companies, MBIA and Ambac, which were particularly at risk, had seen sharp falls in their share prices as investors began to realise that they faced the prospect of having to pay out billions of dollars to cover the losses suffered by investors in these products. Just like any other insurance companies they prosper when their premiums far outweigh their payouts. Clearly, when the payouts are larger than the premiums the insurance companies make losses.

The article states that 'the industry's tormentor-in-chief is William Ackman, who runs Pershing Square, a hedge fund. Mr Ackman has spent the last five years, no less, telling anyone who will listen that the monolines are doomed.' It was certainly true that the main beneficiaries from the problems at the monolines had been the hedge funds which had made some spectacular financial gains as they bet large amounts on a sharp fall in the share prices of these companies. They had been holding short positions in Ambac and MBIA shares. What does this mean in practice?

The hedge fund would be using the futures market. They would sell a set amount of shares in the monoline companies at a fixed price for delivery on an agreed date in the future. Their hope is that by the time they would actually have to deliver the shares the prices would have fallen below the level at which they sold them. They could buy them more cheaply in the open market and pocket the difference. This is a classic example of a short trading strategy in which the hedge funds specialise.

There was a growing concern that developments in the international bond markets could even result in the bankruptcy of one or more of the monolines. Three of the monoline businesses most at risk, Ambac, MBIA and FGIC, had made their money and grown their businesses by focusing on the structured credit markets. These include the mortgage-backed securities market and various other CDOs. The monolines had been largely successful until the shock impact of the total loss of confidence in the US sub-prime mortgage market since the summer of 2007. There had been a resulting sharp fall in liquidity in these markets as most investors became reluctant to attach themselves to any high risk financial market products This has had a knock-on effect in terms of a sharp rise in the credit risk spread between risky bonds and the much lower-risk bonds including those issued by governments such as those of the United States, the United Kingdom and

Germany. The widening in spreads had resulted in an increase in the premiums payable to underwrite new insurance contracts in the bond markets. This was at least one factor that was moving in a favourable direction for the finances of the monolines.

■ Key terms

1. **US sub-prime mortgage (tempest)**

   The prime lending rate is the rate of interest charged to creditworthy companies and individuals in the US. The sub-prime market refers to the lending of money to much higher risk individuals at a higher rate of interest.

2. **Monolines (often known by their full name, 'monoline insurance companies')**

   These are financial institutions that use their high credit ratings to provide insurance on debt issues by relatively risky borrowers. As a result, a borrower rated at just a single A might be able to issue some bonds rated at triple A. The advantage to the borrower is that they will save an enormous amount of interest on their bond issues.

3. **Municipal bonds**

   These are debt securities issued in the US by states or municipal authorities to fund the difference between local taxes and expenditure; they will help to fund transport or education services.

4. **Structured credit markets**

   This term is used in financial markets to cover a whole raft of new and highly innovative financial market products. Their common characteristics are:

   a) The combining of various financial assets – for example, in the mortgage-backed securities a whole group of mortgages will be combined to make a large package that can be traded.

   b) The creation of various tranches supported by the group of financial assets. Each tranche will be allocated into a different risk category.

   c) There will be a clear divide between the credit risk of the original issuer and the credit risk of this particular group of financial assets. This will be done through the creation of a short-lived special purpose vehicle (SPV).

5. **Collaterised debt obligations (CDOs)**

   These are complex financial market securities which are backed by a pool of bonds, loans or some other assets.

   You should see the Analysis section in Topic 15 to see this term fully explained.

6. **Rating agencies**

   There are a number of large international companies that are used to assess the risk of various bond issuers. They produce a formal rating measure for each of them.

7. **Hedge fund**

   This refers to a particular type of investment management where the fund manager will employ a range of different investment tools in an attempt to maximise the returns or try to make gains even in a falling market. The fund will rely on large amounts of borrowing and will use derivative markets and short selling to achieve these aims.

■ What do you think?

1. In financial markets what is the role of a monoline?

2. Why had there been a sharp deterioration in the share price of the leading monolines like Ambac and MBIA?

3. Explain how the problems in the US sub-prime market have caused problems for the monolines. Hint: discuss the domino effect.

4. Explain clearly explain what is meant by the term 'structured products'.

5. Why would the collapse of the monolines cause such severe problems in the US municipal bond market? Hint: would it be possible for these bonds to be issued without some form of insurance against default?

6. What is a short-trading position? Explain how the hedge funds used this technique in relation to their investments in monolines.

■ The Web

Go to the website for MBIA at **www.mbia.com**.
Go the FAQs section.
Find out what is meant by a 'Structured Investment Vehicle'.

■ Research

This type of financial institution receives little coverage in the main textbooks. The best place to learn more about them and the market that they deal in is to read the *Financial Times* regularly. You will find lots of good articles on new financial institutions and the various products that they use.

Boakes, K., (2008) *Reading and Understanding the Financial Times*, Harlow: Financial Times Prentice Hall. You should read Topic 12 to see more about structured investment vehicles.

Go to **www.pearsoned.co.uk/boakes** to access Kevin's blog for additional analysis of recent topical news articles and to post your own comments. Download podcasts containing short audio summaries of the main issues relating to each article and check your understanding of in-text questions with the handy hints provided.

Financial institutions, featuring the demise of Bear Stearns

In Topic 10 we introduced the role that money and interest rates play in the economy. We also set out the key functions of money including its primary use as a medium of exchange. In this section of the book we will build on those key themes introduced at that earlier stage. In economics a financial institution is seen as an agent that provides a range of important financial services for its various clients. The most common financial institutions include the retail banks, building societies, investment banks and central banks. We should start this section by setting out what these all do:

1. Retail banks

    These are the well-known high-street banks like HSBC, NatWest and Barclays. They take deposits from their retail clients and then lend this money out to their individual and commercial customers. The banks also offer a range of other services including foreign exchange facilities, investment advice and secure deposit facilities.

2. Building societies

    These days it is increasingly difficult to differentiate between the roles of banks and building societies. In the past the main difference was that building societies were mutual organisations owned by their members who held savings accounts with them. In addition, the main role of a building society used to be the provision of mortgages to enable people to buy their homes. In recent years we have seen many building societies turn themselves into public companies through share issues. Also, building societies have now diversified the range of their activities to include many new services.

3. Investment banks

    Whenever a large company needs to raise finance the first port of call will be to approach an investment bank. As a classic example of a financial intermediary they act between the issuers of capital (governments and companies) and the investors in capital (pension funds and insurance companies). Most investment banks are split into two main divisions. The first helps companies with the issue of new equity market securities. The second offers companies the chance to issue new bond market securities.

4. Central banks

    Just about all countries now have a national central bank and it is normally their most important financial institution. They have two primary functions. The first is to oversee the workings of the financial system and ensure that all other financial institutions are operating securely. The second key role of the central banks in most countries is to determine the correct stance of monetary policy. In practice this means that they set the level of short-term interest rates in the economy. In doing this they must achieve the economic goals that are set by the national government. The central bank in the United States is called the Fed. The central bank for the Eurozone is called the European Central Bank. Finally, in the UK the central bank is called the Bank of England. It is not clear where this leaves Scotland, Northern Ireland and Wales!

This topic was all over the news at the time of writing this book because the news agenda was dominated by the plight of many financial institutions that were facing financial problems. The first three articles in this section focus on the demise of the US investment bank Bear Stearns. This event sent shock waves through the financial community worldwide. How could one of the oldest names on Wall Street come so close to a total financial meltdown? Perhaps one of the most remarkable features of this whole crisis was the speed and efficiency of the rescue action led by the US Federal Reserve. Many commentators contrasted this with the protracted attempts by the UK authorities to solve the crisis at Northern Rock. Its eventual nationalisation was a final option taken when all other possible solutions had failed.

In the final article in this section we stay with the central banks, but this time focusing on the European Central Bank. This provides a detailed evaluation of the various techniques that it uses to supply liquidity to the commercial banks in the Eurozone.

The following articles are analysed in this section:

Article 26
Fed leads Bear Stearns rescue,
Financial Times, 15/16 March 2008.

Article 27
JPMorgan lifts Bear offer fivefold,
Financial Times, 24 March 2008.

Article 28
Bear and the moral hazard,
Financial Times, 24 March 2008.

Article 29
Eurozone set to receive more liquidity,
Financial Times, 29/30 March 2008.

These articles address the following issues:

- The role of investment banks
- The role of central banks
- The rescue of a financial institution
- Mergers and acquisitions
- Valuing a business
- The economics of moral hazard.

Bear is all over the six o'clock news

Back in the early 1980s I was sent off on a whistle-stop tour of Wall Street with the remit of gathering first-hand knowledge on the health of the US economy. In my four days I visited over twenty different US investment banks. This trip was especially memorable because on my last day a violent storm was forecast to hit New York City and I was advised to keep off the streets to avoid any risk of injury. So, I spent most of that day in the safest place I could imagine. That was in the Bloomingdale department store. I survived in one piece although my credit card took a severe bashing. Among the various banks that I visited that week was one called Bear Stearns. I cannot say that I had thought much more about this bank in the years following my trip until it hit the headlines in March 2008. It had become the first US financial institution other than a commercial bank to be forced to go to the Federal Reserve for emergency finance.

| Article 26 | *Financial Times*, 15/16 March 2008 |

Fed leads Bear Stearns rescue

Francesco Guerrera, Ben White, Krishna Guha and Michael Mackenzie

The credit crisis yesterday engulfed one of Wall Street's most important banks as the Federal Reserve and JPMorgan Chase combined to provide emergency finance for 85-year-old Bear Stearns and prevent further upheaval in global markets.

The decision by the monetary authorities to throw a temporary lifeline to Bear followed a night of negotiations with regulators, led by Timothy Geithner, president of the New York Fed, and came after a slump in its shares amid concerns over its liquidity. It is likely to pave the way for a sale or liquidation of the company in the coming weeks.

The move underlines the Fed concerns at the depth of the credit crunch and its determination to prevent a major bank failure. A Fed official told the Financial Times that the central bank had acted because of the systemic risks involved in the potential failure of the fifth biggest investment bank at a time when markets were extremely fragile.

Investors sought the safety of gold and short-term US government debt. Stocks initially fell as much as 2.8 per cent before paring back their losses. The S&P 500 closed down 2.1 per cent at 1,288.15. Financial stocks were among the worst performers, with the S&P Investment Banks index down 5 per cent. In London, the FTSE 100 closed down 1.07 per cent at 5,681.7.

Shares in Bear plunged as much as 53 per cent as the market opened. They closed down 47.4 per cent at $30 in New York. The stock has lost more than three-quarters of its value over the past year. The crisis at Bear, which has brought forward the announcement of first-quarter results to Monday, has left some of its largest shareholders with sizeable losses.

Joseph Lewis, a UK-born billionaire who had been building a large stake in

→

Bear, is estimated to have lost about $1bn (£495m) on his investment since the summer. Jimmy Cayne, Bear's chairman and former chief executive, is believed to have shouldered paper losses of more than $800m.

Bear yesterday said its liquidity position had 'significantly deteriorated' and that it would tap the Fed's emergency finance facility – known as the discount window – through an arrangement with JPMorgan. The Fed took on the credit risk involved in the loans, which are secured against collateral.

As an investment bank, Bear does not have access to the window, which is only open to commercial banks, so JPMorgan will act as a go-between.

The move marks a dramatic extension of the Fed's role of lender of last resort for the financial system but Fed officials stressed there was no policy to provide emergency liquidity to investment banks in general.

The last time the Fed agreed to offer emergency finance to any financial institution other than a regulated deposit-taking bank was in the 1960s, and Fed officials said the last time cash was disbursed may have been in the 1930s.

Alan Schwartz, Bear's chief executive, said the investment bank had fallen victim of a crisis of confidence in which counterparties in its core fixed-income markets were no longer willing to provide financing given widespread rumours that Bear could fail. On Wednesday, Mr Schwartz had told CNBC that the bank's balance sheet had 'not weakened at all'. Yesterday he said that demands for cash had accelerated on Thursday.

Mr Schwartz said Bear would continue to work with advisers at Lazard to pursue strategic transactions that would protect customers and counterparties and maximise shareholder value.

Such alternatives include a sale of the bank as a whole or in parts. JPMorgan is viewed as a potential buyer of pieces of Bear including its prime brokerage and asset management businesses.

Copyright The Financial Times Limited 2008

■ The analysis

How did the crisis at Bear Stearns develop?

We start with the sub-prime crisis. The crisis at Bear Stearns was the most significant casualty of the global credit crisis that began to dominate our lives in early 2008. Before we focus on the specific problems at Bear Stearns we should explain the origins of the credit crunch.

The story began with the so called sub-prime crisis. In an attempt to restore some confidence in financial markets after the terrorist attacks in New York on 11 September 2001 the Federal Reserve Bank made a series of interest rate cuts which culminated in their main short-term interest rate, the Federal Funds Rate, hitting a low of just 1% in June 2004. The result of this easing in monetary policy was that US economic activity hit record levels fuelled by the availability of very cheap credit. It was a time when it seemed that everyone could borrow almost unlimited amounts of cash at very cheap rates of interest. The banks were awash with money and just desperate to lend it out. The concept of credit risk had been long forgotten. This was a band wagon that everyone was invited to join. From ordinary families right through to the largest sovereign borrowers they could all borrow enormous amounts of money. The banks were open and keen to do business.

The US housing market was one of the main beneficiaries of these conditions, with homeowners seeing sharp rises in house prices throughout the country. As word spread of the 'easy' gains to be had, everyone wanted to join in and take advantage as this new 'gold rush' spread from the West Coast to the East Coast and from the North to the South. Everyone was riding on the roller coaster that was the housing market boom. At the top of the market some of the lowest income groups were invited to borrow as the US banks were running out of other groups to lend to. In the past such people might have been considered to be far too risky a proposition to lend to. But these were no ordinary times. The economy was red hot and for the banks no risk was too great.

However, like all good things this could not last. The economic boom soon gave way to a slowdown as the Fed's policy of monetary policy easing reverted to a more prudent tightening in monetary policy. The resulting increase in mortgage rates caused many homeowners to be forced into defaults on their loans. In the wake of record number of mortgage repossessions, the US housing market crashed and the 'sub-prime crisis' was born.

The question is how did these problems get to impact on the large financial institutions? Surely they were not so heavily involved in the sale of mortgage-based products? The problem was that these mortgages had been pooled together and sold as 'mortgage-backed securities' to international banks across the world. This meant that any of the large financial institutions in almost any country was potentially a victim of the sub-prime crisis. They were all involved but it was not clear which of them had the greatest exposure to the risks associated with the global turmoil. These were exacerbated as a wide range of financial institutions had been involved in the creation of a range of complex financial products including collaterised debt obligations (CDOs). These are fully explained in Exhibit 15.1. Many of the investment banks owned hedge funds that had purchased these instruments that soon turned toxic as their underlying value fell way below their original levels. As a result these funds acquired massive losses that made them and their parent investment banks financially vulnerable.

The warning signals were there back in June 2007 when Bear Stearns became one of the first US investment banks to be forced to admit that it had made substantial losses in its hedge funds as a result of bad investments in these products. This contagious risk soon spread to other banks including BNP Paribas in France and eventually Northern Rock in the UK. You will find a detailed review of the Northern Rock collapse in Topic 12 in my book *Reading and Understanding the Financial Times* (see the Research section)

15

FINANCIAL INSTITUTIONS, FEATURING THE DEMISE OF BEAR STEARNS

Exhibit 15.1 The role of complex financial products

For example, collaterised debt obligations (CDOs)

These are complex financial market securities which are backed by a pool of bonds, loans or some other assets. How are they created?

Most CDOs are manufactured by a leading investment bank. The banks are as usual acting as intermediaries between the owners of the financial assets and the investors in the CDOs, which might be a pension fund or an insurance company. The investment banks charge management fees as well as an upfront percentage of the total stock of financial assets in the particular CDO.

The first stage sees the investment bank acquiring the CDO's stock of financial assets which might be normal income bonds, credit card loans, mortgages or some other financial assets. Then the creator of the CDO will sell the rights to the cash flows that are generated from these various assets (debt interest, mortgage repayments, etc.). These rights will be sold in various tranches ranging from the senior tranche CDOs (AAA-rated), through to the mezzanine tranche (AA- to BB-rated) and then, finally, the equity tranche (which are unrated).

The highest risk applies to the equity tranche and the next highest to the mezzanine tranche with the lowest risk attached to the senior tranche. As a result the highest coupons will apply to the equity tranche and then the next highest to the mezzanine tranche with the lowest coupons reserved for the senior tranche. As usual in financial markets those investors willing to take the highest risk can expect the best returns.

The CDO market had suffered very badly due to the problems in the sub-prime market in the US. CDOs backed by low-quality home loans were hit by a wave of defaults as the borrowers were not able to maintain their mortgage payments.

■ How did we get from sub-prime to the credit crisis?

Any economics textbook will tell you that the banks play a crucial role in any modern economy. Their activities are vital in driving economic activity forward. The banks are involved in many complex financial activities each day that result in large amounts of cash flowing in and out of their accounts. For example, if a significant number of customers withdraw cash to spend in the shops through their cashpoint cards this will result in that bank seeing a significant reduction in liquidity. At the same time another bank might see an exceptional number of customers making cash deposits, which results in an increase in their liquidity. These daily cash imbalances are not a serious problem and they are largely alleviated through the commercial banks lending cash to each other to meet their short-term needs. This is done through the key interbank markets where the main product is the London Interbank Offered Rate (Libor). This is simply the rate of interest charged by one bank when it lends to another. It is normally considered to be a riskless transaction as the banks involved are viewed as being perfectly safe counterparties.

This all changed in the wake of the sub-prime crisis. This was now a very different world that the banks inhabited. It was a financial community rife with rumours about the relative financial security of one bank or another. In this environment no bank was considered to be completely secure, particularly as many had substantial holdings of financial products like CDOs that, as we have seen, were now worth only a fraction of their original value. As a result the banks started to look rather suspiciously at each other and finally refused to lend money to certain other banks, fearing that they would not be able to repay their loans. The key characteristic of the wholesale money markets is normally their liquidity. This now dried up as the banks became unwilling lenders to each other. The markets that were used to seeing billions of pounds of daily trading had been reduced to a trickle of activity. In a matter of a few short months the mantra of the financial institutions had changed. Cash was now king and the banks were putting all their efforts into securing funds rather than lending them out. It was a good time to be a saver and a very bad time to be a borrower.

We had moved on from the sub-prime crisis to the new and even more frightening credit crisis. The banks which are normally lenders were themselves finding it impossible to borrow. The interbank markets had stopped functioning and there was a frantic scramble for liquidity among the banks.

■ And finally to the financial collapse of some banks

In the first article in this section we see that in one weekend in mid March 2008 the crisis hit one of Wall Street's most prestigious investment banks, Bear Stearns. The problem back in June 2007 had now escalated to such a point that other banks were no longer willing to lend them any more money. This was one bank that could fail any day. As a result the US Federal Reserve and JPMorgan Chase were forced to step in and save it to prevent a further loss of confidence in financial markets. For the first time in forty years the Federal Reserve had been forced to support a financial institution other than a normal commercial bank. The motivation for its speedy rescue was clear. It was worried that the collapse of this investment bank could have resulted in carnage on Wall Street, setting off a chain of events which it would not have been able to control. Using its lender of last resort facility the Fed made substantial funds available through the use of its discount window loans. This was done indirectly through JPMorgan because the facility is not open to investment banks.

15

FINANCIAL INSTITUTIONS, FEATURING THE DEMISE OF BEAR STEARNS

JPMorgan lifts Bear offer fivefold

Ben White and Francesco Guerrera in New York

JPMorgan Chase quintupled its original bid for *Bear Stearns* to $10 a share on Monday after its initial offer for the beleaguered Wall Street bank was undone by legal snags and furious opposition from Bear shareholders who viewed it as far too low.

The new all-share offer, coupled with surprisingly strong home sales data, helped spark a broad market rally in the US when investors hoped the worst fallout from the subprime mortgage crisis might be at an end. All three big US stock market indices were up at least 2 per cent in midday trade.

The five-fold increase in the offer for Bear represents a remarkable turnround for JPMorgan executives. Late last week they suggested privately that they had no plans to increase their bid, which they said represented the best possible outcome for Bear. They said then that if the offer failed they would let Bear shareholders fend for themselves in bankruptcy court.

The new offer, which values Bear at about $1.2bn, raises questions about the role of the Federal Reserve, which has been careful to avoid being seen as bailing out Bear's shareholders.

Jamie Dimon, JPMorgan chief executive, said he raised the offer for several reasons, including the need to close the deal more quickly. He said that would encourage Bear's best employees and clients to stay with the bank.

Mr Dimon said he listened to concerns from Bear shareholders that the initial offer was too low and wanted to improve the language of the merger agreement to eliminate several unwanted provisions, including one that would have made JPMorgan liable for Bear's trades for a year, even if the offer had failed.

'We wanted to get something more certain, more definitive. I don't mind being responsive to reasonable requests from the other side,' he said in an interview.

Under the initial agreement, the Fed agreed to fund up to $30bn of illiquid assets on Bear's balance sheet. Under the new agreement, JPMorgan is responsible for the first $1bn of these assets with the Fed funding the remaining $29bn. In addition, JPMorgan will guarantee Bear's borrowings from the Fed under a new facility extended to investment banks.

Under the revised agreement, Bear will sell JPMorgan 95m newly issued shares, representing 39.5 per cent of the bank's outstanding stock, at $10 a share. Bear's board, which controls about 5 per cent of the shares, has agreed to vote in favour of the deal. That leaves JPMorgan near the majority it will need to close the deal. The 95m share purchase is to close on April 8.

In theory, JPMorgan could buy the rest of the shares it needs to close the deal on the open market, but the bank could face legal issues if it did so at a different level than the offer price.

Bear shares, which rose last week on expectations of a higher offer, nearly doubled on Monday, closing 89 per cent higher at $11.25. JPMorgan shares ended the session 1.3 per cent higher at $46.55.

The new agreement came after JPMorgan discovered several errors in the initial merger agreement, which was completed early on the morning of March 17 after a frenetic weekend of talks between executives of both banks and federal officials.

■ The analysis

Rescuers of Bear Stearns see an opportunity

As part of the rescue package put in place to save Bear Stearns, JPMorgan Chase offered to take over the crippled investment bank with an initial offer of just $2 per share. As the second article suggests, this was a very low bid, particularly as the shares had been trading at over $100 per share back in 2007. This derisory offer was not surprisingly met with incredulity by Bear's shareholders. A few days later JPMorgan Chase was forced to increase the offer price to $10 per share. This represented quite a climb-down for the senior staff at JPMorgan as originally they had stated that the $2 offer was a one-off and final bid and if the shareholders were not willing to accept this they would be left to their own devices in the bankruptcy court. The justification for the raised offer included the view that it would 'encourage Bear's best employees and clients to stay with the bank'.

The second article also reports that 'the Fed agreed to fund up to $30bn of illiquid assets on Bear's balance sheet'. The revised agreement made JPMorgan now take responsibility for the first $1bn of these assets with the Fed left to fund the remaining $29bn. JPMorgan was now also required to guarantee the ailing investment bank's borrowings from the Fed.

Article 28	*Financial Times*, 25 March 2008

Bear and moral hazard

A week ago everything was binary. If *Bear Stearns* went under there was a huge systemic risk for financial markets. If not, order could be restored. Meanwhile, if Bear imploded, its shares were worthless. Under the rescue terms from *JPMorgan* and the Federal Reserve, however, they have significant value. Indeed, now, as a solvent business, Bear is worth a lot more than the $2 a share imposed on it during a shotgun wedding with JPMorgan. Once markets returned from the brink, it also became clear that JPMorgan, as it rushed to sign the deal, did not tie up all the loose ends. And by engineering such a lowball offer, JPMorgan gave Bear shareholders a credible argument that they had nothing to lose by voting the offer down.

JPMorgan blinked. Quintupling its offer still leaves Bear cheap. And JPMorgan has done its legal work better this time – with a clear right to buy 39.5 per cent of Bear for $10 a share. But that will face legal challenges and, now that investors have sensed weakness, they will try to push the price yet higher.

Where does this leave the Fed? Outwardly better off. Under the new deal, JPMorgan guarantees the first $1bn of losses on the $30bn of illiquid Bear assets the Fed originally took on. But it also means that the Fed loses its sacrificial Bear. Its intervention has given shareholders $10 a share instead of zero. (Lehman shareholders did even better from the Fed. Lehman's shares soared from their lows in large part because its future was guaranteed by the Fed's decision to give investment banks access to the discount window.)

Moral hazard is returning to the fore. When the smoke clears, the Fed must get its pound of flesh by regulating Wall Street, and doing it more aggressively, to make sure this never happens again.

FINANCIAL INSTITUTIONS, FEATURING THE DEMISE OF BEAR STEARNS

15

■ The analysis

Has the Fed's action increased the risk of moral hazard?

This refers to the concern that because of the actions of the US authorities in rescuing Bear Stearns it might encourage other banks to attempt to adopt a similarly risky business model.

The third article chosen to tell the story of Bear Stearns was taken from the *Financial Times*'s Lex column which appears on the back of the main section of the paper each day. It is a highly influential part of the newspaper where the writers give their analysis of the key financial and economic stories. This particular column starts with the suggestion that

> 'A week ago everything was binary. If Bear Stearns went under there was a huge systemic risk for financial markets. If not, order could be restored. Meanwhile, if Bear imploded, its shares were worthless.'

This effectively means that the Lex view was that had Bear Stearns been allowed to fail this would have presented a massive risk for all financial assets. However, if it could be saved there was a chance of restoring order back into financial markets.

However, under the revised and much-improved offer of $10 per share JP Morgan had been forced to accept that the investment bank still had some substantial monetary value even in its stricken state. The new terms also left the Fed in a more secure position. The bank was guaranteeing the first $1bn of Bear's losses that the Fed had originally taken over. However, if the Fed's losses had been reduced there was a much greater risk that its actions had injected a severe risk of moral hazard into financial institutions for years to come. Put simply, there is the chance that the investment banks would once again return to risky business practices safe in the knowledge that in the event of any dire consequences the Fed will always be there to step in and rescue them. As the FT's Lex column says, 'when the smoke clears, the Fed must get its pound of flesh by regulating Wall Street, and doing it more aggressively to make sure this never happens again'. This suggests the banks will never be as free as they were in the first few years when they made short-term fortunes for many of their staff at the expense of the longer-term health of the financial markets.

■ Key terms

1. **Credit crisis**

   This refers to the cost and availability of credit. It might be a government borrowing (in the government bond market), a company borrowing (in the corporate bond market), a house owner (with a mortgage) or a consumer (with a credit card). We have a 'credit crunch' when the cost of borrowing is considered to be prohibitively expensive by historic standards or it is simply very difficult for more-risky borrowers to obtain finance at all. During 2008 the credit crunch hit home when the banks stopped lending and instead spent all their time sourcing liquidity.

2. **Investment bank**

   An investment bank acts as an intermediary between the issuers of capital (governments and companies) and the investors in capital (pension funds and insurance companies). The staff employed in an investment bank will work either in the Investment Bank Division (IDB) which deals with the new issues of debt and equity capital or the Markets Division which deals with the investors in new bond and equity deals.

3. **Federal Reserve**

The Federal Reserve is the Central Bank of the United States. The key part of the Fed is the Federal Open Market Committee (FOMC) that decides on changes in US monetary policy. It is made up of twelve individuals. The core seven come from the Central Federal Reserve Bank (based in Washington) and the other five represent the various Federal District Reserve Banks.

4. **New York Fed**

This is the most important of the Federal Reserve District Banks. It has a permanent place on the Federal Open Market Committee which determines the level of short-term interest rates in the US.

5. **Commercial banks**

These are the 'high-street' banks that have ordinary people as their customers. They will take deposits from the general public and use these funds to offer loans to both ordinary customers and small companies.

6. **Systematic risk (also called 'market risk')**

This refers to the type of risk that applies to an entire group of financial assets. For example, if interest rates are increased this might impact negatively on the entire stock market. In contrast, unsystematic (or specific) risk applies to only one particular financial asset. For example, if a company loses a particular contract with a customer its share price only will be affected.

7. **S&P 500**

The S&P composite index is based on the market movements of 500 companies that are listed on the New York Stock Exchange. This index is one of the most widely used measures of US equity performance.

8. **FTSE-100**

The FTSE-100 is the most widely quoted UK stock market index. It is based on the value of the 100 largest UK companies in terms of their market capitalisation. It started with a base level of 1000 in January 1984. This index is now quoted in real time on the various news information systems that serve the City traders.

9. **Credit-rating agencies**

There are a number of large international companies that are used to assess the risk of various bond issuers. They produce a formal rating measure for each of them.

For example, they can assign the following ratings:

AAA = Capacity to pay interest and principal extremely strong.
AA = Differs only in a small degree.
A = More susceptible to adverse changes in circumstances.
BBB = Adequate capacity.
BB, B = Speculative.
C = No interest being paid.
D = In default.

10. **Investment-grade status**

Any rating that is at BBB or above is considered to be of investment grade. This means that the credit-rating agencies regard their issuer as having sufficient quality to be able to meet the obligations to the bond holders. If you buy a bond with a below-investment-grade rating you must accept that it is a speculative investment.

11. **Liquidity position**

In terms of banks this normally refers to the proportion of their assets that can easily be converted into cash. In times of uncertainty there will be a significant premium on banks holding large amounts of cash.

12. **Discount window**

This is a special emergency lending facility made available by the Federal Reserve to US commercial banks. Under this arrangement banks can borrow funds from the Fed to help them through short-term financial difficulties. This can cover an unexpected increase in loan activity, technology failure or a period when a bank is in trouble. The discount window loans are not open to investment banks, so Bear Stearns could access this facility through J.P. Morgan.

13. **Sub-prime mortgage crisis**

The prime lending rate is the rate of interest charged to creditworthy companies and individuals in the US. The sub-prime market refers to the lending of money to much-higher risk individuals at a higher rate of interest. When US house prices were rising sharply a number of people were encouraged to take out very large loans (at a very high multiple of their salary) which meant that they had little prospect of ever being able to meet the interest payments let alone any eventual repayment of the out-standing debt. As a result many were forced to default.

14. **Merger agreement**

This is where two companies decide that it would be to their joint benefit to come together to form a new business entity. With a merger the process is normally friendly with the full consent of both sets of shareholders.

15. **Binary**

The technical definition for this term is a two-digit system of numbering. In this context it is used to suggest that there had only been two possible outcomes. Either

Bear Stearns would fail, which would cause a crisis for financial markets, or it would be rescued in which case everything would return to normal.

16. **Moral hazard**

This is an economic term used to cover the risk that an insured person might take less care over their goods. Similarly, in the case of the banks' finance the concern is that because of the actions of the US authorities in rescuing Bear Stearns it might encourage other banks to attempt to adopt a similarly risky business model. This is termed 'moral hazard' and it is a worry that this has been injected into the financial system.

17. **Low-ball offer**

This is a US term for any situation where an offer is made for a product or service that is recognised to be extremely low. I associate the term with baseball where a low-ball pitch to a hitter (batter) can be seen as an attempt to entice the hitter to go for a poor choice of pitches in the hope that the hitter will swing and miss or hit a ground ball that can be easily fielded and the hitter would be put out.

■ What do you think?

1. Explain what factors led to the sub-prime crisis in the United States.

2. A number of influential economic commentators came to blame the former Chairman of the Federal Reserve, Alan Greenspan, for the sub-prime crisis. He had been largely responsible for the significant easing in monetary policy following the 2001 terrorist attacks. Do you think it was fair to blame him or should he have reasonably foreseen the later consequences of his actions?

3. What were the main activities of the Federal Reserve Bank in trying to minimise the impact of the sub-prime crisis?

4. What is meant by the term 'Fed's discount window'? In what situations are banks allowed to use this facility?

5. What were the main factors that caused the credit crisis to develop?

6. What are collaterised debt obligations?

7. It has been claimed that in bailing out Bear Stearns the Federal Reserve ran the risk of injecting moral hazard into the operation of US investment banks in the future. What is meant by this term and do you agree that this is a serious risk?

8. What factors motivated JPMorgan to mount a joint rescue of Bear Stearns with the help of the Federal Reserve?

■ The Web

Go to the Federal Reserve Bank's website at **www.federalreserve.gov**.
Go to the Monetary Policy Section.
Now select Policy Tools.

15

FINANCIAL INSTITUTIONS, FEATURING THE DEMISE OF BEAR STEARNS

Now select the Discount Rate.

You are required to fully explain this facility. In particular, explain what it is used for and what financial institutions can apply for funds at the discount window?

■ Research

Begg, D. and Ward, D., (2007) *Economics for Business*, 2nd edition, Maidenhead: McGraw-Hill. You should look at Chapter 11. The topic of the banking system is discussed on pages 259–265.

Begg, D., Fischer, S. and Dornbusch, R., (2008) *Economics*, 9th edition, Maidenhead: McGraw-Hill. You should look at Chapters 22 and 23. 'Lender of last resort' is discussed on page 453.

Boakes, K., (2008) *Reading and Understanding the Financial Times*, Harlow: Financial Times Prentice Hall. You should read Topic 12 to see a detailed review of Northern Rock.

Gillespie, A., (2007) *Foundations of Economics*, 1st edition, Oxford: Oxford University Press. You should focus on Chapter 28. There is a good discussion of the role of banks and financial institutions.

Mathews, K. and Thomson, J., (2008) *The Economics of Banking*, 2nd edition, Chichester: Wiley. There is a good chapter on bank regulation that starts on page 187.

Sloman, J. and Hinde, K., (2007) *Economics for Business*, 4th edition, Harlow: Financial Times Prentice Hall. You should look at Chapter 28.

Watching the ECB inside the Eurozone

I am sometimes a bit embarrassed when I go into my local newsagent on a Saturday morning and buy a copy of the weekend's FT. I sometimes wonder if I should not ask him to have it ready for me under the counter in a plain brown bag. It is not that the weekend FT is not a superb paper. It most definitely is. In fact it is probably the best read of the week with so many extra sections and a great magazine. It is rather that I worry that the other people in the shop might view me as being quite sad in reading about the world of finance even at the weekend. As I leave the shop I always place the weekend FT firmly under my Saturday *Guardian*.

Sitting down to the FT with a coffee I have no difficulty in identifying why it is such a good read: it is because it has some great articles on economics. This one is a perfect example as Ralph Atkins takes us through the latest developments in the economics of the Eurozone. We saw the problems that faced the European Central Bank (ECB) at a time when great uncertainty in the money markets argued for lower official interest rates while rising inflationary pressures suggested the reverse was necessary. Such dilemmas are among the constant worries of central banks right across the world.

Article 29

Financial Times, 29/30 March 2008

Eurozone set to receive more liquidity injections

Ralph Atkins in Frankfurt

Fresh measures to combat financial market tensions were unveiled by the European Central Bank yesterday but scares about eurozone inflation further reduced the scope for cutting its main interest rate.

Extending its armoury, the ECB announced its first injections of six-month money into eurozone markets. A €25bn ($39bn, £20bn) operation is set to be launched next week, while a second in July will extend beyond the end of this year.

The Frankfurt-based institution will also continue additional injections of three-month money.

The moves followed surges in market interest rates and pointed to heightened ECB concerns about the unfolding global financial crisis. The measures were aimed 'at supporting the normalisation of the functioning of the euro money market,' it said.

However, an unexpected acceleration in German inflation yesterday suggested that the ECB's main interest rate would remain firmly at 4 per cent – where it has stayed since last June – despite sweeping cuts by the US Federal Reserve.

Axel Weber, president of Bundesbank, Germany's central bank, expressed alarm about recent inflation trends and hinted that interest rate increases could not be ruled out. The ECB would 'act if

→

necessary' to secure price stability, he said in Luxembourg.

However, the ECB knows that tougher talk on interest rates could lead to further upward pressure on the euro, which is already at record levels against the dollar and on a trade-weighted basis.

Eurozone inflation data on Monday could show the annual rate for the 15-country region hitting a 16-year high of 3.5 per cent this month, economists said. Eurozone growth figures for the first quarter could also be better than expected, said Jürgen Stark, an ECB executive board member.

Reinforcing Mr Weber's hawkish tone on interest rates, Mr Stark said in a speech in South Africa that central banks had to act in 'a timely and pre-emptive manner'.

Since the start of the financial crisis last August, the ECB has drawn a clear distinction between its actions to ease market tensions and its main interest rate policy, aimed at combating inflation.

Even though the ECB believed the current level of interest rates would suffice, 'the bank is under huge pressure to explain why it is not responding to this surge in inflation,' said Jacques Cailloux of the Royal Bank of Scotland.

■ The analysis

One of the main roles of the ECB is ensuring that the commercial banks in the Eurozone have enough liquidity in order to operate. With their many daily activities there are always going to be some banks that are short of cash while others might be awash with funds. Normally this is sorted out in the interbank markets with the banks with surplus cash lending money to the other banks in need. However, there are some occasions when the banking system as a whole needs an injection of liquidity. This is an important function of any central bank.

This article examines a new emergency measure that was being employed to deal with the liquidity crisis in the money markets in the wake of the credit crunch which had seen the near-demise of both Northern Rock and Bear Stearns. The unusual feature was that it was a relatively long-term funding instrument in the context of these markets. This would now give the ECB three main instruments to inject more liquidity into the money markets. What were they?

a) Firstly, the ECB's **main refinancing operations** remained the weekly money market operations although these were actually carried out by each of the national central banks (acting on behalf of the ECB) across the Eurozone. With this facility the ECB invites the commercial banks to bid for the funds that they make available.

This is in the form of either fixed- or variable-rate tenders to secure the one week funding available. How does this work? Put simply, a fixed rate tender is where the commercial banks bid for funds at a set interest rate so that they have no chance to influence the cost of these funds. It is a 'take it or leave it' auction with only one available price. So, in a fixed-rate tender the ECB sets the interest rate.

In contrast, with a variable-rate tender the ECB invites bids for funds with the final cost of the funds dependent on the level of the bids that come in. If the banks are desperate for funds they will offer to pay very high-interest rates and this will drive the cost of these funds upwards. At other times a lack of interest in the facility will result in fewer bids and a downward move in the cost of these funds. So, in a variable-rate tender the market has a role in setting the interest rate.

So how does the ECB allocate the money available at these tenders? If the ECB is using a fixed-rate facility the process is as explained in Exhibit 15.2. The ECB sets a total amount of liquidity that is available and invites the banks to make their bids. When the total of the banks' bids exceeds the amount of finance made available then a 'pro rata' system is used to decide how much each bank receives. This means that in this case each of the three banks would get 75% of their total bid satisfied. The important point is that each bank is treated equally.

Exhibit 15.2

Example of a fixed-rate facility

The ECB decides to make €105bn available.
This is a fixed-rate facility at a rate of 4%.
In this case three banks submit the following bids:

	Bid (€ bn)	Allocation
Bank 1	30	22.5 (75%)
Bank 2	40	30.0 (75%)
Bank 3	70	52.5 (75%)
Total	140	105

Each bank gets a 'pro rata' allocation.

The percentage allotment is set by dividing the total amount of liquidity available (€105bn) by the total of the bids (€140bn). This means that each bank gets 75% of its bid accepted.

In contrast, if the ECB is using a variable-rate tender then the bids at the highest interest rates will be allocated first. This is followed by the next highest bid and so on until the full amount of liquidity has been allocated. At the final accepted interest rate the pro rata system is again used to allocate the money if there is not enough left to fully satisfy these bids. In this process there will be a range of accepted bids with each bank paying the interest rate that it bids, assuming it is at least partially accepted.

This is the key ECB money market instrument because whether it is a fixed- or a variable-rate tender the weekly refinancing facility is used to signal the direction of monetary policy. The Governing Council of the ECB sets the interest rate in advance for a fixed rate tender or sets the minimum bid for a variable-rate tender.

b) The second method of injecting cash into the Eurozone money markets comes when the ECB offers a **three-month facility**. This was only being made available each quarter.

c) Finally, this article discussed a new ECB facility as it was just about to embark on the first of **a new six-month facility**.

These additional measures were designed to bring some kind of normality back to the Eurozone money markets where there had recently been a sharp spike in interest rates. At the time of this article the 'Euro Libor rate' was trading at around 4.75%, compared to an official minimum bid rate of 4% in the weekly refinancing operations. In normal circumstances these two rates would be much closer together (maybe just a few basis points difference). With the credit crunch severely damaging confidence in the banks, it was clear that they were finding it very difficult to secure funding from the money markets. Liquidity was very tight and the confidence in the banking system was at an all-time low. The success of the ECB's new measures would be judged in terms of how quickly the money market rates returned to a level more in line with the ECB's official interest rate.

One thing was certain at that time, and that was that unlike other central banks the ECB looked to be stuck with 4% official interest rates for many months to come. This is because inflation remained stubbornly high, with the latest figures for Germany showing an unexpected rise. Indeed, if anything, there seemed to be a risk that the next move in Eurozone interest rates might actually be in an upward direction. It was not surprising that money market investors were keen to invest in the euro as they sought to take advantage of the growing interest rate differential in favour of the Eurozone compared to the US. As Table 15.1 shows this differential had changed from minus 125 basis points back in September 2007 to stand at plus 175 basis points in favour of the euro by the spring of 2008. Against this background it was not surprising that the euro remained very strong, particularly against the dollar.

Table 15.1

	Sept. 2007	End-March 2008
Eurozone official interest rate (Min bid at weekly refinancing)	4%	4%
US official interest rate (The Fed Funds Rate)	5.25%	2.25%
Differential (Euro minus US rates)	−1.25%	+1.75%

■ Key terms

1. European Central Bank

This is the Eurozone's central bank. It sets the level of short-term interest rates for all the countries that have adopted the euro. The main policy objective of the ECB is to maintain price stability in the medium term. This is defined as a 0−2% target range for consumer price inflation. The key part of the ECB is the Governing Council which meets every fortnight on a Thursday.

2. Six-month money injection (new ECB facility)

This was a new money market facility being used to add liquidity to the Eurozone money markets. It was a response to the prolonged credit crisis that started in the summer of 2007.

3. Money market interest rates

This is the financial market where short-term borrowing takes place mainly between banks. The key financial market instrument trade here is the London interbank offered rate (Libor). You can get a Libor rate for a wide range of money market maturities as well as currencies. The main money market interest rate in the Eurozone is called Euro 3m (3 months).

4. Inflation (German consumer price index)

This is the monthly data for the consumer price index (CPI) which shows the change in the price of a basket of goods and services for the German economy. The provisional figure is normally published on the 25th of each month and then this is finalised around ten days later. Financial markets focus on the first estimate as any later revision tends to be very small.

5. Main ECB interest rate

This is the weekly refinancing operation carried out by the national central banks on behalf of the ECB. It is fully explained in the analysis of the article above.

6. Federal Reserve Bank

The Federal Reserve is the central bank of the United States. The key part of the Fed is the Federal Open Market Committee (FOMC) which decides on changes in US monetary policy. It is made up of twelve individuals. The core seven come from the Central Federal Reserve Bank (based in Washington) and the other five represent the various Federal District Reserve Banks. One of these, New York, has a permanent place on the FOMC. The other eleven banks share the remainder of the votes on a complex rotation system. The FOMC reviews the outlook for the economy before deciding on the next move in interest rates.

7. Bundesbank

The Bundesbank is the central bank of the Federal Republic of Germany. Due to its sheer size and economic strength the Bundesbank is the most important member of the European System of Central Banks. Both the ECB and the Bundesbank are located in Frankfurt.

8. Eurozone inflation

This is simply a weighted average inflation rate for the whole Eurozone. The ECB is charged with keeping this figure at an annual rate 'of below but close to 2%'.

9. Executive Board (ECB)

This is a key part of the European Central Bank. It consists of the President of the ECB and five other members. The Executive Board is responsible for the ECB's day-to-day activities. For example, it implements the monetary policy directive of the Governing Council and it determines the daily money market operations.

■ What do you think?

1. At the time of this article there were considerable tensions in the Eurozone money markets. As a result the rate of interest on Euro Libor 3-month interest rates was around 4.75%. This was some 75 basis points above the minimum bid at the ECB's main refinancing operations. What impact would this have on the Eurozone economy?

2. Describe the three measures being used by the ECB to add liquidity to the Eurozone money markets.

3. Why might the unexpected increase in German inflation have prevented the ECB from reducing official interest rates at this time?

4. What are the main economic objectives of the ECB?

5. Why might the ECB be described as being one of the least transparent of the main central banks?

6. Explain how the ECB allocates liquidity at the weekly refinancing operations. You should contrast the process for fixed-rate and variable rate tenders.

7. At this time the fall of the dollar versus the euro had seen some commentators claim that the US currency would lose its status as the world's reserve currency. Explain what this term means and discuss the significance of such a move.

■ Data exercise

You will need the **Companies and Market Section** of the *Financial Times*. Go to the **Market Data Section** and look at the middle right-hand side of the page. In this section you will see various data on interest rates. You need to examine the section that looks at the level of **Market Rates**.

   Answer these questions:

1. What is the current level of Euro Libor overnight?

2. What is the current level of Euro Libor three months?

3. What is the current level of Euro Libor six months?

4. What is the current level of Euro Libor one year?

   Now compare this to the official ECB interest rate (you will see this in the FT on the same page in the 'Official Rates' section. Based on this information, how successful has the ECB been in returning the interest rates in the Eurozone to a more normal level.

■ The Web

Go to the ECB's official website **www.ecb.int/home/html/index.en.htm**.
Now find the pdf document titled 'the Monetary Policy of the ECB'.
Go to section 3) The ECB's Monetary Policy Strategy.
You are now required to write a short summary of the ECB's view on 'the role of monetary policy and the benefits of price stability'.

■ Research

The best places to learn more about central banks are the official websites from the major central banks. They are all fantastic learning resources with a great deal of material on monetary policy and the key roles of the central banks. You will also see a wide range of current data on inflation and interest rates.

For reference you will find these at:

www.federalreserve.gov

www.ecb.int/home/html/index.en.html

www.bankofengland.co.uk

It is also essential to read the *Financial Times* just after the major meetings of the central banks. These articles appear in the main section of the paper.

(Hint: look in the headlines for references to the FOMC, the MPC or the key interest rates.)

Begg, D. and Ward, D., (2007) *Economics for Business*, 2nd edition, Maidenhead: McGraw-Hill. You should look at Chapter 10. The topic of inflation targeting is discussed on page 235–236.

Begg, D., Fischer, S. and Dornbusch, R., (2008) *Economics*, 9th edition, Maidenhead: McGraw-Hill. You should look at Chapter 35. The ECB is discussed on pages 679–680.

Gillespie, A., (2007) *Foundations of Economics*, 1st edition, Oxford: Oxford University Press. You should focus on Chapter 28, page 377.

(Hint: look at the 'Economics in Context' box.)

Mathews, K. and Thomson, J., (2008) *The Economics of Banking*, 2nd edition, Chichester: Wiley. There is a section on the economics of central banking from pages 244–264.

Sloman, J., (2007) *Essentials of Economics*, 4th edition, Harlow: Financial Times Prentice Hall. You should look at Chapter 10, pages 372–373.

Sloman, J. and Hinde, K., (2007) *Economics for Business*, 4th edition, Harlow: Financial Times Prentice Hall. You should look at Chapter 28.

Go to **www.pearsoned.co.uk/boakes** to access Kevin's blog for additional analysis of recent topical news articles and to post your own comments. Download podcasts containing short audio summaries of the main issues relating to each article and check your understanding of in-text questions with the handy hints provided.

Glossary

Activist investors We use this term in finance to cover groups of shareholders that range from private investors with small stakes in the business right up to the large financial institutions that often own a significant percentage of the equity of a business. It is normally among these larger shareholders that we find the activist shareholders. These are the shareholders who believe that the managers are not doing a good job and as a result they will attempt to alter company policy and even possibly seek to replace existing senior managers with new people who they think will do a better job.

Appreciation (of the currency) This is simply where we see an increase in the value of one currency relative to another currency.

Association of British Insurers The ABI (Association of British Insurers) was formed in 1985 and it has the task of giving the view of the UK's insurance industry on a number of issues. The work of the ABI is split into four main departments: General Insurance, Life and Pensions, Financial Regulation and Tax and Investment. The ABI has a membership of around 400 companies and is located in the City of London.

Average cost This can be defined as the cost per unit of production.

Average earnings This is the average amount of pay in a particular economy. There is strong interest in this figure as it is seen as a very important factor in determining the level of inflation.

Bank of England This is the UK's central bank. It was made independent from the UK government in 1997. Since then it has been in charge of setting short-term interest rates in the UK money markets. The key part of the Bank of England is the Monetary Policy Committee which meets monthly to set the level of short-term interest rates.

Bank of Japan's Governor This is the head of the Bank of Japan.

Bear market (bottom) This refers to a sustained period in which the prices of financial securities (especially shares) have been falling. This creates a very pessimistic financial market mood with most investors unable to see when there will be a recovery in prices. This situation is normally associated with an economic recession. The period in the 1930s in the US is a perfect example of a prolonged bear market.

Binary The technical definition for this term is a two-digit system of numbering. In this context it is used to suggest that there had only been two possible outcomes.

Biofuels These are types of fuel made from crops like sugar cane, corn or rapeseed. One of the main factors driving their development was the view that they were more environmentally friendly than traditional fossil fuels.

Bond insurers These are financial institutions (called 'monolines') that use their high credit ratings to provide insurance on debt issues by relatively risky borrowers. As a result a borrower rated at just a single A might be able to issue some bonds rated at triple A. The advantage to the borrower is that they will save an enormous amount of interest on their bond issues.

Bond markets Many of the borrowers need to obtain funding for much more than one year. This will include governments, companies and banks that can all access the bond markets to issue longer-term securities.

Book value Put simply, this is what a company would be worth if it went out of business immediately. It is normally calculated as total assets minus any liabilities and intangible assets such as goodwill.

British Chambers of Commerce From their website: 'The British Chambers of Commerce is a non-political, non-profit making organisation, owned and directed by its members, democratically accountable to individual businesses of all sizes and sectors throughout the UK.'

Budget (forecast) This is an annual event where the Chancellor sets out the government's spending and tax plans for the next few years.

Budget deficit A budget deficit is where the government spends more than it receives in tax revenue. The reverse is a budget surplus where tax receipts exceed government spending.

Building societies These days it is increasingly difficult to differentiate between the roles of banks and building societies. In the past the main difference was that building societies were mutual organisations owned by their members who held savings accounts with them. In addition, the main role of a building society used to be the provision of mortgages to enable people to buy their homes. In recent years we have seen many building societies turn themselves into public companies through share issues. Also, building societies have now diversified the range of their activities to include many new services.

Bullish (sign) This refers to the opposite of a bear market. It is a sustained period in which the prices of financial securities (especially shares) have been rising. This creates a very optimistic financial market mood with most investors unable to see when there will be any downturn in prices. This situation is normally associated with an economic boom. The period in the mid to late 1990s in the US is a perfect example of a bull market.

Bundesbank The Bundesbank is the central bank of the Federal Republic of Germany. Due to its sheer size and economic strength the Bundesbank is the most important member of the European System of Central Banks. Both the ECB and the Bundesbank are located in Frankfurt.

Business plan This is a document that is written by a company's senior managers to give details of the future course of the business. It is frequently prepared by a company in preparation for a new or a first issue of capital. It will usually include a detailed financial forecast showing plans for several years in the future.

Capital adequacy This is a very important measure of risk for any bank. It is normally measured as a ratio of a bank's capital to its assets. The Bank for International Settlements (based in Basel) stipulates that banks must operate with a capital adequacy ratio no lower than 8%.

Capital inflows These are the inflows of capital that are recorded in a country's balance of payments. These can be borrowing from overseas, sales of overseas assets or foreign investment into the country.

Capital investment This term is used to cover any money that is invested in a business to buy new fixed assets like machinery, technology or industrial buildings. The aim of this expenditure is to enable the company to increase production of goods or services and generate higher income in future years. Economists see this type of investment as being vital in terms of securing higher rates of economic growth in the future.

Capital markets This refers to the financial markets where companies can access additional finance to fund new investment projects.

Capital spending There is a very important distinction made between two types of government spending. The first is current spending which covers spending on items that will have a short life. For example, this could be the purchase of stationery items for a school. In contrast capital expenditure is going on assets that will have a long life. This could include new school buildings, transport systems or hospitals.

Carry trade This was a very popular foreign exchange trading technique which is possible due to the existence of significant interest rate differentials between different countries. In this strategy an investor will sell a currency from the low-interest-rate zone and then invest the funds to buy another currency in a high-interest-rate zone. The investor is using this technique to exploit the difference between interest rates in these two zones. This strategy is far from risk-free as there is a chance that an adverse movement in the currency markets can more than offset any income gains.

Cash flow This refers to the amount of cash that a company generates and spends in a set time period. The cash flow available to a business is a crucial measure of liquidity for a company.

Central bank Just about all countries now have a national central bank and it is normally their most important financial institution. They have two primary functions. The first is to oversee the workings of the financial system and ensure that all other financial institutions are operating securely. The second key role of the central banks in most countries is to determine the correct stance of monetary policy. In practice this means that they set the level of short-term interest rates in the economy.

Central Bank of Iceland This is an independent central bank which has the task of operating monetary policy with the aim of maintaining price stability. Like most central banks it is required to support the other economic objectives (reasonable economic growth and high employment) as long as they do not conflict with its primary target.

Central government spending This covers all the spending made by central as opposed to local government. It will cover areas like defence, health and education.

Chairman In most companies the role of chairman is separated from that of chief executive officer. This is to ensure effective corporate governance with the non-executive chairman ensuring that the interests of the shareholders are fully protected.

(a) Non-executive chairman

This is supposed to be a person who is independent of the core management team. They will normally be employed on a part-time basis and will chair the main board of directors. In addition the CEO can look to them for advice and guidance.

You will also see the term NED, which stands for non-executive director. Most public companies will employ a number of part-time NEDs to give independent advice on the running of the company's operations.

(b) Executive chairman

This refers to a situation where a company has a full-time chairman who also takes the role of chief executive of the business.

Chief executive (officer) This is the top person in the company who will have the main responsibility for implementing the policies of the board of directors on a daily basis. Put simply, they are running the business.

Civil Aviation Authority (CAA) The CAA is the UK's independent regulator of the aviation sector. According to its website its activities include economic regulation, airspace policy, and safety regulation and consumer protection.

Claimant count This is the key official measure of unemployment used in the UK. It is based on the number of people who are out of work and actually claiming the state benefit currently called 'job seekers allowance'. During the 1980s the Labour Party used to criticise this figure, claiming that the then government (Conservative) had manipulated the definition of unemployment many times to massage the official unemployment rate. When Labour came to power in 1997 it said it would put a greater emphasis on a broader measure of unemployment which is based on all those people who are looking for work rather than just those claiming benefits. This measure, based on a survey of the labour force, tends to show a much higher level of unemployment than the claimant count.

Collaterised debt obligations (CDOs) These are complex financial market securities which are backed by a pool of bonds, loans or some other assets.

Commercial banks These are the 'high-street' banks that have ordinary people as their customers. They will take deposits from the general public and use these funds to offer loans to both ordinary customers and small companies.

Competition In economics we use this term to refer to the battle between companies to win market share. For this to be the case there have to be enough buyers and sellers in a market to ensure that no single player has so much power that they can influence the price of the good or service. Economists define perfect competition as existing where many companies operate, there are no barriers to entry into the sector, the product or service is identical and the companies must all be price-takers. In contrast to this we sometimes have a monopoly.

Competition Commission This is an official UK body that investigates whether a monopoly or possible monopoly acts against the public interest. It replaced the Monopolies and Mergers Commission in 1999. It can only make investigations following referrals by the Office for Fair Trade or the Secretary of State for Trade and Industry.

Confederation of British Industry (CBI) The Confederation of British Industry (CBI) is widely described as the employers' organisation. It is a voluntary group made up of around

1500 UK-based manufacturing companies. It carries out a wide range of surveys to gauge its members' views on the current state of economy activity. It provides a useful overview of the state of manufacturing industry.

Conglomerate This refers to a company that is made up of several different businesses. The attraction of this type of set-up is that it provides a diversification of risk. This means that if one part of the company hits any financial problems this might be offset by the performance of the others. In addition, a multinational conglomerate has the advantage of having markets in a range of countries. This can again allow the company to diversify its risk.

Consumer price inflation Until 2003 the UK government's target for inflation was set in terms of the percentage annual increase in the average prices of goods and services as measured by the retail price index (RPI). There was some controversy in 2003 when the relevant inflation measure was changed to the consumer price index (CPI) which excludes certain important costs such as council tax and mortgage interest payments.

Consumer service companies Put simply these are businesses that make their living by supplying services to their customers. In this article good examples include hairdressers and gym instructors.

Consumption Put simply, this is something most of us enjoy doing – spending money. Economists make a distinction between consumption by the private sector (you and me) and the public sector (the government).

Consumption good Economists use this term to define the purchase of certain goods or services that give pleasure in their own right. The consumer does not purchase these items in order to derive any future gains. For example, I might spend £20 on a ticket to go and see my favourite football team. In contrast, I could use this money to buy a new textbook that promises to increase my knowledge of economics and improve my chances of securing a well-paid job in the future.

Core inflation This simply refers to the annual rate of CPI excluding certain especially volatile prices including seasonal food and energy. It is also sometimes called the 'underlying' rate of inflation.

Corporate bond market (widening spreads) The corporate bond market refers to the issue of debt securities by companies. These bonds represent a debt that must be repaid normally at a set date in the future. Most corporate bonds pay a set interest rate each year, called the 'coupon'. The other key characteristic of a bond is its maturity. This is the date that the bond will be redeemed.

Corporate debt (investment grade) The corporate bond market refers to the issue of debt securities by companies. These bonds represent a debt that must be repaid normally at a set date in the future. Most corporate bonds pay a set interest rate each year, called 'the coupon'. The other key characteristic of a bond is its maturity. This is the date on which the bond will be redeemed.

Corporate finance firm (boutique) This term is normally used to describe a small investment bank that acts as an adviser but does not trade in financial market securities on its own behalf. The advantage of such a firm is that its advice can be seen to be completely impartial.

Corporate governance (code) This is a general term used to describe the relationship between the owners of a business (the shareholders) and the managers of the business. It covers the various mechanisms by which the shareholders can try to make sure that the managers act in their interest. This should ensure that the managers are open, fair and fully accountable for all their actions.

Corporation tax A direct tax charged on the profits made by limited companies. In the UK this is split into a main corporation tax rate (charged at 28%) and a small company's corporation tax rate (charged at 21%).

Correlation (tight) This is defined as a measure of the strength of the relationship between two economic variables.

Cost inflation This simply refers to the higher charges being faced by the oil exploration companies. This would include labour (wages) as well as materials and transport costs.

Cost of capital This is simply the cost of finance for a company looking to make a new investment. It is normal to break this down into the cost of equity finance and the cost of debt finance.

Credit crisis This refers to the cost and availability of credit. It might be a government borrowing (in the government bond market), a company borrowing (in the corporate bond market), a house owner (with a mortgage) or a consumer (with a credit card). We have a 'credit crunch' when the cost of borrowing is considered to be prohibitively expensive by historic standards or it is simply very difficult for more risky borrowers to obtain finance at all. During 2008 the credit crunch hit home when the banks stopped lending and instead spent all their time sourcing liquidity.

Credit crunch This refers to the crisis that first affected financial markets in the summer of 2007. This was caused by the sub-prime crisis that started in the US. As a result banks became very reluctant to lend to each other and the interbank markets saw their liquidity dry up.

Credit indices We need to start with the idea of a credit default swap. This is a financial market instrument that is designed to offer a bond investor complete protection against the risk of default. Essentially, the seller of the swap takes over the risk of default on the bond issuer for a one-off payment. So, in the event of any default the seller of the swap will be fully liable to pay the par value of the bond and any due interest payments to the credit swap buyer. A credit index is created to allow investors to trade credit market risk without having to buy and sell individual credits. Instead they trade one of the credit default indices based in the US, Europe or one of the emerging markets.

Credit markets This refers to the financial markets where debt securities are first issued (the primary market) and then traded (the secondary market). The issuers of these debt instruments will be mainly companies and governments and the investors will be pension funds and insurance companies.

Credit spreads This is a measure of the relative cost of issuing more risky bonds. It is best seen with an example. Let us assume that the United States government has close to zero risk of default. As a result a 10-year US Treasury bond might have a yield of 4.5%. In contrast a 10-year issue from Ford Motor Company which has significantly more risk of default might have a yield of 6.5%. This gives us a credit yield spread of 6.5% minus 4.5% which is 200 basis points difference. In this case investors were selling lots of the higher-yielding (more risky) bonds which caused 'credit spreads to balloon' as the relative cost of these bonds rose.

Credit-rating agencies There are a number of large international companies that are used to assess the risk of various bond issuers. They produce a formal rating measure for each of them.

For example, they can assign the following ratings:

AAA = Capacity to pay interest and principal extremely strong.
AA = Differs only in a small degree.
A = More susceptible to adverse changes in circumstances.
BBB = Adequate capacity.
BB, B = Speculative.
C = No interest being paid.
D = In default.

Currency intervention This is where a government, or more often its central bank, engages in foreign exchange trading in order to influence the value of its currency on the international currency markets. In simple terms, they will sell their currency and buy some foreign currency in order to bring about a fall in the value of the domestic currency. In contrast, they will buy their currency and sell some foreign currency in order to bring about a rise in the value of their currency.

Current account deficit The current account records trade in goods (the visible balance) and the other side made up of services, transfers and interest, profits and dividends (the invisible balance). If it is in deficit a country is earning less income from its exports than it is spending on its imports.

Default This is where a borrower takes out a loan but fails to keep to the original agreed schedule of interest payments and final capital repayments. A bond issued by the United States or United Kingdom government is generally regarded to be free of default risk. In contrast a bond issued by a company might well have significant risk of default. For example, a company might not be able to keep up with the interest payments on the loan as a result of a downturn in its profitability.

Demand and supply In economics we define demand as the quantity of a good or service that a consumer wishes to buy at a particular price. In the same way the supply is defined as the quantity of a good or service that a producer wishes to make available at a particular price.

Depreciation This represents the reduction in the value of long-term assets due to wear and tear etc.

Deposit ratios These measure the amount of the banks' loans compared to their deposits. For example, one bank might have loans amounting to £100m compared to total deposits of £800m. This gives them a deposit ratio of 12.5%. If they increase their loans to £150m with the same amount of deposits the ratio increases to 18.75%.

Derivative markets These are the financial instruments which have been developed to allow investors to manage and exploit risk. The name 'derivative' is used because they derive from the fundamental financial products. The most common examples are futures, options and swaps.

Diminishing returns (law of) If we start with the production process being made up of fixed and variable units. For example, for a particular company the factory might be the fixed factor and the supply of labour might be the variable factor. If the company adds extra labour (more staff or existing staff working overtime) this will result in an increase in the amount being produced. However, in the end the company will reach a certain production level where as they add an additional unit of the variable input this starts to result in less and less extra output being produced. Put simply, their level of total output is still increasing but now it is at a reduced rate. This is the impact of the law of diminishing returns in action.

Discount window This is a special emergency lending facility made available by the Federal Reserve to US commercial banks. Under this arrangement banks can borrow funds from the Fed to help them through short-term financial difficulties. This can cover an unexpected increase in loan activity, technology failure or a period when a bank is in trouble.

Earnings premium In simple terms this is the wage differential enjoyed by one person compared to another. It is used to calculate the value of different stages of educational attainment. For example, you can calculate the earnings premium enjoyed by graduates compared to non-graduates.

Economic downturn This is simply any slowdown in economic activity. In an extreme case this can result in a recession (defined as two or more successive quarters of negative economic growth) or even a depression (a severe economic downturn that lasts several years).

Economic growth This can be defined as an increase in the general level of production of goods and services in a country. We normally measure this each quarter, although most attention will be focused on the annual data because the quarterly data are too volatile.

Economic regulation This refers to some form of government intervention that is intended to impact on the behaviour of firms and individuals in the private sector.

Economic uncertainty This is when there the future course of economic activity cannot be predicted with any degree of confidence. There might be a strong chance of a severe downturn but there is a doubt about the timing and the severity of this outcome.

Economies of scale This is the reduction in unit costs that comes about from an increase in production.

Emerging economies This term is used to denote the generally fast-growing economies of the newer nations around the world. They tend to be characterised by high growth but much greater political and social risk.

Engineering and Manufacturing Support and Employment Advice for Business (the EEF manufacturers' organisation) This is an organisation that offers a range of business services to over 6000 manufacturing, engineering and technology companies. These cover things like advice on health and safety, legal advice, environmental services and current data on pay levels. In addition it represents the interests of this sector at a national and European level. To this end it has offices in London and Brussels

Equity markets These allow the lenders to contribute risk capital to a range of different businesses. They lend their money to these companies without a guarantee of any capital repayment or dividend income in the future. This makes it a risky form of investment but with the possibility of securing very high rates of return at some stage in the future.

Euro and sterling term money markets This is where the banks that have too much money lend cash to the banks which lack funds. The main financial market product traded in the money markets is the London Inter-bank offered rate (Libor) which is the rate used for loans made to low-risk banks in the London money markets. You can get a Libor rate for a wide range of money market maturities. It starts with overnight money and then goes to one month, three months, six months and one year.

European Central Bank This is the Eurozone's central bank. It sets the level of short-term interest rates for all the countries that have adopted the euro. The main policy objective of the ECB is to maintain price stability in the medium term. This is defined as a 0–2% target range for consumer price inflation. The key part of the ECB is the Governing Council which meets every fortnight on a Thursday.

Eurozone inflation This is simply a weighted average inflation rate for the whole Eurozone. The ECB is charged with keeping this figure at an annual rate 'of below but close to 2%'.

Excess profits Economists measure these as any profits earned by a company that are above the normal level of profits. This normal level offers a fair return on capital employed. It is accepted that a major cost for companies is the opportunity cost of not using their time and money in doing something else. They are taking far more risk than they would be if they simply left their money in a bank. So economists allow for this cost when they decide on a reasonable rate of return for them to earn. The normal profit will be made up of the riskless return plus some extra amount to offset this risk they take. Any level of profit above this normal level is termed excess in the sense that it is more than can be justified by the costs incurred by the business.

Executive Board (ECB) This is a key part of the European Central Bank. It consists of the President of the ECB and five other members. The Executive Board is responsible for the ECB's day-to-day activities. For example, it implements the monetary policy directive of the Governing Council and it determines the daily money market operations.

Externalities These occur when the actions of either consumers or producers have an impact on people other than themselves. These consequences for others are sometimes referred to as 'third-party or spin-off effects'.

Fed Funds Rate This is the most important short-term interest rate in the United States. It refers to the overnight inter-bank lending that takes places in the United States money markets. The money that one bank lends to another comes from any excess reserves held at the Fed. A target level for the official Fed Funds Rate is set by the Federal Open Market Committee.

Federal Reserve Bank The Federal Reserve is the central bank of the United States. The key part of the Fed is the Federal Open Market Committee (FOMC) which decides on changes in US monetary policy. It is made up of twelve individuals. The core seven come from the Central Federal Reserve Bank (based in Washington) and the other five represent the various Federal District Reserve Banks. One of these, New York, has a permanent place on the FOMC. The other eleven banks share the remainder of the votes on a complex rotation system. The FOMC reviews the outlook for the economy before deciding on the next move in interest rates.

Federation of Small Businesses The FSB is a body that represents the interests of small businesses in the UK.

Financial distress In corporate finance we use the term 'financial distress' to describe a position where a company is failing to meet its commitments to its creditors. This means that it is not making timely interest or redemption payments. More often than not financial distress will result in the bankruptcy of a business.

Financial liabilities This is where one party (the debtor) is required to make some kind of financial payments to another party (the creditor).

Fiscal deficit This is where a government is spending more than it is receiving in tax revenue. We normally measure this as a percentage of a country's total income.

Fixed costs Economists use the term 'fixed costs' to denote those that must be paid by a company no matter what their level of production. For example, a company might employ a member of staff to deal with all health and safety issues in all their factories. Her salary must be paid no matter what the production levels might be. Indeed even if the factory's production ceases all together she will continue to be paid until the company decides that this position can be terminated

Floating currencies This describes the process of allowing a currency to float freely on the foreign exchange markets without any official foreign exchange intervention.

Floating rate (bank loans) With these loans the interest rate that is charged will not be fixed in advance. It will instead be set in terms of some benchmark market or official interest rate with a fixed additional spread. The benchmark might be an official central bank interest rate (like the Fed funds rate) or a money market rate (like Libor).

For example, the floating-rate bank loan might have an interest rate set at Libor plus 25 basis points. So, if Libor is 6.75% when the interest rate is next set, the interest rate for the loan will be set at 6.75% plus 25 basis points, that is 7%.

Foreign exchange markets These allow people to convert one currency into another. For example, a Japanese investor can exchange their yen for US dollars and use the proceeds to buy some government bonds issued by the United States Treasury. You will see this discussed in detail in Topic 12 which covers international economics.

Foreign reserves (intervention) These are the reserves of foreign currency that are normally held by a country's central bank. It sometimes uses these reserves to intervene in the foreign exchange markets in order to have an impact on currency values. It can sell these reserves of foreign currency and buy domestic currency to try to strengthen its own currency. Or it can buy more reserves of foreign currency by selling its own currency to try to cause depreciation in its domestic currency.

FTSE-100 The FTSE-100 is the most widely quoted UK stock market index. It is based on the value of the 100 largest UK companies in terms of their market capitalisation. It started with a base level of 1000 in January 1984. This index is now quoted in real time on the various news information systems that serve the City traders.

FTSE Eurofirst 300 This is one of the FT's more recently created stock market indices. It attempts to track the performance of the leading European stock markets. It is shown on the front of the FT each day in the World Market's Data section.

Futures market In the money markets there is a well-established futures market that allows banks to deal at a set interest rate for a transaction on a specified future date. For example, a bank could arrange to lend £10m to another bank at a set interest rate on a specific date in the future. The attraction of this deal is that both parties know now what the interest rate is going to be. There is no uncertainty as this transaction will not be affected by any subsequent rise or fall in money market interest rates.

Global acquisitions An acquisition is where one company buys a controlling interest in another company. When it is global it simply means that the acquiring company is buying a business in another country. It becomes a cross-border deal.

Global financial conditions This refers to the current state of financial markets. If they are relatively stable they might be deemed to be 'favourable'. In contrast, financial markets can be said to be 'in turmoil' when financial institutions are themselves facing funding difficulties. This was the case with Northern Rock (in the UK) in late 2007 and Bear Stearns (in the US) in March 2008.

Government bonds The United States has the world's largest government bond market. The Treasury market is backed by the US government and as a result is seen as having no default risk. It sets the standard for all other dollar-denominated bonds. As a result other dollar issues will see their yields set in relation to the equivalent US Treasury issue. The market can be split into three divisions:

(a) Treasury bills:

This covers three months to one year maturity issues.

(b) Treasury notes:

This covers 2–10-year maturity and coupon bonds.

(c) Treasury bonds:

This covers bonds with a maturity of 10 years plus.

Green budget Economists use the term 'green budget' to refer to any measures that are designed to have a beneficial impact on the environment. This could include policies to discourage the frequent use of air travel or to encourage greater use of recycling.

Gross domestic product This is a measure of the total level of income earned within a country's national boundaries.

Hard economic landing This is where economic activity comes to an abrupt halt. The result is severe economic disruption with many companies failing and widespread unemployment.

Hedge This term is widely used in financial markets to indicate that an investment in a financial market product is being made to minimise the risk of any unfavourable movement in the price of a particular financial asset. In the context of this article it seems that some investors have been specifically investing in commodities (like oil) to protect themselves against a rise in inflation.

Hedge fund This refers to a particular type of investment management where the fund manager will employ a range of different investment tools in an attempt to maximise the returns or try to make gains even in a falling market. The fund will rely on large amounts of borrowing and will use derivative markets and short selling to achieve these aims.

House depreciation The term 'depreciation' is used to measure the declining value of an asset over time. For example, a company can claim the annual reduction in value of a piece of industrial machinery as a legitimate business expense. For most periods in the UK housing market we have tended to think more of appreciation rather than depreciation. However, if there is no annual capital growth in house prices then depreciation in house values become a more relevant concept. It measures the decline in the value of a house as certain fittings become outdated or wear out.

ICEX Benchmark stock market index This is the main measure of the performance of the stock market in Iceland. It is based on the performance of 15 leading companies.

Incremental revenue This refers to the extra revenue that a company generates by going ahead with a new investment project.

Industrialisation (emerging economies) This refers to an economy that has a very well-developed industrial sector. At this time we were seeing many former emerging economies go through this process and as a result become large users of oil as well as other commodities.

Inelastic and elastic demand In economics these terms are used to provide a measure of how responsive demand is to any given change in the price level. Certain goods are expected to have a high elasticity of demand, which means that demand for them will fall sharply as their price rises. This might include items like expensive cars and other luxury products. In contrast other goods will have an inelastic demand, which means that their demand will be relatively insensitive to any price change. This could include basic food items and essential heating and light.

Inflation This is normally defined as any sustained increase in the general level of prices for goods and services. It is normally measured by a consumer price index that records the monthly changes in a basket of goods and services reflecting typical spending patterns across different time periods and in different countries.

Inflation (German consumer price index) This is the monthly data for the consumer price index (CPI) which shows the change in the price of a basket of goods and services for the German economy. The provisional figure is normally published on the 25th of each month and then this is finalised around ten days later. Financial markets focus on the first estimate as any later revision tends to be very small.

Inflation expectations This refers to the situation where people within a country start to take account of inflation in their decisions. For example, wage negotiators will start to build in a certain level of price inflation before agreeing to a new wage settlement.

Inflation target (Bank of England's) When the government made the Bank of England independent (free to set interest rates without any political interference) in May 1997 it also gave it a target for controlling inflation. This target is currently 2% and is set in terms of the CPI. It is argued that maintaining low inflation is essential in order to achieve sustainable long-term economic growth.

Inflationary expectations This is a key concept in economics; it attempts to measure what people believe will happen to inflation in the foreseeable future. The significance of inflationary expectations is that they will influence everybody's decisions. This might include the level of wage demands or any investment decisions.

Initial public offer (IPO) An IPO refers to the situation where a company first sells its shares by listing on the stock exchange. This gives it a much wider access to increase its shareholder base. In addition it provides much greater liquidity in terms of the trading of the shares in the company. Companies considering a new IPO will appoint an investment bank to manage the process. The bank will meet the company and be heavily involved in valuing the shares, preparing a prospectus and getting investors interested in the new issue. The investment bank will be very well rewarded for this work with substantial fees often being paid to ensure a successful IPO.

Institute for Public Policy Research This is a UK-based think tank founded in the late 1980s which has strong links with the UK Labour Party. On its website it describes itself as 'The UK's leading progressive think tank, producing cutting edge research and innovative policy ideas for a just, democratic and sustainable world'.

Institutional investors These are the large pension funds and insurance companies that are the key investors in financial markets. They look to invest in long-term assets to match their long-term liabilities (paying out pensions). These investors have flourished in recent years due to the greater wealth of the private sector. In contrast the private clients refer to the individuals who invest on their own behalf.

Integrated suppliers In terms of the energy market this refers to vertical integration. This is where a firm owns its upstream suppliers and its downstream buyers. So you have Centrica that both owns production platforms in the North Sea (upstream) and supplies its retail gas customers. This is very common in other markets. For example, BP is involved in oil exploration and supply while at the same time owning petrol stations supplying retail customers.

Interest rates When an individual or a company borrows money there is a cost that they have to pay in order to obtain the funds. If it is a short-term loan (up to one year) this is normally referred to as an 'interest rate'. So we might take out a one-month bank loan with an annual interest rate of say 8.5%. This is the interest rate, or the cost of obtaining the funds.

Interest rates (Iceland) All central banks have one major interest rate that is used to signal changes in their monetary policy. In Iceland this rate is called the 'policy rate'. This was raised to 15% in response to the economic crisis experienced in March 2008.

International Energy Agency (IEA) The IEA has the role of providing independent advice to its twenty-seven member countries. It was founded as a result of the 1973 oil crisis in an attempt to co-ordinate the supply of oil in emergencies.

International Monetary Fund (IMF) This international body was set up in the 1940s with the aim of running the new fixed exchange rate system. These days it has a membership that runs to over 180 countries. The IMF plays an important role in terms of working with these economies and advising them on their fiscal and monetary policies.

Investment (growth) This is where a business spends money now in the expectation that it will result in an increase in output or income at some stage in the future.

Investment banks This is a classic example of a financial intermediary that acts between the issuers of capital (governments and companies) and the investors in capital (pension funds and insurance companies). Most investment banks are split into two main divisions. The first helps companies with the issue of new equity market securities. The second offers companies the chance to issue new bond market securities.

Investment good Economists use this term to define the purchase of certain goods or services that they hope will result in a significant future financial gain. It can be compared to similar investments in physical capital (a new machine) or some kind of financial assets (some shares).

Investment-grade status Any rating that is at BBB or above is considered to be of investment grade. This means that the credit-rating agencies regard their issuer as having sufficient quality to be able to meet the obligations to the bond holders. If you buy a bond with a below-investment-grade rating you must accept that it is a speculative investment.

Japan's Finance Minister This is the head of the Japanese Ministry of Finance and a key member of the Cabinet.

Krona Iceland uses the term 'krona' (meaning 'crown') for its national currency. This is also true in most of the other Nordic states (including Sweden, Denmark and Norway).

Leveraged takeover This term is used in the context of management buyouts and it suggests that the new company will be financed largely with debt capital.

Liquid (trading market) A liquid trading market refers to the level of trading that takes place in this market. The more trading there is, the more liquid the market.

Liquidity (banking system) In financial markets this normally refers to how easily an asset can be converted into cash. Therefore notes and coins are the most liquid financial asset. In general the more liquid an asset the lower is its return.

Liquidity (extra) In economics this normally refers to how much money is flowing around in the economy. The more liquidity that is in existence the more the risk of rising inflation as excess demand forces prices up.

Liquidity position In terms of banks this normally refers to the proportion of their assets that can easily be converted into cash. In times of uncertainty there will be a significant premium on banks holding large amounts of cash.

Liquidity valuation There are a number of financial techniques that are used by economists to correctly value a company's share price. One of the most common is the dividend valuation model. With this we take the future cash flows which will be earned by a company and multiply them by an appropriate discount factor to get their present value.

Long-run costs Economists define the long run as being the time period when all the factors of production can be changed. So, in the long run a company can look to expand its warehouse or factory capacity without any problems.

Low-ball offer This is a US term for any situation where an offer is made for a product or service that is recognised to be extremely low. I associate the term with baseball where a low-ball pitch to a hitter/batter can be seen as an attempt to entice the hitter to go for a poor choice of pitches in the hope that the hitter will swing and miss or hit a ground ball that can be easily fielded and the hitter would be put out.

Low pay commission From their website:

'The Low Pay Commission (LPC) is an independent statutory non departmental public body set up under the National Minimum Wage Act 1998 to advise the Government about the National Minimum Wage. Our permanent status was confirmed by Government in 2001 and we were given a Terms of Reference for a programme of longer-term research.'

Macroeconomics This takes a look at the economy as a whole. For example, it covers important economic themes including the total number of people unemployed or the general level of price inflation in a particular country. In essence it is concerned with the bigger picture.

Main ECB interest rate This is the weekly refinancing operation carried out by the national central banks on behalf of the ECB.

Margin calls (at hedge funds) A margin call refers to the request, normally from a brokerage house, that a particular investor must supply additional cash to their account. In this case this is where the bank has lent large amounts of cash to the hedge funds. This particularly extreme form of fund manager will employ a range of different investment tools in an attempt to maximise the returns or try to make gains even in a falling market. The funds are highly dependent on large amounts of borrowing from the banks. If the banks now start to 'call' this money back the hedge funds will be in financial trouble and they will be forced to make immediate sales of financial assets, often incurring serious losses as a result.

Marginal cost This can be defined as the additional cost of producing one extra unit of production.

Market failure This occurs when the allocation of goods and services that is achieved through market forces is not efficient.

Maturity transformation In the banking system lenders and borrowers have very different requirements in terms of the length of time that they want the funds for. On the one hand the lenders are often reluctant to tie up their money for long periods of time while on the other the borrowers might be looking for very long-term funding for new investment projects. The banks can manage this process relatively easily. They are quite willing to lend to borrowers for long time periods while taking their customers' money for potentially much shorter periods. We call this process 'maturity transformation'.

Mercantilism An economic policy that dates back to the time of the famous economist Adam Smith (1770s) that argues for a more interventionist policy from governments as they try to increase the level of exports and minimise the level of imports. This viewpoint sees any one country only making gains at another's expense. In other words, to have a winner you must have as loser.

Merger agreement This is where two companies decide that it would be to their joint benefit to come together to form a new business entity. With a merger the process is normally friendly with the full consent of both sets of shareholders.

Merit (and demerit goods) Merit goods can be defined as any that are more highly valued by society than they are by individual consumers. As a result the government would like people to consume them in much larger quantities than they would if they were left to their own devices. A good example of a merit good might be art and culture. In contrast demerit goods are those items that we tend to consume without taking full account of their negative impacts. Examples of demerit goods include smoking or drinking to excess.

Microeconomics This covers all the aspects that deal with the behaviour of individuals and companies as economists try to explain how markets operate. For example, it shows us how the supply and demand for a particular good or service determines its price.

Minimum wage This is legally the lowest wage that an employer is allowed to pay an employee. It is normally stated as a rate per hour with different bands according to the age of the employee.

Minority shareholder This is where a shareholder has less than fifty per cent of the company.

Monetary policy When you see the term 'monetary policy' in the context of central banks it refers to interest rate policy. A central bank tightens monetary policy when it raises interest rates. A central bank eases monetary policy when it cuts interest rates.

Monetary Policy Committee The Bank of England's Monetary Policy Committee (MPC) is in charge of setting UK interest rates. It is made up of nine members: the Governor of the Bank of England, two Deputy-Governors, two Bank of England and two non-executive Directors and four independent members. The MPC is required by the government to ensure that the UK economy enjoys price stability. This is defined by the government's set inflation target of 2%.

Money market This allows the banks with surplus cash to lend these funds to the banks with a financial deficit. The key characteristic of this market is its short-term nature. Money market securities are defined to have a maturity of anything up to one year. The key interest rate that is traded in this market is called the London Inter-bank Offered Rate (Libor). This is the rate used for loans made to low-risk banks in the London money markets. You can get a Libor rate for a wide range of money market maturities. It starts with overnight money and then goes to one month, three months, six months and one year. This is the market that saw a sharp reduction in liquidity in the wake of the credit crunch.

Money market interest rates This is the financial market where short-term borrowing takes place mainly between banks. The key financial market instrument trade here is the London interbank offered rate (Libor). You can get a Libor rate for a wide range of money market maturities as well as currencies. The main money market interest rate in the Eurozone is called Euro 3m (3 months).

Money supply definitions There are many different measures of money supply that are used by most countries. In the UK we start with a narrow definition such as M0 which includes only cash deposits held at the central bank plus all the liquid cash circulating in the economy. This measure is often referred to as 'narrow money'.

M2 is a broader definition of money. It includes M0 plus all retail sight deposits held at banks and building societies. Sight deposits can be withdrawn with no notice (current accounts).

M4 is wider still as it equals M0 plus all sterling deposits held with the banks and building societies. This will include various time deposits that are tied up for a fixed period.

Money supply growth This is defined as the total amount of money that is in circulation in a particular country's economy at a set time. In practice there is no single definition of money supply. Instead we have various measures depending on how widely we define the concept of money.

Monolines (often known by their full name, 'monoline insurance companies') These are financial institutions that use their high credit ratings to provide insurance on debt issues by relatively risky borrowers. As a result, a borrower rated at just a single A might be able to issue some bonds rated at triple A. The advantage to the borrower is that they will save an enormous amount of interest on their bond issues.

Monopoly In economics a pure monopoly exists where only one single supplier exists in the marketplace. This gives them considerable control over the price that is being charged. It should not be confused with the monopsony, where there is only one buyer of a particular good or service.

Moral hazard This is an economic term used to cover the risk that an insured person might take less care over their goods.

Mortgage interest payments (MIPs) These are the monthly payments made by house owners to service their outstanding mortgage debt. The amount of the MIPs will depend on the size of the mortgage and the level of mortgage interest rates.

Mortgage principal This is the total amount of mortgage debt that is owed by an individual. The mortgage interest payments service this debt.

Mortgage-backed securities A mortgage-backed security is created where a large pool of mortgages are collected together and traded between various large investors.

Municipal bonds These are debt securities issued in the US by states or municipal authorities to fund the difference between local taxes and expenditure; they will help to fund transport or education services.

Mutual fund (tracker money) This term is used mainly in the United States for some form of collective investment fund. It can invest a range of assets including shares, bonds and money market securities. When it is organised as a tracker fund this simply means that the fund will attempt to match the performance of some particular financial market index. This could be a stock market index like the FT-SE 100. In this case it would have to make sure that its holdings perfectly matched the index. So, if Tesco plc made up 10% of the FTSE100 the fund would have to hold the same percentage in the fund.

Net investment This can be defined as investment net of any depreciation.

Net national product This is GDP *minus* Capital Consumption.

NETA (pronounced 'neater') (New electricity trading arrangements) This was a new market mechanism that replaced the 'Electricity pool of England and Wales'. Under this older system all electricity generators had to put all their electricity into a central pool. The retail suppliers would then place bids to obtain the amount that they wanted at this price. A 'system marginal price' was arrived at. This was the highest price that you needed to go to in order to obtain all the electricity that was needed. All the electricity generators then received this higher price for all the electricity that they supplied. This system was felt to be inflexible and uncompetitive and was replaced by NETA in 2001.

New York Fed This is the most important of the Federal Reserve District Banks. It has a permanent place on the Federal Open Market Committee which determines the level of short-term interest rates in the US.

Nikkei 225 This is the most-closely followed index of Japanese share prices. The index is quite broad as it is based on Japan's top 225 blue-chip companies quoted on the Tokyo Stock Exchange.

Nominal and real investment The term 'nominal' means before we allow for inflation. The term 'real' means after allowing for inflation.

For example, a company might spend £500m more on new investment this year compared to last year. However, if the costs of investment have increased by £400m over this time period, the real increase in investment is only £100m.

Non-bank financial institutions This covers any financial institutions that are not officially defined as banks. It will include building societies, most insurance companies and investment banks.

Non-domiciles These are people who are granted 'non-domiciled' status by the UK tax authorities. They will normally be from abroad but be living and working in the UK. They must pay tax on any UK earnings but not on any money earned overseas. It is estimated that there are as many as 110,000 such people in the UK.

Office for National Statistics (ONS) The Office for National Statistics (ONS) is a department of the government that has the function of producing official data on the UK as a country and as an economy. The remit of the ONS is wide-ranging as it publishes statistics on so many areas, from births to deaths and everything in between, including marriages, divorces and travel to the UK as well as the standard economic data like inflation and unemployment.

OFGEM This is the body that regulates the UK's gas and electricity companies. It is supposed to protect the interests of consumers, ensuring that the supply of energy remains competitive.

Oil futures Like most other commodity markets there is a very liquid futures market for oil trading. In these markets the buyer agrees to take delivery and the seller agrees to supply a fixed amount of oil for some set dates in the future and at a set location. The most commonly traded futures contract in the oil market would be for delivery in the next month. The minimum size of contract is 1000 barrels.

OPEC and non-OPEC (oil production) OPEC is the most important example of a cartel operating in practice. This is where a group of suppliers come together to create a formal agreement to control the volume delivered into the market. The members of OPEC have been meeting in Vienna since the mid-1960s to set the level of their output and to influence the level of world oil prices. Each OPEC member is allocated a specific quota that they are allowed to produce. The members include Algeria, Indonesia, Iran, Iraq, Saudi Arabia and Venezuela.

Non-OPEC producers include Mexico, Russia and Norway.

Open economy This term is used to describe an economy that is largely free of any barriers to free trade. As a result it is an economy that is highly dependent on foreign trade in terms of its economic growth prospects.

Opportunity costs This is simply the cost of doing something measured in terms of what must be sacrificed in order to do this activity. For example, if you decided to undertake some paid bar-work this evening you would make a financial gain; however, there would be an opportunity cost because you would be forgoing the chance to have some leisure or possibly study time.

Pension funds and insurance companies These are the large financial institutions that are the key investors in financial markets. They look to invest in long-term assets to match their long-term liabilities (paying out pensions). These investors have flourished in recent years due to the greater wealth of the private sector.

People's Bank of China (PBOC) This is the central bank of China which was created in 1948. The PBOC is in charge of monetary policy within China as it has the responsibility of maintaining financial stability.

Pre-emption rights This refers to one of the longest-standing principles of corporate law. It gives all shareholders the first right to buy any additional shares being sold by companies. The new shares would be offered to existing holders in direct proportion to their existing holdings. So, if you owned 10% of the existing shares in a company you would be given the right to buy 10% of the new shares being sold via a rights issue. These additional shares are normally sold at a significant discount to the existing market share price to ensure a successful completion of the transaction.

The shareholders involved face three choices:

(a) They can exercise their right which means that they agree to buy the additional shares.

(b) They can formally renounce the right, which will result in the company selling their rights on their behalf.

(c) Finally, they can do nothing. In this case the company will still normally sell the rights on behalf of the shareholder anyway.

Price-cap The main tool used to regulate former publicly owned utilities now operating in the private sector. It is effectively a price ceiling placed with a limit imposed on the highest price rise allowed to be made by these companies. The aim of this type of regulation is to encourage these companies to seek efficiency savings as they can take advantage of any additional gains to their shareholders.

Price–earnings ratio The P/E ratio is calculated by taking the market share price and dividing it by company's earnings per share. This ratio is often used to compare the current stock market value of a company.

Price-insensitive The elasticity of demand is an important concept for economists. This measures how sensitive demand is to a given price change. There are some products where demand is highly inelastic. For example, a consumer will be reluctant to stop buying basic food or heating for their home no matter how high these prices become. In contrast the demand for more luxury products will generally be more price-sensitive.

Principal–agent situation This exists in large companies where there is a clear split between the owners and the managers of the business. The shareholders are the owners and we refer to them as the 'principals'. In contrast, the managers of the company are the 'agents' employed to work on behalf of the owners.

Private and state schools In the UK we use the term 'private' to cover schools that are not funded by the government. As a result they generally require the parents to pay fees before their children can be educated in these schools. In contrast state schools are fully funded by the government so that their pupils can be educated free of charge.

Privatisation (state companies) This term is generally used where a whole business has its ownership transferred from the government to the private sector. However, it can also cover the introduction of the private sector into some parts of a publicly provided service. For example, the National Health Service might use a private company to undertake services like catering or cleaning.

Public goods These are products where one person's consumption does not result in less being available for others. In addition, it is impossible to exclude certain individuals from the consumption of these goods.

Public-sector net borrowing (PSNB) This is one way of measuring the difference between the government's spending and revenue. It is the difference between the revenue the government receives each month and its spending on schools, prisons, defence, etc.

Purchasing power Economists normally use this term to define the value of money in terms of the quantity and quality of goods it can be used to purchase. In this article it is being used to refer to the shift in national wealth from the rich industrialised countries of the 1970s (like the United States) to the oil producers (like Saudi Arabia).

Randomness This is where the outcome of some event lacks any predictability or pattern. In this context many local authorities introduced a lottery to determine which pupils would be accepted into a particularly popular school. This meant that the schools could no longer use set entry criteria such as religious affiliation, academic ability or location to influence their selection decisions.

Rating agencies There are a number of large international companies that are used to assess the risk of various bond issuers. They produce a formal rating measure for each of them.

Rationalisation In a business context this refers to a major reorganisation of a company. This will normally aim to improve the efficiency and profitability of a business. In this case it is likely to result in job cuts in the UK as the new owners look to find cheaper costs of production elsewhere.

Real exchange rate This is the nominal exchange rate adjusted for relative price change between countries involved.

Recession A severe economic slowdown normally defined as two or more successive quarters of negative economic growth.

Reserve requirements This is where the commercial banks are forced to hold deposits with the central bank. The amount that they are required to hold is normally a percentage of eligible liabilities. What are the eligible liabilities? These are simply the value of the deposits held in their accounts in a certain period. The larger a bank's deposits, the more reserves it will have to hold.

Retail banks These are the well-known high-street banks like HSBC, Nat West and Barclays. They take deposits from their retail clients and then lend this money out to their individual and commercial customers. The banks also offer a range of other services including foreign exchange facilities, investment advice and secure deposit facilities.

Retail-price index (RPI) This was the main measure of UK inflation used in the UK until 2003. The RPI measures inflation by looking at the prices of a wide group of goods and services. Unlike the consumer price index (CPI) it includes certain important costs such as council tax and mortgage interest payments.

Retailers' margins This is simply the difference between the price that a retailer pays for a product and the price that is charged to the customer in the shop. When the economy is very active retailers will try to increase these margins to enhance their profitability.

Risk aversion This is the natural desire for an investor to avoid taking any unnecessary risks unless the amount of return that is on offer fully compensates for the additional risk. So, in times of financial market uncertainty it is normal to see a 'flight to quality' with investors in bonds preferring to buy high-quality issues.

Savings All the income we do not consume we save. We often measure the level of savings in an economy by looking at the country's savings ratio. For example, the UK savings ratio is defined as the proportion of gross disposable income households save rather than spend. It was around 6% at the time of the article.

Shareholder In most companies the shareholders provide the bulk of the long-term finance. This makes them the key stakeholders in the business. They are the owners of the business and the managers must always remember that they are merely acting as agents working on behalf of the shareholders who are the principals. The shareholders range from private investors with small stakes in the business right up to the large financial institutions that often own a significant percentage of the equity of a business.

Short-run costs Economists define the short run as being the time period when at least one of the factors of production is completely fixed. For example, for a particular company this might mean that they have reached full capacity in a warehouse or at a factory site.

Short-term bank finance Normally in economics we define this as any bank loans that must be repaid within a year. In practice many of these loans will be even shorter-term. The banks can withdraw the finance at very short notice.

Six-month money injection (new ECB facility) This was a new money market facility being used to add liquidity to the Eurozone money markets. It was a response to the prolonged credit crisis that started in the summer of 2007.

Small and medium enterprises (SMEs) In most cases the key criterion used to define SMEs is the number of staff that they employ, with other supplementary factors including the firm's turnover and the size of its balance sheet. For example, the UK's Department for Business, Enterprise and Regulatory Reform (BERR) defines a small enterprise as one with less than 50 employees, and a medium enterprise as one with at least 50 but less than 250 employees. Finally, large enterprises have more than 250 employees.

Sole proprietorship This is in many ways the simplest form of business organisation. In this the individual and their company are one single business identity. The big advantage of such a business is that it is easy to set up and is accountable only to the sole proprietor and no one else. The downside is that it does not enjoy limited liability.

Stagflation This is the nightmare combination for macroeconomists. An economy goes through a period of very weak economic growth combined with high unemployment. This is accompanied by a continued significantly high level of price inflation.

Standard and Poor's (S&P) 500 The S&P 500 composite index is based on the market movements of 500 companies that are listed on the New York Stock Exchange. This index is one of the most widely used measures of US equity performance.

Standard of living A key economic goal for most countries is to raise the standard of living of their population. This equates to the average spending per person. It is usually measured by looking at total gross domestic income per person. One drawback of this measure is that it does not show how the total income is actually distributed. It is widely thought that the UK economy is becoming more and more financially divided with the rise of the super-rich taking an increasing share of national income at the expense of the poor.

Start-up This is a brand new business venture that is at the first stage of development. Such business ventures have a notoriously bad chance of success with very few surviving beyond a year or two.

Stock market bubble This term is used to describe any situation where the price of financial assets rises to a level far above any realistic value based on fundamental values like dividends or a company's earnings.

Stock market listing This is the process of a company selling its shares on a recognised stock market. The company in question will be required to sign a listing agreement which commits its directors to certain standards of behaviour especially in relation to reporting to their shareholders.

Strong yen This is the reverse of a weak yen. It occurs when the yen can be exchanged for larger amounts of foreign currency. As a result it will require less yen to purchase goods or services from overseas. At the same time it will be more expensive for other countries to import Japanese goods and services.

Structured credit markets This term is used in financial markets to cover a whole raft of new and highly innovative financial market products. Their common characteristic are:

a) The combining of various financial assets – for example, in the mortgage-backed securities a whole group of mortgages will be combined to make a large package that can be traded.

b) The creation of various tranches supported by the group of financial assets. Each tranche will be allocated into a different risk category.

c) There will be a clear divide between the credit-risk of the original issuer and the credit-risk of this particular group of financial assets. This will be done through the creation of a short-lived special-purpose vehicle (SPV).

Sub-prime The sub-prime market refers to the lending of money to much higher risk individuals at a higher rate of interest. When US house prices were rising sharply a number of people were encouraged to take out very large loans (at a very high multiple of their salary) which meant that they had little prospect of ever being able to meet the interest payments let alone any eventual repayment of the outstanding debt. As a result they were forced to default in large numbers.

Sub-prime mortgage crisis The prime lending rate is the rate of interest charged to credit-worthy companies and individuals in the US. The sub-prime market refers to the lending of money to much-higher-risk individuals at a higher rate of interest. When US house prices were rising sharply a number of people were encouraged to take out very large loans (at a very high multiple of their salary) which meant that they had little prospect of ever being able to meet the interest payments let alone any eventual repayment of the outstanding debt. As a result many were forced to default.

Subsidies This is a financial inducement that governments can offer to encourage the consumption of particular goods or services. They can also be used for a number of other purposes:

(a) To keep the prices of some basic food items as low as possible.

(b) To maintain the production of a particular good or service. For example, in agriculture or certain industries.

(c) To encourage the employment of a particular group of individuals. For example, the long-term unemployed.

Supply factors In economics, supply and demand are the fundamental factors that are important in determining price changes. If there is a fall in supply of a particular good or service economists would predict that the resulting scarcity would result in a price rise. In this case there has been a sharp fall in the supply of mainly food products such as pork caused by factors like 'blue-ear disease'. This has caused a 63% increase in pork prices.

Systematic risk (also called 'market risk') This refers to the type of risk that applies to an entire group of financial assets. For example, if interest rates are increased this might impact negatively on the entire stock market. In contrast, unsystematic (or specific) risk applies to only one particular financial asset. For example, if a company loses a particular contract with a customer its share price only will be affected.

Tariffs (gas and electricity) In economics the term 'tariff' is normally associated with some form of government tax or duty imposed on imported products. In recent years the move towards free trade has seen the elimination of most tariffs. However, this term can also refer to certain system of prices. In this context 'gas and electricity tariff' simply means the charges for these products from the various energy supply companies in the UK.

Term Auction Facility This was an emergency facility used by the Federal Reserve to inject large amounts of liquidity (cash) into the US money markets during the period of the credit crunch.

Tightening (monetary policy) When you see the term 'monetary policy' in the context of central banks it refers to interest rate policy. Central banks tighten monetary policy when they raise interest rates.

Total cost This can be defined as the sum of total fixed costs and total variable costs.

Trades Union Congress (TUC) This is the trade union umbrella group representing over six and a half million union members based in the UK. They campaign for better working conditions as well as the broader aim of social justice.

Trading platform In finance we use the term 'trading platform' to describe the market where buyers and sellers can operate. It might be an official market place like the official list (London Stock Exchange) or a less structured market.

Unemployment and non-farm payroll employment release This economic release is made up of three parts. The first figure is the percentage rate of unemployment which is based on a random survey of people. The second part tells us the change in thousands each month in the number of people on companies' payrolls. It excludes various special categories such as farm workers (hence the 'non-farm'), the self-employed, unpaid family workers and the armed forces. The final measure looks at the current trends in employee wage costs. It can provide early evidence of any rising cost-push inflation.

US sub-prime mortgage (tempest) The prime lending rate is the rate of interest charged to credit-worthy companies and individuals in the US. The sub-prime market refers to the lending of money to much higher-risk individuals at a higher rate of interest.

US Treasury Secretary This is the Head of the US Department of Treasury. It is the part of the US Administration that deals with financial and economic policy making.

Variable costs In contrast to fixed costs, these are the costs that are entirely dependent on the level of production. For example, for a company manufacturing curtains and other textile products these costs will come mainly from the factory's inputs like material and cotton. If the company receives a new large order from a customer the resulting increase in production will see a sharp rise in the variable costs.

Vehicle-Excise tax An annual charge levied by the UK tax authorities on car drivers. There are now thirteen different tax bands with the annual charge varying from £0 to £950 per year.

Weak yen This is where the yen can only be exchanged for smaller amounts of foreign currency. As a result it will require larger amounts of yen to purchase goods or services from overseas. At the same time it will be cheaper for other countries to import Japanese goods and services.

Weaker pound This refers to a fall in the value of the pound sterling. For example, as measured in pounds per dollar, the exchange rate might fall from $2.10/£1 to $1.90/£1 which means customers will get fewer dollars for their pound.

West Texas Intermediate (WTI) There are many different types of crude oil. They are differentiated in terms of their specific gravity and sulphur content which is largely determined by the origin of the oil. WTI is a light crude oil and it is the standard benchmark for oil trading and pricing in the US.

Wholesale market (energy) We use the term 'wholesale' to refer to the supply of energy to the retail energy companies. These companies purchase gas and electricity from the wholesale markets.

Winning bid When a company is put up for sale or is the subject of a takeover approach the winning bid is the one that secures the company. It should be noted that sometimes the bidder can end up paying more than the business is worth. Economists call this phenomenon 'the winner's curse'.

Working Tax Credits These credits are part of a complex system of welfare reforms introduced in 2003. Under the credits scheme those people who are in low income work receive extra payments from the state. It is a means-tested benefit designed to provide such individuals or families with an incentive to work rather than just rely on government aid.

Index